BARRON'S

6 GRE®
PRACTICE TESTS
2ND EDITION

David Freeling and Vince Kotchian

BARRON'S

®Graduate Record Exam and GRE are registered trademarks of Educational Testing Service (ETS). This publication is not endorsed or approved by ETS.

About the Authors

David Freeling, a graduate of Columbia University, has worked as a teacher and tutor since 1997, helping students of all ages improve their fundamental math and English skills. He prepares students for a wide range of standardized tests including the GRE, GMAT, SAT, ACT, SSAT, and HSPT. His other book titles include *Barron's GRE Math Workbook, 2nd Edition, Vocabmonster,* and the self-published classic *First Fun SAT Book.* Connect with his educational material online by visiting *NoeValleyTutor.com,* which features eight short videos presenting important GRE math test-taking tips, or by logging onto *Vocabmonster.com,* where you can learn to master advanced English vocabulary with funny, full-color cartoons and creative mnemonic devices. Mr. Freeling is currently completing his first novel, *The Bug to End All Bugs.*

Vince Kotchian grew up in Connecticut and completed the honors program at Boston College, graduating with a B.A. in English Literature. He has been privately tutoring standardized tests in San Diego for the past several years, and has helped hundreds of students get into the schools of their choice. He has authored nationally published books on the SSAT/ISEE and GRE. He teaches a GRE prep course at UCSD and has an official 170V 166Q score on the GRE. When he's not working, Vince enjoys playing and watching sports, reading and writing fiction, and running (which is enjoyable at least some of the time). Vince can be found online at *vincekotchian.com.*

All inquiries should be addressed to:
Barron's Educational Series, Inc.
250 Wireless Boulevard
Hauppauge, New York 11788
www.barronseduc.com

Library of Congress Catalog Card Number: 2015935135

ISBN: 978-1-4380-0629-1

PRINTED IN THE UNITED STATES OF AMERICA

9 8 7 6 5 4 3 2 1

10%
POST-CONSUMER
WASTE
Paper contains a minimum of 10% post-consumer waste (PCW). Paper used in this book was derived from certified, sustainable forestlands.

CONTENTS

Introduction 1

Overview of the GRE 1

How Is the GRE Scored? 2

A Closer Look at GRE Verbal Reasoning 3

A Closer Look at GRE Quantitative Reasoning 10

Basic Test-Taking Strategies for the GRE 15

Tips for Taking a Computer-Based Exam 16

Guessing Strategies 16

Practice Test 1 19

Section 1—Analytical Writing 23

Section 2—Verbal Reasoning 29

Section 3—Quantitative Reasoning 37

Section 4—Verbal Reasoning 44

Section 5—Quantitative Reasoning 52

Answer Key 58

Answer Explanations 59

Practice Test 2 75

Section 1—Analytical Writing 79

Section 2—Verbal Reasoning 85

Section 3—Quantitative Reasoning 92

Section 4—Verbal Reasoning 97

Section 5—Quantitative Reasoning 104

Answer Key 110

Answer Explanations 111

Practice Test 3 125

Section 1—Analytical Writing 129

Section 2—Verbal Reasoning 135

Section 3—Quantitative Reasoning 143

Section 4—Verbal Reasoning 149

Section 5—Quantitative Reasoning 156

Answer Key 162

Answer Explanations 163

Practice Test 4 177

Section 1—Analytical Writing 181
Section 2—Verbal Reasoning 187
Section 3—Quantitative Reasoning 195
Section 4—Verbal Reasoning 201
Section 5—Quantitative Reasoning 209
Answer Key 216
Answer Explanations 217

Practice Test 5 231

Section 1—Analytical Writing 235
Section 2—Verbal Reasoning 241
Section 3—Quantitative Reasoning 249
Section 4—Verbal Reasoning 256
Section 5—Quantitative Reasoning 264
Answer Key 271
Answer Explanations 272

Practice Test 6 287

Section 1—Analytical Writing 291
Section 2—Verbal Reasoning 297
Section 3—Quantitative Reasoning 306
Section 4—Verbal Reasoning 311
Section 5—Quantitative Reasoning 320
Answer Key 327
Answer Explanations 328

Acknowledgments 341

Introduction

OVERVIEW OF THE GRE

The GRE is the most widely accepted graduate admissions test worldwide, and taking it can bring you closer to achieving your academic goals. A wide range of graduate schools and business schools use GRE scores as a major factor in determining student admissions.

The test is designed to measure your skills in the following three areas:

Verbal Reasoning

You must be able to

- ☑ Analyze and draw conclusions from written material; identify an author's assumptions and point-of-view; understand meaning on multiple levels, such as literal and figurative
- ☑ Understand the structure of a text; distinguish between major and minor points
- ☑ Understand the meanings of words, both in sentences and in relationship to an entire text

Quantitative Reasoning

You must be able to

- ☑ Analyze numerical and quantitative information
- ☑ Solve mathematical problems
- ☑ Model and solve problems with quantitative methods
- ☑ Understand basic math concepts in arithmetic, algebra, geometry, and data analysis, including probability and statistics

Analytical Writing

You must be able to

- ☑ Effectively articulate complex ideas in a logically organized way
- ☑ Support ideas with relevant examples
- ☑ Analyze arguments and critically evaluate evidence used in an argument
- ☑ Sustain a focused, coherent essay
- ☑ Demonstrate proficiency in the usage of standard written English

In most areas of the world, the GRE is administered as a computer-based exam. Hence, this introduction and the format of the practice tests in this book are designed to be consistent with the experiences of taking the computer-based test. However, the academic content of the exam is the same for both test formats, so by studying this book, you will be well prepared for either the computer- or paper-based test. Mastering the concepts covered herein is the best way to prepare for the GRE. Every practice test has been carefully created to match the structure and content of the actual test.

The first section of the GRE is always the Analytical Writing section, which consists of two separately timed writing tasks: a 30-minute "Analyze an Issue" task, and a 30-minute "Analyze an Argument" task. Strategies and sample responses for this section are outside the scope of this book. However, typical writing questions, or "prompts," are presented within each practice test for completion.

The GRE always contains two scored Verbal Reasoning sections, often Sections 2 and 4. These are 30-minute timed sections with about 20 questions. The GRE always contains two scored Quantitative Reasoning sections, often Sections 3 and 5. These are 35-minute timed sections with about 20 questions.

HOW IS THE GRE SCORED?

Both the Verbal and Quantitative sections are scored from 130 to 170, in one-point increments. Subtle factors involving the adaptive difficulty level of the questions influence your final score. But a rough estimate of your score can be obtained as follows: on a section of 20 questions, 20 correct would result in a perfect score of 170. For every problem that is not correct, deduct 2 points from your score. So 12 correct, for example, would mean 8 incorrect answers, and your score would be roughly $170 - 8 \times 2 = 170 - 16 = 154$.

The Analytical Writing is scored from 0 to 6, in half-point increments, and is the only part of the test scored by human graders. Two trained readers will read each essay and assign it a score from 0 to 6; your score will be the average of these two scores. In rare cases when the scores differ by more than a point, a third reader will score the essay.

When you get your official scores, be sure to note what percentile your scores fall into. This measure will give you an idea of how you performed compared to other applicants.

ONLINE RESOURCES: REGISTER AND PRACTICE

The main online resource for the GRE is the official website of the Educational Testing Service, ETS, which you can visit at either *www.ets.org/gre* or *www.gre.org*. There you can find test-center locations, register for the test, and familiarize yourself with its contents. We strongly recommend that you download the free *PowerPrep II* software, which enables you to practice two computer-based tests and become familiar with the use of all onscreen tools and icons, including the built-in calculator.

A CLOSER LOOK AT GRE VERBAL REASONING
Question Types and Strategies

The Verbal sections of the GRE have three question types: Reading Comprehension, Text Completion, and Sentence Equivalence. Within each Verbal section, these questions may appear in any order.

READING COMPREHENSION QUESTIONS

Reading Comprehension questions appear in sets of one to four questions and relate to a given reading passage. There are five types of reading comprehension questions:

Multiple choice: You will be asked to select one answer from five choices.

Multiple answer: You will be asked to select one or more answers from three choices.

In-passage selection: You will be asked to highlight a sentence within the passage.

Logic: You will be asked to make a logical conclusion about a passage.

Structure: You will be tested on your knowledge of the components—assertions, conclusions, supporting evidence, etc.—of a passage.

When answering a multiple-answer question, you will need to select all possible correct answers in order to receive credit for the question; there is no partial credit given.

The GRE selects reading passages from the sciences, from the arts and humanities, and from everyday life. The passages you'll see on the test can range from one to five paragraphs in length.

GENERAL READING COMPREHENSION STRATEGIES

- Read the passage selectively, just noting the author's main topic and purpose. Write these two things down in your own words. For now, ignore details—you can always go back for them later if a question asks about something specific. In particular, pay attention to the content after shifts in the passage. Signposts for shifts include words such as: however, despite, but, although, etc.
- After reading a question, take a moment to paraphrase the question in your own words, and write your paraphrase down. This will make it easier to think about.
- When asked about a specific topic within a passage, re-read the section containing that topic. Jot down notes that include a guessed answer to the question.
- Eliminate answer choices that are wrong instead of looking for the correct answer. Many incorrect answer choices may seem correct at first. Watch out for the following ways that the test writers try to trick you:
  - including mixed-up facts
  - including true but irrelevant statements
  - including statements not literally supported by the passage
  - using poorly chosen adjectives
  - using absolute wording (always, never, etc.)

Overall, don't worry about complete comprehension of the passage as you work with questions: a partial understanding will usually be enough to answer the question correctly. Reading a section or passage until you have complete understanding is time-consuming and can overwhelm you with details that might be unnecessary. Focus on the parts of a passage you do understand, rather than the parts you don't.

Sample Multiple-Choice Question

Sample Questions 1 to 3 are based on this passage:

Line
(5)

(10)

(15)

Neurofeedback is a method for training of the self-regulation of physiological, especially neurophysiological, body signals. It became popular in the 1970s when the first devices for relaxation training were offered. The self-regulation training was mediated by visual or acoustical real-time display of, for example, the muscular tension measured by the electromyogram or the amplitude of the alpha rhythm activity measured by the electroencephalogram. The measurements required that electrode sensors be attached to the brain or other body parts. The feedback era began after Kamiya published his studies on conditioning of the alpha rhythm, finding the alpha amplitude to be connected to the state of relaxation. Since then, many biofeedback devices have appeared on the market, and, often, these devices have been applied in nonscientific settings. The scientific investigations of brain physiological self-regulation conducted by Sterman in 1974 described the application of neurofeedback for the therapy of patients with epilepsy. Birbaumer and his group demonstrated the human ability for self-regulation of the slow cortical potentials. They also successfully applied feedback training to patients with intractable epilepsy for reduction of their seizure frequency.

DIRECTIONS: For the following question, select *one* answer choice.

---

1. The passage implies which of the following about commercial biofeedback devices?

   Ⓐ Commercial biofeedback devices were highly profitable for their manufacturers due to the popularity of relaxation training.
   Ⓑ Nonscientific applications of biofeedback devices detracted from the neurofeedback field's academic reputation.
   Ⓒ Many commercial biofeedback devices were designed to help people induce alpha rhythms.
   Ⓓ Commercial biofeedback devices were primarily marketed to mental health professionals.
   Ⓔ Biofeedback devices that were popular on the commercial market were of lower quality than those used by Sterman and Birbaumer.

Answer: (C) The assertion that commercial biofeedback devices were intended to induce alpha rhythms is supported by the passage. The passage states that Kamiya "(found) the alpha amplitude to be connected to the state of relaxation," then proceeds to say that "since then," commercial biofeedback devices have been sold, implying that the reason these devices were marketed was their ability to help people achieve relaxing alpha rhythms.

Sample Multiple-Answer Question

> **DIRECTIONS:** For the following question, consider each of the choices separately and select *all* that apply.

2. The passage suggests which of the following about the application of biofeedback training to patients suffering from epilepsy?

    Indicate *all* that apply.

    A   Birbaumer's biofeedback treatment for patients with epilepsy was more successful than Sterman's.
    B   At least some of Birbaumer's patients were able to reduce their seizure occurrences through use of biofeedback.
    C   Sterman's use of biofeedback in the treatment of epileptic patients required less active patient participation than did Birbaumer's.

Answer: (B) The passage states that "(Birbaumer's group) also successfully applied feedback training to patients with intractable epilepsy for reduction of their seizure frequency," which directly suggests that some of his patients successfully reduced their seizure occurrences with the training.

Sample Select-In-Passage Question

3. Select the sentence that distinguishes ways by which a user of a biofeedback device might receive data from the device.

Answer: "The self-regulation training . . . electroencephalogram." This sentence indicates that a user of a biofeedback device had a "visual or acoustical" display of information about muscle tension or alpha rhythm activity—i.e., two different ways of receiving information from the device.

SAMPLE LOGIC QUESTION

Logic questions usually fall into two types: strengthen or weaken an argument, or resolve an illogical situation or paradox. It is important to note that logic questions can appear after a short passage or as part of the question set for a longer passage.

GENERAL LOGIC QUESTION STRATEGIES

- For "strengthen or weaken an argument" questions, paraphrase the argument and include the reason(s) the argument uses to support its claim.
- To strengthen an argument, look for an answer choice that eliminates a potential objection to the argument.
- To weaken an argument, find an answer choice that raises a good objection to the argument.
- The opposite of the correct answer choice should weaken the argument if you're trying to strengthen it, and vice versa.
- For "resolve a paradox" questions, paraphrase the argument and find a choice that allows both conflicting facts (the paradox in the passage) to remain true.

Astronomers have long held the view that the planet Saturn was first discovered by the ancient Greeks, but some recently discovered ancient Hindu drawings that predate Greek civilization depict the planet, even though the planet is not visible by the naked eye from the Indian subcontinent.

Line
(5)   Therefore, it is now argued that the ancient Hindus who made the drawings must have copied the artwork of another civilization that could have observed the planet directly, especially since the ancient Hindus were known to have copied the drawings of other civilizations.

DIRECTIONS: Read the passage above. For the following question, select *one* answer choice.

4.   Which of the following, if true, most weakens the recent argument about the ancient Hindus?

Ⓐ The question of who first discovered the planet Saturn is still a topic of debate among astronomers due to the lack of concrete evidence.

Ⓑ In ancient times, the distance of Saturn from the Earth was slightly smaller than it is today.

Ⓒ Only two ancient Hindu drawings are known that depict the planet Saturn.

Ⓓ Most hypotheses regarding ancient civilizations are never proved due to the difficulty of procuring evidence.

Ⓔ Though only four planets are visible to the naked eye from the Indian subcontinent, the ancient Hindus believed there must be a fifth planet that represented an important deity.

Answer: (E) The argument that the ancient Hindus discovered Saturn would be weakened if a plausible objection to that argument was raised. Choice E raises a plausible objection by providing an alternate reason why the ancient Hindus might have drawn a fifth planet—to represent one of their deities.

Sample Structure Question

Many scientists attribute the decline in mosquito populations in Airdale to the use of pesticides alone. However, bats have also contributed to the decline. Since they were named a protected species, the population of bats in the town has risen in recent years, and examinations of dead bats nearly always show that they had recently ingested mosquitoes.

TIP

Like Logic questions, Structure questions can also appear after a short passage or as part of the question set for a longer passage.

DIRECTIONS: Read the passage above. For the following question, select *one* answer choice.

5. In the argument, the portion in **boldface** plays which of the following roles?

Ⓐ It is the argument's overall conclusion.

Ⓑ It is a discovery that the argument seeks to explain.

Ⓒ It is an explanation that the argument concludes is accurate.

Ⓓ It provides evidence in support of the argument's conclusion.

Ⓔ It introduces a judgment that the argument opposes.

Answer: (E) It is useful to categorize each sentence of the argument, so its components can be isolated. The first sentence is an opinion not shared by the argument's author. This is evident since, after the first sentence, the author shifts direction with "However" and then writes an opinion statement, which can be thought of as the argument, or as its conclusion. The third sentence is used to provide evidence that supports the author's argument.

TEXT COMPLETION QUESTIONS

Text completion questions involve short passages of one to five sentences with one to three blanks. Each blank has three answer choices, unless there is only one blank, in which case five answer choices are offered. There is only one correct answer choice for each blank, and you must complete all blanks correctly to receive credit for the question.

GENERAL TEXT COMPLETION STRATEGIES

- Read the passage, simply noting the main idea. Jot this main idea down in your own words.
- Pick one of the blanks, and use context clues (descriptive phrasing, adjectives, shifts, etc.) to invent your own word for the blank before looking at the choices. Write your invented word(s) down. If there are multiple blanks, it is often easier to begin with the second or third blank.
- Eliminate choices that are not literally supported by the passage.

Overall, do not spend much time either trying to figure out what unfamiliar words mean, or re-reading the passage again and again. Just use your level of understanding, and guess quickly among vocabulary words that you can't define. Make sure each answer choice you choose has literal support. If you are confused by a sentence, try paraphrasing all or part of it, making sure you write down your paraphrase.

Sample Text Completion Questions

> **DIRECTIONS:** For the following questions, select *one* entry for each blank from the corresponding column of choices. Fill all blanks in the way that best completes the text.

1. Although he was undoubtedly beholden to corporate interests due to his sponsors' sizable contributions to his campaign, the candidate presented a platform that belied any _____ those companies' agendas.

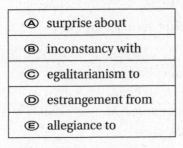

Ⓐ	surprise about
Ⓑ	inconstancy with
Ⓒ	egalitarianism to
Ⓓ	estrangement from
Ⓔ	allegiance to

Answer: (E) The candidate is *beholden* (obligated) to corporations. Since the word "although" indicates that the direction of the sentence will either shift or be surprising, choosing *allegiance* (loyalty) creates that surprise because the candidate's platform *belied* (gave a false impression of) his corporate loyalty.

2. Rather than exhibit the (i) _____ that marked so many animals treated cruelly in the name of sport, the greyhound displayed (ii) _____ that made many remark about his even composure.

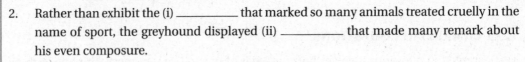
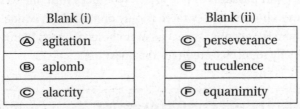

Blank (i)	Blank (ii)
Ⓐ agitation	Ⓒ perseverance
Ⓑ aplomb	Ⓔ truculence
Ⓒ alacrity	Ⓕ equanimity

Answer: (A, F) The second blank is *equanimity* (an even-tempered nature) because many "remark(ed) about his even composure." The word "rather" creates a shift in the sentence, so the first blank must contrast with "even composure" and be supported by a quality that might appear in "animals treated cruelly." Therefore, *agitation* (restless anxiousness) would work.

SENTENCE EQUIVALENCE QUESTIONS

Sentence Equivalence questions have one sentence, one blank, and six answer choices, of which you must select two. You must select both correct answers to receive credit for the question.

> ### GENERAL SENTENCE EQUIVALENCE STRATEGIES
>
> - Read the sentence, taking a few seconds to paraphrase it and to write down your paraphrase.
> - Invent a word for the blank that takes the sentence's descriptive clue(s) into account, and write your word down. Look for descriptive language and shifts.
> - Select two choices that are synonyms. Make sure the meanings of both choices are as alike as possible.
>
> Overall, keep an open mind when looking at the answer choices. Often, one choice will work well in the sentence, but none of the other choices will be a close synonym to it. The two right choices will both be literally supported by the sentence AND be very close synonyms. Like text completion questions, do not spend too much time trying to figure out what unfamiliar words mean.

SAMPLE SENTENCE EQUIVALENCE QUESTION

> **DIRECTIONS:** For the following question, select the *two* answer choices that, when used to complete the sentence, fit the meaning of the sentence as a whole and produce completed sentences that are alike in meaning.

1. Although his youth was marked by bouts of intemperance, as an adult, Higgs was widely known for his _____.

    - A moderation
    - B harmony
    - C mellifluousness
    - D measure
    - E sagacity
    - F wisdom

Answer: (A, D) If Higgs's youth was marked by *intemperance* (excess), he will exhibit a nearly opposite quality in adulthood, since the word "although" signifies a shift in meaning. Both *moderation* and *measure* (a moderate degree) create an appropriate shift.

A CLOSER LOOK AT GRE QUANTITATIVE REASONING

Sometimes you may be able to do a math problem in your head or by using the onscreen calculator, but usually it will really help you to copy the important information onto paper. The first step is to make a rough diagram of the question on a sheet of scrap paper. If the problem is algebraic, look to manipulate or transform the given information in some way. For example, a common step in a GRE math problem might be to take an equation such as $m + 2n = 5$ and multiply both sides by 3 to obtain $3m + 6n = 15$. Or suppose you see a question such as this:

If $\frac{x}{y} = 4$, and x is 6 more than y, what is the value of y?

When you copy the given equation onto paper, you may notice that multiplying both sides by y yields $x = 4y$. This resulting equation is equivalent to the original but easier to work with. Next, translate the phrase "x is 6 more than y" as $x = 6 + y$. Because of your earlier transformation, you can now substitute for x in this latter equation to obtain $4y = 6 + y$. Solving from here is relatively easy: subtract $1y$ from each side to obtain $3y = 6$, and $y = 2$. *The key point* is that jotting the information down on paper allows you to work through the steps necessary to find an answer.

If you are working on a geometric problem, look to add additional lines to your diagram or cover up part of the picture. For example, suppose you face a Quantitative Comparison question such as the following:

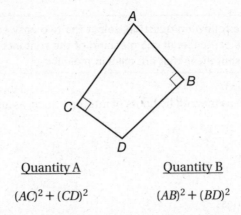

Quantity A	Quantity B
$(AC)^2 + (CD)^2$	$(AB)^2 + (BD)^2$

In this type of question, you are asked to compare the values in the two columns, according to these directions:

Select one of the following four answer choices.

- Ⓐ Quantity A is greater.
- Ⓑ Quantity B is greater.
- Ⓒ The two quantities are equal.
- Ⓓ The relationship cannot be determined from the information given.

In the problem above, no numbers are given, so many students would select choice (D), which you can think of as standing for, "it depends." But look what happens when segment AD is drawn.

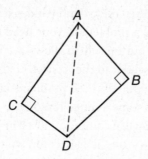

TIP

1. Your rough diagram, plus the lines and notes you add to it, are indispensible in solving the problem.
2. Look out for hidden right triangles, which can be used to find lengths in figures.

Do you see that two right triangles are formed? The Pythagorean theorem (which states that $a^2 + b^2 = c^2$, if a and b are leg lengths in a right triangle and c is the length of the hypotenuse) can now be applied to show that both quantities equal $(AD)^2$ and are thus equal to each other, choice (C).

Top Six Strategies for Tackling Quantitative Reasoning Questions

1. **WATCH THE WORDING.** It is easy to get close to the right answer, but make sure you close the deal. In other words, follow through to the final step! Always double-check what the problem is asking for. Often you may solve for x, but the question may be asking for the value of y or $x + 2$. A common mistake is to make false assumptions or misinterpret a key word. For example, consider this question:

   If a square has a perimeter equal to 36, what is the length of its diagonal?

   Begin by finding the side length of the square. Many of you will take the square root of 36 to obtain $s = 6$ as the first step, because you are familiar with the fact that $6^2 = 36$, which means that a square with a side length of 6 has an area of 36. The error is that the *perimeter*, not area, is given as 36. Since the perimeter of a square is four times the side length, $s = 36 \div 4$, which is 9, not 6. From the side length of a square, you would be able to apply the Pythagorean theorem to find the diagonal length, which is $9\sqrt{2}$ here, as will be explained later in the book. *The key point* is that if your first assumption is wrong, you will do a lot of additional work with the incorrect side length of 6 in place.

   Now try this one:

   The length of a rectangle is 2 more than its width. If the rectangle's length is 6, what is its area?

   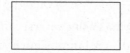

   This is a *numeric-entry* question, which allows you to type in virtually any number as your answer, and thereby allows the test-makers to make sure you really know your math.

   The rectangle question above is one of the easier ones that you will encounter; yet many students would get it wrong. Did you remember to draw the picture? If you thought the rectangle measured 6 × 8 and marked 48, you read "2 more" too quickly. The width must be 2 less than the given length, so the area = length × width = 6 × 4 = **24**.

2. **USE THE CALCULATOR.** The GRE exam includes a built in calculator. Use it. There is no extra credit for doing a problem in your head or longhand. A nice feature of the calculator is the *transfer* button, which allows you to transfer the number showing on the calculator's display screen to the answer box, in a numeric-entry type problem. Suppose you are solving one of these problems and find, for example, that $x = 190$. Suppose further that for some strange reason the problem asks, *what is the value of 2x*? You may think that you can compute 190×2 in your head, but it is easier and more accurate to simply type $\times 2$ on the calculator, which will apply the operation to your last answer. Then, by pressing *transfer*, you can automatically transfer your result to the answer box, without having to risk mistyping or miscalculating it.

That said, there will be situations when using the calculator is ill-advised.

Consider the following quantitative comparison question:

Quantity A	Quantity B
The number of minutes in one thousand days	The number of seconds in 25 thousand minutes

After careful consideration, you determine that Quantity A is $60 \times 24 \times 1,000$, and that Quantity B is $60 \times 25,000$. If you study these quantities, you will notice that $60 \times 25,000 > 60 \times 24,000$, so Quantity B is greater. Typing these large values on the calculator would waste time and would likely lead to an error.

3. **PICK A NUMBER.** It is often helpful to pick a number for one or more unknowns in a problem. Make sure to jot this choice (or choices) on a sheet of paper and substitute the same value for every occurrence of the variable. The idea is that working with a specific model is easier than working with a general situation. Here is an example:

Ann is 4 years older than Bob and 6 years older than Carla.

Quantity A	Quantity B
The median age of Ann, Bob, and Carla	The average (arithmetic mean) age of Ann, Bob, and Carla

Simply pick an age for Ann, such as $A = 10$. This makes Bob $10 - 4 = 6$ years old and Carla $10 - 6 = 4$ years old. The median of 4, 6, and 10 is the middle value, 6. The average of 4, 6, and 10 is $\frac{4+6+10}{3} \approx 7$, so Quantity B is greater. The key is to work with the specific numbers, rather than using several variables. Yes, you could also represent the three ages as x, $x - 4$, and $x - 6$, but why force yourself to use the algebraic method when picking numbers is so much easier? Of course, sometimes you will have to think carefully about whether the answer you get with one choice of values will hold in general.

For most questions, use the algebraic method if you know it. But picking numbers can get you through a few hard problems or help you get started.

Here is a different type of example:

$$4 < x < 5$$

Quantity A	Quantity B
$\dfrac{x}{6}$	$\dfrac{7}{10}$

Pick a number such as 4.1 for x, and the calculator shows that Quantity A is roughly .68, which is less than $\dfrac{7}{10} = .7 = .70$. Pick a number such as 4.9 for x, and Quantity A is roughly .82, which is greater than $\dfrac{7}{10}$. Therefore, (D) is correct. Picking a wide range of values for x was the key here.

4. **LOOK FOR CANCELLATION.** Tough-looking problems can often be simplified by finding something that cancels out.

   If $\dfrac{2x}{7} \times \dfrac{3y}{x} \times \dfrac{7}{2} = 12$, and $x \neq 0$, then what is the value of y?

   This problem is much easier than it looks if you are familiar with the concept of "cross-canceling." When multiplying fractions, numbers that duplicate in the top and bottom may be canceled. This is the same as reducing a fraction and means that the left side of the equation above can be simplified to $\dfrac{2\!\!\!/x}{7\!\!\!/} \times \dfrac{3y}{x\!\!\!/} \times \dfrac{7\!\!\!/}{2\!\!\!/} = 12$. So $3y = 12$, and $y = \mathbf{4}$.

   In problems involving addition, look for pairs of numbers such as 4 and -4, whose sum is 0, to cancel out. For example, suppose you encounter an expression such as $N + -4 + -3 + -2 + -1 + 0 + 1 + 2 + 3 + 4$. Because a number plus its additive inverse is 0, this whole expression would simplify to $N + 0$, or just N.

   In problems with square roots, look for "squaring" and "taking the square root" to cancel out, because they are inverse operations. For example, $\sqrt{89^2} = 89$. No calculator needed!

5. **ESTIMATE AND ELIMINATE.** On many questions, the answer choices are widely spread in value. You may be able to estimate the answer to a problem you don't know how to solve and then eliminate any choices that are far from your estimate. Guess from the remaining choices. This strategy works best in traditional multiple-choice problems.

6. **TEST THE ANSWER CHOICES.** You can sometimes work with the given choices to find the right answer, even if you don't know how to do a problem. This is equivalent to "working backwards." Consider this one:

   $$4^{x+1} = 8^{x-1}$$

   What value of x satisfies the equation above?

   (A) 4
   (B) 5
   (C) 6
   (D) 7
   (E) 8

Suppose for a moment that choice (A), $x = 4$, is correct. Then the exponent $x + 1$ would equal 5, the exponent $x - 1$ would equal 3, and the equation would read $4^5 = 8^3$. We will test this on the calculator. The expression 4^5 means 4 multiplied by itself 5 times, so type $4 \times 4 \times 4 \times 4 \times 4$ to obtain 1,024. Now type $8 \times 8 \times 8$ for 8^3, which equals 512. Since $1{,}024 \neq 512$, choice (A) is incorrect. Next, test choice (B), $x = 5$, which would make the equation read $4^6 = 8^4$. Find 4^6 by multiplying 4^5 by one more 4, and find 8^4 by multiplying 8^3 by one more 8, to utilize the work you've already done. That is, $4^6 = 1{,}024 \times 4 = 4{,}096$, and $8^4 = 512 \times 8 = 4{,}096$. Since choice (B) makes the two sides match in value, (B) is correct.

Let's compare this to the algebraic method. Exponent equations can often be solved by finding a common base. Since $4 = 2 \times 2$ and $8 = 2 \times 2 \times 2$, we can replace 4 with 2^2 and 8 with 2^3 in the original equation. Substitution yields $(2^2)^{(x+1)} = (2^3)^{(x-1)}$. The *power to a power* rule applies, dictating that the exponents are multiplied: $2^{(2x+2)} = 2^{(3x-3)}$ (by the distributive property). Since both sides now have the same base, the exponents may be set equal, implying that $2x + 2 = 3x - 3$. Finally, subtract $2x$ and add 3 to both sides to find $x = 5$ again.

Notice that by testing the choices, you were able find the correct answer even if you had forgotten the rules of exponents.

The following hard problem can be solved most efficiently by testing the answer choices:

A train rode from Town X to Town Y at 20 miles per hour and returned by the same route at 30 mph. If the train's total traveling time was 10 hours, what was the one-way distance between the two towns?

- Ⓐ 90 miles
- Ⓑ 120 miles
- Ⓒ 150 miles
- Ⓓ 180 miles
- Ⓔ 200 miles

This type of motion problem hinges around the idea that distance equals rate × time, or $D = rt$. Let's imagine for a moment that choice (C) is correct. *You can often narrow down more quickly by first testing the middle value, which is almost always answer choice (C).* If (C) is correct, then the one-way distance is 150 miles. For the trip to Town Y, use 20 as the rate in $D = rt$ formula: $150 = 20t$. Divide by 20 to obtain $t = 7.5$, meaning that at 20 mph it would take 7.5 hours to travel 150 miles. Similarly, the return trip at 30 mph would require $150 \div 30 = 5$ hours. But 7.5 hours + 5 hours does not match the 10 total hours of traveling time given. Therefore, (C) is incorrect, and you may also eliminate (D) and (E) because a larger distance between the towns would require even more traveling time.

Test choice (B) next, using the $D = rt$ formula again. If the distance were equal to 120 miles, then the trip to Town Y at 20 miles per hour would require 6 hours, because $120 = 20 \times 6$, and the return trip at 30 mph would require 4 hours, because $120 = 30 \times 4$. Since 6 hours to Town Y plus 4 hours return equals 10 total hours, choice (B) is correct. Here, working with the choices makes a long and challenging problem manageable.

TIP

Remember that if you do get stuck on one hard problem during the exam, your best strategy is to guess randomly and bank your time for problems within your range of ability.

For extra practice, we recommend that you attempt this train problem using the algebraic method. You should be able to get $D = 120$ without using the choices. Here is an outline of the solution:

1. Let t_1 and t_2 represent the time to Town Y and the return time, respectively. Note that $t_1 + t_2 = 10$.
2. Use the given rates (speeds) in the $D = rt$ formula to obtain the equations $D = 20t_1$ and $D = 30t_2$.
3. Because the train took the same route each way, the distance there equals the return distance, so the Ds can be set equal to each other. That is, $20t_1 = 30t_2$.
4. Divide both sides by the common factor, 10, to get $2t_1 = 3t_2$.
5. Isolate t_1 or t_2 in the equation $t_1 + t_2 = 10$ from step (1) above, and substitute this expression into the equation $2t_1 = 3t_2$ from step (4), above.
6. Solve for t_1 or t_2; you should get 6 or 4.
7. Finally, substitute your known t_1 or t_2 back into the appropriate equation to find the distance, D.

Because of the time limit, most students would benefit by attempting this problem with the Testing Answer Choices method.

BASIC TEST-TAKING STRATEGIES FOR THE GRE

Here are a few tips for making the structure of the computer-based GRE work for you.

- **WRITE THINGS DOWN.** Use your pencil and paper as much as possible. This will reduce the amount of work you have to do in your head, reducing your fatigue and increasing your accuracy. A seemingly impossible math problem, for example, becomes straightforward when a simple diagram is drawn. A typical GRE math problem requires several steps, and very few people could work through them all in their head. On reading passages, it's a good idea to jot down a key short phrase summarizing each paragraph.

- **DON'T OVER-REVIEW.** You can review any question at any time, but don't over-review. Try to make one pass through all the questions first and then begin to review, starting with the marked ones.

- **FOCUS ON THE QUESTION TYPES AT WHICH YOU'RE MOST SKILLED.** Many students who struggle with vocabulary, for instance, can benefit by spending more time on the reading passages. It is wise to spend very little time on a problem that you know is too hard for you and to allocate your time to the questions you have the greatest chance of getting correct.

- **NEVER LET A SECTION END WITH BLANK QUESTIONS.** Make sure to practice bubbling in quickly with the *PowerPrep* software available through *www.gre.org*, so if you are running out of time, you can bubble your answers efficiently on test day. Any unanswered question is automatically wrong.

- **IGNORE THE ADAPTATION.** After you take the first scored Verbal and Quantitative sections, the second scored sections will adapt based on your score of the first. If you do well, the second scored section will contain harder questions, and if you do poorly, you will face easier questions. That said, there is no point trying to guess whether or not you are doing well based on the difficulty level of the problems you receive. Simply try your

TIP

You can also jot down ideas for the Writing section. Type your notes directly onscreen. Then just cut-and-paste them directly into the body of your essay.

best to answer every question correctly. *In this book, some sections may be very slightly harder than those that appear on your actual GRE.* This simulates a section that has adapted to a student who is doing well and enables advanced students to practice the challenging types of problems they will face.

TIPS FOR TAKING A COMPUTER-BASED EXAM

If you've used a computer before, you should have no problem with the computer-based GRE interface. The onscreen instructions will guide you through the test—just point and click with your mouse. However, there are a few things worth mentioning.

- In all sections (except for the Analytical Writing section), you have the ability to skip forward and backward through the questions. This will enable you to come back to any questions you skip within a section and skip forward to the questions that are easiest for you.
- You have the ability to mark questions for review. This feature lets you keep track of questions you initially skipped or ones you want to go over again.
- Certain questions in the Verbal and Quantitative sections will require that you select a sentence in a passage or type in a numerical answer.
- Some questions require you to select more than one answer. A good way to recognize these questions is the shape of the answer bubbles—they will be square-shaped instead of the usual oval shape.
- Don't forget: you may have to complete an additional Verbal or Quantitative section in addition to the two scored sections of each type. This experimental, unscored section will be indistinguishable from the scored ones and may be any of the Verbal or Quantitative sections you take. The GRE uses this section to test questions for future tests.
- When the test is completed, you'll have the chance to report your scores or cancel them. Unless you're 100% sure you bombed the test (due to illness, etc.), it's a good idea to report the scores. You can probably take the test again if you did do poorly, and many students have an inaccurate perception of how many questions they answered correctly. In most cases, you won't want to enter school codes to send scores to before you start the test, since you can send scores after you get your results (for a fee).
- The scores you receive at the end of the test will range from 130 to 170 for both Verbal and Quantitative. You'll receive your essay score, along with an official score report, a few weeks after you take the test.

GUESSING STRATEGIES

As you work through each section, make sure to answer each and every question. There is no guessing penalty, so there is no point leaving any questions blank. Your score is based on the total number correct.

If you are unsure of how to answer a question and have to guess, your guessing strategy should be guided by elimination. Are there any answer choices you can eliminate? Try to knock out a couple of clearly wrong choices and guess *quickly* from the remaining ones, so you don't lose much time. For example, suppose you are working on a sentence completion question, and you know the meaning of only two of the five words presented in the answer choices. If neither of these two words fits well in the sentence, just guess randomly from the three hard words, and save your time for questions that you have a better chance of getting right.

If you do guess on a problem, "mark" the problem, using the icon labeled *Mark* at the top of the screen. Then, when you have finished all the questions you do know how to answer, you can easily find and review the ones you guessed on. Of course, if you find a question so challenging that your guess is purely random, do not mark it, because further review of this problem will only be time wasted.

In general, only mark a question when you think you might be able to improve your guess with more time, or when you "know" the answer but feel you need to double-check your work. For the paper-based GRE, "marking" would simply mean circling the problem number in your test booklet.

When you notice that there is about one minute left in any section, start guessing on all the questions you haven't reached yet. This should be enough time to very quickly scroll through every remaining question, filling in the first answer bubble that you can reach with your mouse. Again, make sure that you have not left any blanks earlier in the section.

Make sure that you fill in an answer, even if it's a guess, for every question as you go along. Never leave a blank.

Practice Test 1

SECTION 1—ANALYTICAL WRITING

TIME: 60 MINUTES—2 WRITING TASKS

TASK 1: ISSUE EXPLORATION

TIME: 30 MINUTES

The topic is presented in a one- to two-sentence quotation commenting on an issue of general concern.

Your essay will be judged on the basis of your skill in the following areas:

- response to the specific task instructions
- consideration of the complexities of the issue
- organization, development, and expression of your ideas
- support of your position with relevant reasoning and examples
- control of the elements of standard written English

TOPIC

Students are more responsible for their education than their teachers.

DIRECTIONS: Write a response in which you discuss the extent to which you agree or disagree with the statement and explain your reasoning for the position you take. In developing and supporting your position, you should consider ways in which the statement might or might not hold true and explain how these considerations shape your position.

TASK 2: ARGUMENT ANALYSIS

TIME: 30 MINUTES

Your essay will be judged on the basis of your skill in the following areas:

- identification and assessment of the argument's main elements
- organization and articulation of your thoughts
- use of relevant examples and arguments to support your case
- handling of the mechanics of standard written English

TOPIC

The ancient Oppo tribe has long been thought to have hunted only with wooden spears because none of their cave paintings depict bows or arrows. Recently, however, flint arrowheads have been found among the fossilized bones of ibex, animals thought to be a staple of the Oppo tribe's diet. Since these finds were made on land previously inhabited by the Oppo tribe, it follows that the Oppo used both spears and arrows to hunt.

DIRECTIONS: Write a response in which you discuss what specific evidence is needed to evaluate the argument and explain how the evidence would weaken or strengthen the argument.

SECTION 2—VERBAL REASONING

TIME: 30 MINUTES—20 QUESTIONS

> **DIRECTIONS:** For Questions 1 to 6, select *one* entry for each blank from the corresponding column of choices. Fill all blanks in the way that best completes the text.

1. When genuine _____ is considered to be an aberration, it is no wonder that the cynical belief that everyone is just out for profit is considered to be realism.

Ⓐ cupidity
Ⓑ avarice
Ⓒ altruism
Ⓓ vacillation
Ⓔ determination

2. The bane of many a fund manager, the volatility of the emerging markets index has often _____ investors seeking a stable repository for their funds.

Ⓐ confounded
Ⓑ assuaged
Ⓒ underscored
Ⓓ relieved
Ⓔ enriched

3. The advent of three-dimensional printing has made once (i) _____ fabrication of complicated plastic components possible for many individuals and companies. But is the (ii) _____ of 3-D printers good for the marketplace? The surfeit of manufacturers may drive down prices, making it harder for the very companies the technology initially benefited to compete.

Blank (i)	Blank (ii)
Ⓐ negligible	Ⓓ glut
Ⓑ implausible	Ⓔ dearth
Ⓒ lucid	Ⓕ ambiguity

4. The characteristic (i) _____ of Victorian homes lies in stark contrast to the more modern style of houses designed recently: today's architects are often utilitarian, discarding any architectural embellishments to the point that their style could almost be described as (ii) _____.

Blank (i)	Blank (ii)
Ⓐ ornateness	Ⓓ ascetic
Ⓑ blandishments	Ⓔ concomitant
Ⓒ austerity	Ⓕ labyrinthine

5. Despite the actor's profession that (i) _____ was the antithesis of art, his campy performance on the play's opening night was undoubtedly (ii) _____.

Blank (i)	Blank (ii)
Ⓐ melodrama	Ⓓ laconic
Ⓑ intransigence	Ⓔ maudlin
Ⓒ indigence	Ⓕ immutable

6. The recent Lowbrow art movement of Los Angeles has inarguable (i) _____. Original works by artists such as Mark Ryden, once only collected by a select few, have now garnered greater (ii) _____ and often sell for tens of thousands of dollars at auction. The movement's detractors need not be surprised, then, that more people are clamoring for these works to (iii) _____ more classic pieces at galleries and museums.

Blank (i)	Blank (ii)	Blank (iii)
Ⓐ esteem	Ⓓ deprecation	Ⓖ curtail
Ⓑ panache	Ⓔ approbation	Ⓗ supplant
Ⓒ lassitude	Ⓕ rectitude	Ⓘ contravene

DIRECTIONS: For Questions 7 to 12, select *one* answer choice unless otherwise instructed.

Questions 7 to 9 are based on the following reading passage:

There is some evidence that where sign language was found among Native American tribes it was largely uniform, simply because many tribes had, at one time, been forced to dwell together at peace. A collection of signs that was nearly uniform was obtained
Line from a new delegation of the Kaiowa, Comanche, Apache, and Wichita tribes. How-
(5) ever, the individuals who gave the signs had actually lived together at or near what was known as Anadarko, Indian Territory, for a considerable time, and the resulting unifor- mity of their signs might either have been thought of as jargon or as the natural ten- dency to compromise for mutual understanding—the unification so often observed in oral speech, coming under many circumstances out of former heterogeneity. The rule
(10) is that dialects precede languages and that out of many dialects comes one language. It may be found that other individuals of those same tribes who had, from any cause, not lived in the union may have had signs for the same ideas different from those in the above-mentioned collection. This idea gained currency because some signs of other representatives of one of the component bodies—Apache—had actually been reported
(15) to differ from those ideas given by the Anadarko group. The uniformity of the signs of those who had been secluded for years at one particular reservation was notable, but some collected signs of other Cheyennes and Sioux differed, not only from those on the reservation, but from each other. Therefore, the signs used in common by the tribes at the reservation seem to have been modified and to a certain extent unified.

For Question 7, consider each of the choices separately and select *all* that apply.

7. Which of the following can be inferred from the passage regarding the research about Native American sign language?

   Indicate *all* that apply.

   A   The researchers studying the Anadarko group had a functional understanding of the signs used by the delegation of tribes.
   B   Some of the signs used by the members of the Anadarko delegation differed significantly from those used by other delegation members.
   C   Native American tribes who were not forced to share living space did not share any common signs.

8. Select the sentence of the passage in which the author draws a parallel between two different methods of communication.

9.   In the context in which it appears, "currency" (line 13) most nearly means

     Ⓐ funding
     Ⓑ acceptance
     Ⓒ value
     Ⓓ uniqueness
     Ⓔ contemporaneity

Questions 10 to 12 are based on the following reading passage:

     An organism's color can serve an adaptive function in numerous ecological contexts, including crypsis (the ability to avoid detection), communication, and thermoregulation. As such, it is likely that organismal color reflects a balance among numerous and
Line perhaps competing demands; a color best suited for the performance of one function
(5) (e.g., avoidance of predators) may reflect a trade-off with that suited for another (e.g., attractiveness to potential mates). This trade-off is further shaped by the wavelengths of light available in the organism's natural environment; a color pattern that is cryptic in one environment may be conspicuous in another. In other words, the relative strength of the color signal depends on not only the visual system of the receiver but
(10) also the medium and surrounding environment in which it is transmitted. In fact, a new explanation of color evolution using this concept has been hailed by researchers as a useful way to tie what were competing theories together.

10.   In the context in which it appears, "hailed" (line 11) most nearly means

     Ⓐ signaled
     Ⓑ invoked
     Ⓒ lauded
     Ⓓ spoken
     Ⓔ conflated

For Question 11, consider each of the choices separately and select *all* that apply.

11.   The passage implies which of the following regarding the evolution of an organism's coloring?

Indicate *all* that apply.

    Ⓐ An organism with conspicuous markings will be unlikely to survive long enough to pass its genes to later generations.
    Ⓑ A species with conspicuous markings evolved those markings because they helped its members reproduce.
    Ⓒ Organisms with cryptic markings exist because previous generations with such markings were able to avoid predators better than those without cryptic markings.

12. The author of the passage most likely discusses an organism's "adaptive function" (line 1) in order to

Ⓐ suggest that organisms use color change as a way to meet various biological needs

Ⓑ provide reasoning for the assertion that an organism's coloring can make its survival more difficult

Ⓒ offer an explanation for the phenomenon that some organisms have no natural predators

Ⓓ suggest that organisms that have learned to adapt to their surroundings have a greater chance of survival than those that are less adaptable

Ⓔ provide support for the theory that less conspicuous organisms are more attractive to potential mates

DIRECTIONS: For Questions 13 to 16, select the *two* answer choices that, when used to complete the sentence, fit the meaning of the sentence as a whole *and* produce completed sentences that are alike in meaning.

13. The politician's tendency to _____ left even his most ardent supporters unsure of his position on certain issues.

A corroborate
B equivocate
C disabuse
D venerate
E mitigate
F vacillate

14. In private, the critic insisted that the novel was seriously flawed, citing both its sophomoric premise and lack of structure, but then wrote a review that _____ the work.

A deprecated
B extolled
C complicated
D celebrated
E assuaged
F berated

15. It was ironic that the very professor who urged us to write simply and clearly could not do so himself: his directions were often _____ by layers of ambiguity.

A eschewed
B enervated
C obfuscated
D compounded
E elucidated
F obscured

16. The bursts of gamma-ray radiation generated by the mergers of binary star systems are _____ in nature; scientists have found it difficult to collect meaningful data from such a brief time span.

[A] expedient
[B] protracted
[C] transient
[D] sidereal
[E] fleeting
[F] celestial

DIRECTIONS: For Questions 17 to 20, select *one* answer choice unless otherwise instructed.

Question 17 is based on the following reading passage:

Midwinter in the southern hemisphere comes in June and July, and midsummer comes in December. The opening of spring comes in August and September, and autumn approaches in February and March. But while in the northern hemisphere the differ-
Line ence between the heat of midsummer and the cold of midwinter is somewhat lessened
(5) by the changing distance of the sun, **in the southern hemisphere this effect is intensi-fied, because the earth comes to perihelion in the southern midsummer.** However, on account of the swifter motion of the earth from October to March than from April to September, **the southern summer is shorter enough to compensate for the sun's being nearer**, so that the southern summer is practically no hotter than the northern.

17. In the argument given, the two portions in **boldface** play which of the following roles?

Ⓐ The first is an assertion made by the argument in support of a position; the second states that position.
Ⓑ The first is a claim made by the argument; the second qualifies the claim by presenting another assertion.
Ⓒ The first is the summary of the argument's position; the second provides evidence supporting that position.
Ⓓ The first presents an example that is contrary to the argument's position; the second adds another opposing example.
Ⓔ The first is a concession that the position the argument establishes is not absolute; the second provides an exception to the argument's position.

Questions 18 to 20 are based on the following reading passage:

In his *New York Times* blog in August, 2006, Douglas Coupland lamented the state of Canadian literature as, essentially, a literature in which old biddies talk about their small lives in small towns. Canadian literature is a category, he makes clear, in which he does not fit.

Line

(5) Yet if Coupland and his compatriots do not recognize their place in Canadian literature, Coupland does recognize himself as a Canadian writer who is intent on investigating, as well as helping to create, the culture of his country through his art. Dedicating his book *Souvenir of Canada* to his father, a more Canadian man is hard to imagine, Coupland adds, and to follow in his footsteps is the deepest of honors. Coupland has

(10) created numerous pieces that explicitly give language to the Canadian experience. In the category of non-fiction, *Souvenir of Canada* and *Souvenir of Canada 2* are coffee-table books that use images of daily Canadian life to speak about and to Canadians. *City of Glass* performs this role for Vancouverites specifically. *Terry: Terry Fox and his Marathon of Hope* tells a story that is close to the hearts of most Canadians. And finally,

(15) *Souvenir of Canada*, the documentary, draws viewers into the world of Canadiana and that of the author/filmmaker, therefore defining Coupland himself as the quintessential Canadian. In fiction, Coupland takes a slightly different approach.

Instead of Canadian literature, Coupland perhaps considers his place among the writers of American literature a more adventurous bunch, presumably. Certainly, American

(20) critics have accepted him in their fold. In *Hybrid Fictions*, one of the few in-depth analyses of Coupland's work, for example, Daniel Grassian positions Coupland as an American writer of serious American fiction, to be classed among the American writers David Foster Wallace, Richard Powers, Neal Stephenson, William Vollmann, Sherman Alexie, Michele Serros, and Dave Eggers, all of whom, like the American Modernists

(25) before them, are not being sufficiently studied in their own time, according to Grassian. Grassian does admit that Coupland is Canadian (Canadian by birth, he adds in parentheses in the first of three such confessions), but he insists that despite this geographical aberration, Coupland's writing, even when it is based in Canada, appears almost indistinguishable from American fiction.

18.   The primary purpose of the passage is to

Ⓐ compare Coupland's writing to that of other Canadian authors

Ⓑ investigate whether it is accurate to classify Coupland's fiction as American literature

Ⓒ argue that Coupland, unlike his Canadian contemporaries, deserves to be studied like his American peers

Ⓓ discuss the merits of representing one's country through one's art

Ⓔ provide evidence supporting the opinion that Coupland's work can be classified as Canadian

19. The passage implies that which of the following statements is true?

    Indicate *all* that apply.

    A Canadian literature, despite its unique character, is inferior to American literature.
    B An artist's dismissal of his nationality is not sufficient reason to omit mention of it from criticism of his work.
    C Coupland's writing, due to its artistic merit, deserves further study.

20. Which of the following statements about Douglas Coupland is supported by the passage?

    Indicate *all* that apply.

    A Had Coupland been born in the United States, his work would have received more critical acclaim.
    B Coupland's work has not received the scholarly analyses that its breadth and value indicate.
    C Coupland's claim that his work should not be classified as Canadian is belied by the content of his work.

SECTION 3—QUANTITATIVE REASONING

TIME: 35 MINUTES—20 QUESTIONS

DIRECTIONS: For Questions 1 to 5, compare Quantity A and Quantity B, using the additional information given, if any, and select *one* of the following four answer choices:

Ⓐ Quantity A is greater.

Ⓑ Quantity B is greater.

Ⓒ The two quantities are equal.

Ⓓ The relationship cannot be determined from the information given.

s and t are positive integers greater than 1.

	Quantity A	Quantity B
1.	$s^{\frac{t}{4}}$	s^{t-4}

$$xy = \sqrt{99}$$

	Quantity A	Quantity B
2.	x^2	$\dfrac{99}{y^2}$

$a + 2b = 3$, and $a - b = 12$

	Quantity A	Quantity B
3.	a	b

The revenue, R, that a company earns from offering x promotional discounts is given by the function
$$R(x) = -2x^2 + 32x + 160.$$

	Quantity A	Quantity B
4.	The revenue earned from offering five discounts	The revenue earned from offering 11 discounts

A circle is inscribed in a square of perimeter 36.

Quantity A	Quantity B
The circumference of the circle	27

5.

DIRECTIONS: For Questions 6 and 7, enter your answer in the answer box below the question. Equivalent forms of the correct answer, such as 2.5 and 2.50, are all correct. Fractions do not need to be reduced to lowest terms.

---

6. In a triangle with perimeter equal to 24, the side lengths are three consecutive even integers. What is the triangle's area?

7. In a mixture of nuts, the ratio of almonds to cashews to peanuts by weight is 5:8:11. When 156 pounds of the mixture are made, how many pounds of peanuts are used?

lbs.

8. $400 is placed in an account earning an annual interest rate of 6%. If the account is compounded annually, how much more interest is earned in the second year than in the first?

   Ⓐ $1.22
   Ⓑ $1.33
   Ⓒ $1.43
   Ⓓ $1.44
   Ⓔ $1.54

9. Ann's tree is 76 inches tall and is growing at a rate of 3.6 inches per year. Bob's tree is 58 inches tall and is growing at a rate of 4.8 inches per year. In how many years will Bob's tree reach Ann's tree in height?

   Ⓐ 12
   Ⓑ 14
   Ⓒ 15
   Ⓓ 20
   Ⓔ 25

10. Sam's bowling scores for seven games were, in order played, 54, 35, 89, 76, 48, x, and y. Sam's mode score for the seven games was 76, and his median score was 54. If $x < y$, which of the following could be the value of x?

    Ⓐ 50
    Ⓑ 55
    Ⓒ 70
    Ⓓ 76
    Ⓔ 80

11. A sheet of rectangular paper measures 12 cm by 20 cm. At the edge of the paper, a margin exactly 1-cm wide is painted all the way around. What percentage of the area of the original rectangle remains *unpainted*?

    Ⓐ 95%
    Ⓑ 90%
    Ⓒ 85%
    Ⓓ 80%
    Ⓔ 75%

Questions 12 to 15 are based on the following data, which show the employment break-down of the 80 million person workforce in Country X in the year 2011 and the projected employment breakdown of the 120 million person workforce predicted for the country in the year 2050.

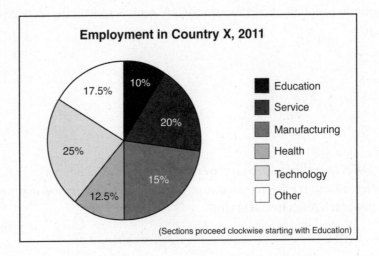

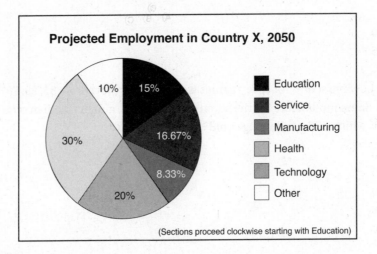

12.   How many more people are projected to be employed in the technology sector in 2050 than in 2011?

    Ⓐ 4 million
    Ⓑ 8 million
    Ⓒ 12 million
    Ⓓ 16 million
    Ⓔ 20 million

For Question 13, enter your answer in the grid below the question. Equivalent forms of the correct answer, such as 2.5 and 2.50, are all correct. Fractions do not need to be reduced to lowest terms.

13. In 2011, for every five people who worked in the health sector, n people worked in the service sector. What is the value of n?

14. For how many of the six employment categories shown will the total number of employees increase from 2011 to 2050?

Ⓐ two
Ⓑ three
Ⓒ four
Ⓓ five
Ⓔ six

15. The total number of people employed in education and manufacturing in the year 2050 will exceed by how many the total number of people employed in education and other in 2011?

Ⓐ 4 million
Ⓑ 5 million
Ⓒ 6 million
Ⓓ 7 million
Ⓔ 8 million

For Questions 16 to 18, consider each of the choices separately and select *all* that apply.

16. "A number squared is equal to at least twice the number." Which of the following numbers satisfy this statement?

Indicate *all* such numbers.

A 10^{-2}
B 0.9
C 1
D 2
E 3
F 10^8

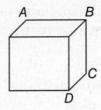

17. In the rectangular solid above, points A, B, C, and D are vertices, $AB = 8$, and all edges meet at right angles. Which of the following statements, *considered individually,* is sufficient to determine the volume of the solid?

Indicate *all* that apply.

- A The solid is a cube.
- B The area of one face of the solid is 64.
- C $BC = CD = AB$.
- D $BD = 8\sqrt{2}$, and triangle BCD is isosceles.
- E $AC = BD$.

18. If g is the function defined by $g(x) = \dfrac{(6x-3)(x+4)}{(x-1)(x+2)(x-3)}$, then $g(x)$ is *undefined* for which of the following values of x?

Indicate *all* that apply.

- A $\dfrac{1}{2}$
- B 1
- C -1
- D -2
- E 3
- F -4

For Questions 19 and 20, enter your answer in the grid below the question. Equivalent forms of the correct answer, such as 2.5 and 2.50, are all correct. Fractions do not need to be reduced to lowest terms.

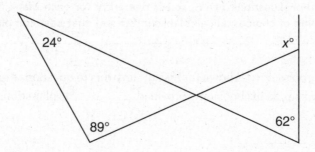

19. In the figure above, what is the value of x?

20. If $\sqrt{2x-3} = x-3$, then what is the value of x?

SECTION 4—VERBAL REASONING

TIME: 30 MINUTES—20 QUESTIONS

> **DIRECTIONS:** For Questions 1 to 6, select *one* entry for each blank from the corresponding column of choices. Fill all blanks in the way that best completes the text.

1. Just as our professor was known for his curt answers to questions during the discussion group, so his book only provided _____ explanations of most concepts.

Ⓐ liberal
Ⓑ summary
Ⓒ fractious
Ⓓ unhelpful
Ⓔ ambivalent

2. Although at first the couple's argument seemed to be about a _____ matter, it soon became obvious that their disagreement stemmed from a fundamental schism.

Ⓐ base
Ⓑ nugatory
Ⓒ officious
Ⓓ lucid
Ⓔ basal

3. I loved the way the movie conveyed its themes with (i) _____, but most critics argued that its subtleties would have been better portrayed in a more (ii) _____ way, so that its powerful message would be accessible to more people.

Blank (i)	Blank (ii)
Ⓐ gallantry	Ⓓ maladroit
Ⓑ vigor	Ⓔ circuitous
Ⓒ nicety	Ⓕ forthright

4. Film is now widely respected as a serious art form: even Westerns, once (i) _____ by most critics as patent escapism, are now commonly lauded as (ii) _____ of creative expression by even the most jaded reviewers.

Blank (i)	Blank (ii)
Ⓐ rhapsodized	Ⓓ exemplars
Ⓑ deflected	Ⓔ anomalies
Ⓒ derided	Ⓕ antitheses

5. That early factory owners extended benefits to female workers (i) _____ the theory that gender equality and the industrial revolution were two movements with (ii) _____ aims.

Blank (i)	Blank (ii)
Ⓐ bolstered	Ⓓ precarious
Ⓑ cheapened	Ⓔ preternatural
Ⓒ adulterated	Ⓕ complementary

6. Pathfinding in games must appeal to player expectations for (i) _____ and naturalness, that is, what natural intelligence might conceivably do. Thus, navigation in games is not necessarily (ii) _____ for maximum machine efficiency or for shortest distance. Indeed, these goals are assumed to be secondary and possibly even undesirable. That is, if they lead to unrealistic, mechanical-looking movement that is lacking in sensori-emotional or aesthetic qualities, movement as such (iii) _____ players and detracts from the game's replay appeal and immersive quality.

Blank (i)	Blank (ii)	Blank (iii)
Ⓐ plausibility	Ⓓ optimal	Ⓖ discomfits
Ⓑ artifice	Ⓔ permeable	Ⓗ abets
Ⓒ comfort	Ⓕ quixotic	Ⓘ emboldens

Question 7 is based on the following reading passage:

To encourage students to make healthier choices, a certain high school cafeteria stopped selling all sodas containing corn syrup. Despite this, a recent survey of the students at the school showed that soda consumption during school hours had risen by 15 percent compared to a survey taken before the cafeteria's change.

7. Which of the following, if true, best explains the contradiction present in the passage?

    Ⓐ In the month before the new survey, several billboards in the school's town displayed ads for popular brands of soda.

    Ⓑ The school's cafeteria, after removing the sodas with corn syrup, began offering sodas made from cane sugar at a lower price than the sodas made with corn syrup.

    Ⓒ Many families in the school district have at least one parent who works at the town's biggest employer, a soda distribution plant.

    Ⓓ In addition to buying sodas at the school cafeteria, students may also purchase sodas from one of the several vending machines on school property.

    Ⓔ To comply with state standards, the school recently implemented a new health program with a focus on nutrition.

Questions 8 and 9 are based on the following reading passage:

Standard model particle interactions obey typical conservation of momentum and energy laws as well as conservation laws. The model has been thoroughly probed and has led to spectacular results such as the precision measurement of the anomalous mag-
Line netic moment of the electron (analogous to measuring the distance between New York
(5) and Los Angeles to the width of a human hair). Despite its success, the standard model does not contain any particle that could act as the dark matter. The only stable, electrically neutral, and weakly interacting particles in the model are the neutrinos. Can the neutrinos be the missing dark matter? Despite having the "undisputed virtue of being known to exist" (as put so well by Lars Bergstrom), there is a major reason why neutrinos
(10) cannot account for all of the Universe's dark matter. A neutrino-dominated universe would have inhibited structure formation and caused a "top-down" formation (larger structures forming first, eventually condensing and fragmenting to those we see today). However, galaxies have been observed to exist less than a billion years after the Big Bang and, together with structure formation simulations, a "bottom-up" formation (stars gal-
(15) axies, then large galaxies, then clusters, etc.) seems to be the most likely. While neutrinos do account for a small fraction of dark matter, they clearly cannot be the only source.

For Question 8, consider each of the choices separately and select *all* that apply.

8. It can be inferred from the passage that a hypothesis using neutrinos for the missing dark matter in the standard model would include which of the following elements?

    Indicate *all* that apply.

    ☐ A A structural model of the universe in which the average distance between galaxies increased over time.

    ☐ B A justification for the "top-down" universe formation that includes a new weakly interacting particle.

    ☐ C An inconsistency regarding the conservation of energy when used for measurements at the atomic level.

9. It can be inferred that the author of the passage mentions "large galaxies" (line 15) primarily in order to

    Ⓐ explain another benefit of using the standard model to explain particle interaction
    Ⓑ identify a probable source of missing dark matter
    Ⓒ help account for the accuracy of the standard model in measuring distance
    Ⓓ indicate how cosmic structures have followed a model in which larger structures disintegrate
    Ⓔ point out a factor that contradicts a model using neutrinos as the universe's missing dark matter

Questions 10 and 11 are based on the following reading passage:

In the final decades of the nineteenth century, railroad expansion and a series of economic crises gave rise in the U.S. to a population of transient, marginally employed workers known as tramps (and later as hobos). The word tramp, which previously had
Line signified a journey taken on foot, now named a distinct social type and an object of
(5) public concern and debate. In the late nineteenth century, tramps were understood by middle- and upper-class Americans in terms of deviancy and criminality; but by World War II, the tramp had entered the realm of nostalgia. The primary reasons for tramping did not change; what changed was the social meaning assigned to the tramp. George M. Baker begins his 1879 novel *A Tight Squeeze* with the question "What is a
(10) tramp?" In detailing his protagonists' travels and observations, Baker provides a survey of common late-nineteenth-century understandings of the tramp. Rather than focusing on socioeconomic conditions, he points to individual character traits in explaining the existence of tramps. This sometimes takes the form of romanticization, as when Baker has his protagonist meet up with a Thoreauvian tramp who states, "I could tramp
(15) forever and forever, with Nature for a companion." More often, however, tramps appear as professional parasites, making up maudlin stories of distraught wives and starving children in order to cadge money off of naive but well-meaning marks. Tramps are also defined as drunkards: underlying the rambling propensities, nay, the very instigator of those propensities was the vice of drunkenness. Last but not least, tramps appear
(20) as recent immigrants with weak work habits, tramping without an object in view or an ambition to prompt them. Describing a crowd of tramps, Baker notes: "There were some Americans . . . but the majority were foreigners."

For Question 10, consider each of the choices separately and select *all* that apply.

10. Which of the following statements about Baker's *A Tight Squeeze* can be inferred from the passage?

    Indicate *all* that apply.

    A The tramps in Baker's novel are usually portrayed as criminals who have been victimized by economic forces beyond their control.
    B Characters in the novel with a propensity for tramping are less likely to be portrayed in a favorable light than are their marks.
    C In the novel, Baker attributes tramping to be an activity undertaken of one's own volition.

11. Select the sentence that uses personification to explain a motivation.

Question 12 is based on the following reading passage:

Many of the features of human cognition can be found in animals as well. These include perception, motor behavior, and memory. But there are also substantial differences between human and animal cognition. Animals, primates included, do not engage in
Line science or philosophy. These are unique human inventions. And yet, we do these things
(5) with a brain that has many features in common with animal brains, in particular that of mammals. These similarities are even more striking in case of the neocortex, which is in particular involved in cognitive processing. It is a task requiring some experience to tell a histological section of the mouse cortex from a human one. Now, it is hazardous to directly relate brain size to cognitive abilities. But the size of the neocortex is a different
(10) matter. There seems to be a direct relation between the size of the neocortex and cognitive abilities. For example, the size of the human neocortex is about four times that of chimpanzees, our closest relatives. This difference is not comparable to the difference in body size or weight between humans and chimpanzees.

12. According to the passage, which of the following is the main difference between a human neocortex and a chimpanzee neocortex?

    Ⓐ shape
    Ⓑ cellular structure
    Ⓒ ability
    Ⓓ histology
    Ⓔ memory

DIRECTIONS: For Questions 13 to 16, select the *two* answer choices that, when used to complete the sentence, fit the meaning of the sentence as a whole *and* produce completed sentences that are alike in meaning.

13. Businesses that merely embrace the status quo and that do not devote a sizable portion of their budgets to research and development are not likely to compete well against more _____ companies that are not afraid to take risks in order to grow.

   - A complacent
   - B aggressive
   - C established
   - D passive
   - E entrenched
   - F intrepid

14. Sunspots, now recognized by scientists as areas of reduced solar surface temperature that are caused by magnetic activity, were once thought to be planets due to the _____ of astronomical knowledge at that time.

   - A reversal
   - B obstruction
   - C lack
   - D scantness
   - E difficulty
   - F polarity

15. Due to the _____ amount of information that most people are deluged with on a daily basis, it is vital to develop a keen eye for what is important and for what can be filtered out.

   - A copious
   - B scarce
   - C exacting
   - D profuse
   - E censored
   - F sparse

16. It is far from apparent and in fact somewhat doubtful that consumers will benefit if state and local governments continue to _____ small businesses, making it possible for those companies to avoid paying more than a modicum of taxes.

   - A rarefy
   - B arbitrate
   - C castigate
   - D propitiate
   - E coddle
   - F decry

Question 17 is based on the following reading passage:

Most car manufacturers now offer hybrid vehicles: cars and trucks, which use both standard gasoline and electricity to power their engines. Therefore, consumers who drive hybrid vehicles are using less gasoline now than before these manufacturers began offering hybrid cars and trucks.

17.   Which of the following, if true, most strengthens the argument?

Ⓐ Hybrid vehicles generally have higher horsepower than non-hybrid vehicles.

Ⓑ Hybrid manufacturers use less gasoline in their manufacturing equipment than non-hybrid manufacturers do.

Ⓒ Most hybrid vehicles get the majority of their power from gasoline combustion.

Ⓓ The number of miles driven in a hybrid vehicle that are attributable to electricity is greater than the equivalent number of miles that could have been driven with the gasoline used to create that electricity.

Ⓔ More electrical power is used driving a hybrid vehicle than an equivalent non-hybrid vehicle.

Questions 18 to 20 are based on the following reading passage:

As is the case with Vernon's first two novels *Eden* (2002) and *Logic* (2004), *A Killing in This Town* comes to readers straight from Vernon's thoughts and pen. In this way, the novel suffers from a certain randomness of development that is likely to frustrate the reader who expects to find a lucidly outlined and logically progressive, even if modernist, plot. Indeed, most of Vernon's writing could benefit from more narrative discipline. Not so paradoxically, however, is the fact that it is through this rejection of narrative discipline and, conversely, through a commitment to a kind of raw artistry that the novel achieves its authenticity.

18.   Which of the following can be inferred from the passage regarding Vernon's *A Killing in This Town*?

Ⓐ Unlike Vernon's earlier work, *A Killing in This Town* suffers from structural problems that may confound readers.

Ⓑ Among Vernon's novels, *A Killing in This Town* stands out as the primary example of her artistry due to its raw subject matter.

Ⓒ *A Killing in This Town* has a narrative structure that both adds to the novel's worth and detracts from its accessibility.

Ⓓ Given its modernist authenticity, *A Killing in This Town* deserves more scholarly attention than it has currently received.

Ⓔ Many reviewers of *A Killing in This Town* have found the novel's structure problematic.

19. In the first sentence ("As is the . . . pen."), the author of the passage is most likely suggesting that

Ⓐ Reviewers of Vernon's novels have benefited from her willingness to forsake a more traditional writing process.

Ⓑ *A Killing in This Town* will outshine her earlier work in terms of critical acclaim.

Ⓒ Vernon will eventually receive more recognition for her narrative structure than for her novels' content.

Ⓓ In lieu of mapping out her novels' plots, Vernon instead opts for a more improvisational writing approach.

Ⓔ To best understand *A Killing in This Town*, it is important to study Vernon's earlier novels.

20. Which of the following best describes the main issue that the author of the passage is addressing?

Ⓐ the lack of narrative development in *A Killing in This Town*

Ⓑ how Vernon uses death as a metaphor in *A Killing in This Town*

Ⓒ whether *A Killing in This Town* is worthy of further critical attention

Ⓓ the relationship between Vernon's earlier novels and her current work

Ⓔ the nature of narrative development in *A Killing in This Town*

TIME: 35 MINUTES—20 QUESTIONS

> **DIRECTIONS:** For Questions 1 to 5, compare Quantity A and Quantity B, using the additional information given, if any, and select *one* of the following four answer choices:
>
> Ⓐ Quantity A is greater.
> Ⓑ Quantity B is greater.
> Ⓒ The two quantities are equal.
> Ⓓ The relationship cannot be determined from the information given.

For the unknown constants a, b, c, d, and e,
$abc = 0$; $bcd = 12$; $cde = 0$.

	Quantity A	Quantity B
1.	a	e

	Quantity A	Quantity B
2.	$\left(\sqrt{3}+\sqrt{3}+\sqrt{3}\right)^2$	$\left(\sqrt{54/2}\right)^2$

$$x^4 = 81;\ 8y^3 = 64$$

	Quantity A	Quantity B
3.	x	y

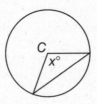

The area of the circle above,
with center C, is 36π, and $x > 90$.

	Quantity A	Quantity B
4.	The area of the triangle	18

S is the set of all integer multiples of 999.

T is the set of all integer multiples of 9,999.

Quantity A	Quantity B
The number of elements in the intersection of sets S and T	9

5.

DIRECTIONS: For Questions 6 to 20, select *one* answer choice unless otherwise instructed.

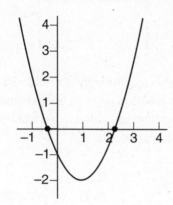

6. A graph of the function $g(x)$ is shown above. $g(x)$ is defined by which of the following equations?

    Ⓐ $g(x) = (x + 1)^2 - 2$
    Ⓑ $g(x) = (x - 1)^2 - 2$
    Ⓒ $g(x) = (x + 1)^2 + 2$
    Ⓓ $g(x) = (x - 1)^2 + 2$
    Ⓔ $g(x) = (x - 2)^2 + 1$

7. A student's average test score in algebra is 88 after eight tests have been taken. When the teacher drops the student's two lowest test scores, the student's average score increases to 92. What is the average score of the two tests that were dropped?

    Ⓐ 72
    Ⓑ 74
    Ⓒ 75
    Ⓓ 76
    Ⓔ 78

8. The sum of the first 100 positive integers is how much greater than the sum of the first 80 positive integers?

    Ⓐ 905
    Ⓑ 1,800
    Ⓒ 1,805
    Ⓓ 1,810
    Ⓔ 1,820

9. In the xy-plane, the distance between the point $P(1,3)$ and $Q(9,y)$ is 17. If $y > 0$, then what is the value of y?

    [ ]

10. The weights of python snakes are normally distributed with a mean of 110 kg and a standard deviation of 8 kg. If 68% of pythons weigh within one standard deviation of the mean and 95% of pythons weigh within two standard deviations of the mean, what percent of pythons weigh from 94 to 102 kg?

    Ⓐ 47.5%
    Ⓑ 34%
    Ⓒ 27%
    Ⓓ 17%
    Ⓔ 13.5%

For Questions 11 to 14, enter your answer in the grid below the question. Equivalent forms of the correct answer, such as 2.5 and 2.50, are all correct. Fractions do not need to be reduced to lowest terms.

11. How many $2 \times 4 \times 6$ boxes will fit in a $14 \times 16 \times 18$ storage locker? (The boxes and locker are rectangular solids, and all units are in feet.)

    [ ]

12. Let m be the 1,003rd digit to the right of the decimal point in the repeated decimal expansion $0.\overline{13579}$, and let n equal the 78th digit to the right of the decimal point in the repeated decimal expansion $0.\overline{2468}$. What is the value of m^n?

13. A jar contains 30 red marbles, 40 blue marbles, 50 green marbles, and no other marbles. After x blue marbles are added to the jar, the probability of selecting a blue marble on a random draw is equal to $\frac{7}{9}$. What is the value of x?

14. At School Y, 60% of all students are male, and 40% of all male students are transfer students. If two students at the school are selected at random from the entire student body of 25 students, what is the probability that both students will be male transfer students?

For Questions 15 through 17, consider each of the choices separately and select *all* that apply.

15. If $\frac{4n^2}{15}$ is an integer, then which of the following *could be n*?

Indicate *all* that apply.

A −75
B −9
C 4
D 135

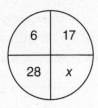

16. Four numbers are placed in the number circle above so that one number is equal to the sum of the other three. Which of the following *could be* the value of *x*?

Indicate *all* that apply.

A 5
B 17
C 39
D 51
E 2,856

Questions 17 to 20 are based on the following data, which shows the amount of money that an average student at College Z spent on tuition, rent, and food from the year 2007 through the year 2010. Figures at left are in dollars.

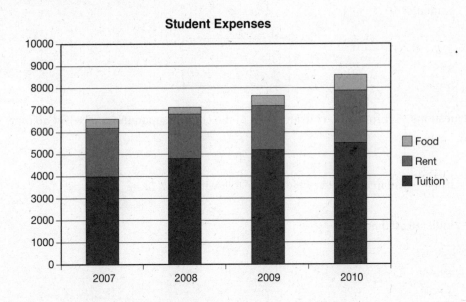

Student Expenses

17. The data supports which of the following statements for the period shown?

Indicate *all* that apply.

A The average student's tuition expenses increased each year.
B The average student's rent expenses increased each year.
C The average student's total expenses for food, rent, and tuition combined increased each year.

18. In which year did the average student spend less on food than in the previous year?

(A) 2007

(B) 2008

(C) 2009

(D) 2010

(E) None of the above

19. By approximately what percent did the average student's tuition increase from 2007 to 2010?

(A) 25%

(B) 27%

(C) 35%

(D) 38%

(E) 41%

20. Considering the costs of *tuition and rent only*, the average student's expenses increased by an average of how much *per year* over the period shown?

(A) $450

(B) $500

(C) $550

(D) $600

(E) $650

ANSWER KEY
Practice Test 1

Section 2: Verbal Reasoning

1. **C**
2. **A**
3. **B, D**
4. **A, D**
5. **A, E**
6. **A, E, H**
7. **A, B**
8. **Sentence 3**
9. **B**
10. **C**
11. **B, C**
12. **B**
13. **B, F**
14. **B, D**
15. **C, F**
16. **C, E**
17. **B**
18. **E**
19. **B**
20. **C**

Section 3: Quantitative Reasoning

1. **D**
2. **C**
3. **A**
4. **C**
5. **A**
6. **24**
7. **71.5**
8. **D**
9. **C**
10. **A**
11. **E**
12. **D**
13. **8**
14. **C**
15. **C**
16. **D, E, F**
17. **A, C, D**
18. **B, D, E**
19. **129**
20. **6**

Section 4: Verbal Reasoning

1. **B**
2. **B**
3. **C, F**
4. **C, D**
5. **A, F**
6. **A, D, G**
7. **B**
8. **A**
9. **E**
10. **B, C**
11. **Sentence 8**
12. **C**
13. **B, F**
14. **C, D**
15. **A, D**
16. **D, E**
17. **D**
18. **C**
19. **D**
20. **E**

Section 5: Quantitative Reasoning

1. **C**
2. **C**
3. **D**
4. **B**
5. **A**
6. **B**
7. **D**
8. **D**
9. **18**
10. **E**
11. **84**
12. **625**
13. **240**
14. **.05 or $\frac{1}{20}$**
15. **A, D**
16. **A, D**
17. **A, C**
18. **B**
19. **D**
20. **D**

ANSWER EXPLANATIONS

Section 2—Verbal Reasoning

1. **(C)** If the cynical belief that everyone just wants profit is thought of as realistic, then it would make sense that *altruism* (helping others) would be an *aberration* (something unusual).

2. **(A)** If the investors are looking for a stable place for their funds, the *volatility* (unpredictability) of the index would *confound* (confuse and frustrate) them.

3. **(B, D)** If the fabrication was once *implausible* (unimaginable), the first sentence makes sense, since that fabrication is now possible. The third sentence talks about the *surfeit* (oversupply) of manufacturers driving down prices, so it makes sense for the second sentence, which is continued by the third with no shifts in direction, to be talking about the same thing—a *glut* (oversupply).

4. **(A, D)** Since without further context both choices (A) and (C) could fit blank (i), it makes sense to begin with blank (ii). The architects are *utilitarian* (only focused on the useful), and they discard *embellishments* (decorations); their style could therefore be termed *ascetic* (severely simple in appearance), especially since given the clue "to the point that," which indicates "to an extreme level." The contrast to such a style would be *ornateness* (decorativeness).

5. **(A, E)** The word *despite* signifies an upcoming shift or contradiction in the sentence. Looking at the choices, *melodrama* (excessive drama) and *maudlin* (overly sentimental) create that shift, because, with those words in the sentence, the actor does something that contradicts what he claims to believe. Knowing the definition of *antithesis* (opposite) helps here.

6. **(A, E, H)** It is easiest to start with blank (ii): if the works were once only collected by a few and now sell for thousands of dollars, then *approbation* (approval) fits. Accordingly, blank (i) should also be complimentary to the art, so *esteem* (high regard) is logical. Blank (iii) should maintain the positive light in which these works are regarded, and if the works *supplant* (replace) old ones, such a tone is supported.

7. **(A, B)** Choice (A) is correct. The researchers studying the Anadarko group had a functional understanding of the signs used by the delegation of tribes because, as the passage mentions, they were able to ascertain that the signs used had a degree of uniformity, a judgment that would have been impossible if they didn't have a working understanding of the signs. Choice (B) is also correct. Since the passage uses qualifying language like "nearly uniform" when describing the signs and says that they were unified "to a certain extent," it can be inferred that at least some of the signs used by delegation members differed significantly from those used by other members.

8. **(Sentence 3: However, the individuals who gave the signs . . . heterogeneity)** Most of the passage is concerned with describing the similarities between different tribes' signs, but the author compares sign language to spoken language in Sentence 3, saying that signs can have "the unification so often observed in oral speech."

9. **(B)** The idea "gained currency" because of the reasoning given later in the sentence, so the word "acceptance" could be substituted for "currency" in this context. The idea gained support.

10. **(C)** If the researchers are calling the explanation a "useful way to tie" things together, it makes sense that "hailed" means *lauded* (praised) in this context.

11. **(B, C)** Like any trait that current organisms possess, conspicuous markings must exist because organisms with them are the offspring of previous generations that survived long enough to reproduce. By saying that there is a "trade-off" in terms of color function, the author implies that any trait would not exist unless it had a corresponding benefit to the organism's survival, and therefore, its reproduction. He also implies that conspicuous markings may be detrimental to an organism, contrasting them with *cryptic* (camouflaging) markings, giving further evidence that being conspicuous must help an organism breed, (B). Choice (C) is also supported by this reasoning.

12. **(B)** By saying that an organism's color is an "adaptive function," the author implies that its color can help the organism in different ways at different times, which supports the assertion that these demands may be "competing," i.e., a color that helps with one demand may be unhelpful for another.

13. **(B, F)** If even the politician's *ardent* (passionate) supporters are unsure of his position, he must not be very clear. *Equivocate* (communicate to allow multiple interpretations) and *vacillate* (waver) both convey the politician's lack of clarity.

14. **(B, D)** The word *but* indicates that the critic's review will be in contrast to his private insistence. Both *extolled* (praised) and *celebrated* create the necessary shift.

15. **(C, F)** Since the professor cannot write simply and clearly, his directions must be the opposite of those characteristics. It is thus logical that his directions are *obfuscated* (made unclear) or *obscured* (hidden) by *ambiguity* (lack of clarity).

16. **(C, E)** If scientists have trouble collecting data due to the brief time span, it follows that the bursts are either *transient* (short-lived) or *fleeting*. The use of "bursts" also conveys a short time span.

17. **(B)** The first portion in boldface makes a claim, or assertion, that "**in the southern hemisphere this effect is intensified**." The second portion provides another assertion that *qualifies*, or restricts, the earlier assertion, by giving a reason that compensates for the sun's greater intensity, i.e., that the southern summer is shorter.

18. **(E)** In paragraph 2, the author provides examples of Coupland's work and says that it "give(s) language to the Canadian experience." He also subtly mocks Grassian, who seems to classify Coupland's fiction as American, which implies that the author disagrees with that classification.

19. **(B)** The author begins with a description of Coupland claiming that his work should not be characterized as Canadian, but then provides evidence that Coupland's work helps create a Canadian identity that is therefore, essentially, Canadian. The word "yet" signifies a shift from Coupland's dismissal.

20. **(C)** In the second paragraph, the author says that by exploring and extending Canadian culture through his writing, Coupland has, ironically, made his work a part of Canadian literature even though he dismisses said literature as of inferior quality. In other words, his claim is *belied* (contradicted) by his work's content.

Section 3—Quantitative Reasoning

*Indicates an alternative way to solve the problem.

1. **(D)** Think of s as a constant, such as 2 or 3, and replace t with various values. If $t = 100$, then Column A reads s^{25}, while Column B reads s^{96}, and Quantity (B) is much greater. If $t = 4$, then Column A becomes s^1, which equals s, while Column B reads s^0, which equals 1, and this time Quantity (A) is greater. Therefore, (D) is correct, since it is possible to make either quantity greater.

2. **(C)** Start with the given equation, $xy = \sqrt{99}$ and divide both sides by y to obtain $x = \dfrac{\sqrt{99}}{y}$. Now square both sides: $x^2 = \dfrac{\sqrt{99}^2}{y^2} = \dfrac{99}{y^2}$. Thus, the two quantities are equal, (C).

3. **(A)** Line up the two given equations vertically, and then subtract to eliminate the variable a, remembering to distribute the negative sign across the second equation:

$$\begin{array}{r} a + 2b = 3 \\ -(a - b = 12) \\ \hline 3b = -9 \end{array}$$

Divide this last equation, $3b = -9$, by 3 on each side, and $b = -3$. Now substitute this value of b into either given equation, say the second, to obtain the value of a. So $a - (-3) = 12$, which means $a + 3 = 12$, yielding $a = 9$. Because $9 > -3$, (A) is greater.

4. **(C)** Obtain the revenue for five discounts by putting in 5 as x into the given function $R(x) = -2x^2 + 32x + 160$. Then $R(5) = -2(5)^2 + 32(5) + 160$. The order of operations dictates that squaring comes before multiplying in the first term, so $R(5) = -50 + 160 + 160 = 270$. Find the revenue from offering 11 discounts similarly. $R(11) = -2(11)^2 + 32(11) + 160 = -242 + 352 + 160 = 270$, and the quantities are equal, (C).

*When a quadratic equation is in the form $y = ax^2 + bx + c$, it graphs as a parabola in the xy-plane, with the parabola's axis of symmetry given by the formula $x = \dfrac{-b}{2a}$.

Here, the axis of symmetry is $x = \dfrac{-32}{2(-2)} = 8$.

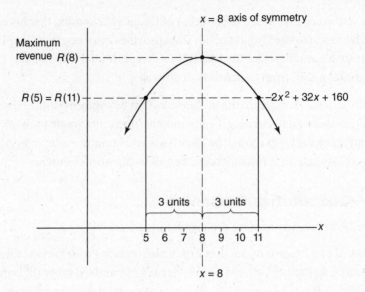

Since the value $x = 5$ is 3 units to the left of the symmetry line, while the value $x = 11$ is 3 units to the right of the symmetry line, the y-values associated with these points must be equal, and (C) is correct.

5. **(A)** Divide the square's perimeter by 4 to obtain the length of one side. $36 \div 4 = 9$. Draw the diameter of the circle and note that this also equals the square's side length, 9.

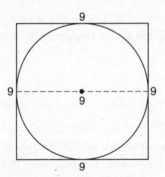

Then the circle's circumference, given by $\pi \times diameter$, equals 9π. Since $\pi > 3$, $9\pi > 9 \times 3 = 27$ and (A) is greater.

6. **(24)** Three consecutive even integers can be represented by x, $x + 2$, and $x + 4$. Set the sum of these side lengths equal to the perimeter: $x + x + 2 + x + 4 = 24$. Combining like terms yields $3x + 6 = 24$. Subtract 6 from both sides, and $3x = 18$, so $x = 6$. This means that the three side lengths are 6, 8, and 10, which you can also obtain with a guess-and-check approach, since $4 + 6 + 8$ equals only 18, but $6 + 8 + 10 = 24$.

If we knew that this were a right triangle, we could treat 8 as the base and 6 as the height, and the triangle's area, given by $\frac{1}{2} \times$ base $\times$ height, would equal $\frac{1}{2} \times 6 \times 8 = 24$.

We can verify that the triangle is, in fact, right by noting that $6^2 + 8^2 = 10^2$ (since $36 + 64 = 100$), which means that the side lengths satisfy the Pythagorean relationship $a^2 + b^2 = c^2$. Then the area *is* 24, by coincidence matching the perimeter.

7. **(71.5)** Start by writing the ratios in an easy-to-read form, using the first letter of each type of nut.

    A:C:P
    5:8:11

    There are 11 pounds of peanuts for every $5 + 8 + 11 = 24$ pounds of the nut mixture. This means that peanuts are $\frac{11}{24}$ of the total weight. Then a 156 pound mix contains $\frac{11}{24} \times 156 = 71.5$ pounds of peanuts.

8. **(D)** In year one, the account earned 6% of $400 in interest. That is, $.06 \times 400$, or $24. When the interest is "compounded," this $24 is reinvested in the account, which will then hold $400 + 24 = \$424$. In year two, the interest is 6% of $424, or $.06 \times 424$, which equals $25.44. The year two interest is greater by $25.44 - 24 = \$1.44$, (D).

9. **(C)** Set up a linear equation to model each tree's growth. Let x be the number of years, and let y, the dependent variable, represent the height of the tree as it varies over time. For Ann's tree, $y = 3.6x + 76$; for Bob's, $y = 4.8x + 58$. When the trees' heights are equal, the y values in each equation will be equal, so we can set $3.6x + 76$ equal to $4.8x + 58$. Then, group like terms together by subtracting $3.6x$ and 58 from both sides:

    $$\begin{array}{r} 3.6x + 76 = 4.8x + 58 \\ -3.6x - 58 \quad -3.6x - 58 \\ \hline 18 = 1.2x \end{array}$$

    Finally, divide both sides by 1.2 to obtain $x = 15$, (C).

10. **(A)** The *mode* of a list is the *most* frequently recurring number on the list. Since 76 is the mode, 76 must appear at least twice on the list. So at least one of the unknown scores must equal 76.

    The *median*, or middle value on a list, is found by first rewriting the given numbers in order from least to greatest. Here, after inserting the second 76, we know these 6 scores: 35, 48, 54, 76, 76, 89.

    ▲

    Since the median is given as 54, draw a triangle below the 54, and think of that as the balancing point. There are three values to the right of the triangle but only two to the left. Therefore, the final missing score must be less than 54, to ensure that 54 is in the middle. Only choice (A), 50, works. Thus, the two missing scores are 50 and 76, and since the problem asks for the smaller of these, (A) is correct.

11. **(E)**

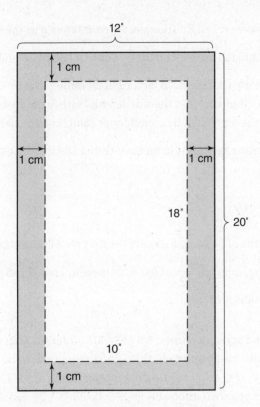

The original area of the 12 by 20 page was $12 \times 20 = 240$ cm². When a 1-cm margin is painted around the edge of the paper, the length and width of the unpainted region are each reduced by 2 cm, because the paint covers both the top and bottom of the page, as well as the left and right of the page. Therefore, the unpainted region now measures $(12 - 2)$ by $(20 - 2)$, or 10 by 18, and its area is $10 \times 18 = 180$ cm². This means that $\frac{180}{240} \times \frac{18}{24} = \frac{3}{4}$, or 75% remains unpainted, (E).

12. **(D)** In 2011, the technology sector consists of 25% of 80 million people, which is 20 million people. In 2050, technology represents 30% of 120 million people, which is $.30 \times 120$ million, or 36 million people. The increase is $36 - 20 = 16$ million people, (D).

13. **(8)** In 2011, the ratio of health employees to service employees was 12.5%:20%, or $\frac{12.5}{20}$. Multiply the top and bottom of the fraction by 2 to create an equivalent ratio of integers, $\frac{25}{40}$. Now divide the numerator and denominator by 5, the greatest common factor of 25 and 40 to obtain the reduced ratio of $\frac{5}{8}$. This means that for every five health employees there were 8 service employees.

14. **(C)** Be careful. The total number of employees increases from 80 million to 120 million between 2011 and 2050, so a decrease in percentage for a category *could* correspond to an increase in actual workers. For example, the service sector in 2011 contains 20% of 80 million employees, which is 16 million employees, while in 2050, the percentage drops to 16.67%, but $.1667 \times 120$ million ≈ 20 million employees, a net increase. In addition to the service sector, the health, technology, and education sectors also see an increase in the number of employees (a higher percentage of a higher total), so there are four such categories in all, (C).

15. **(C)** In 2050, the education and manufacturing sectors account for $15\% + 8.33\% = 23.33\%$ of the 120 million total employees. This equals $.2333 \times 120$ million ≈ 28 million employees. In 2011, education and other account for $10\% + 17.5\% = 27.5\%$ of the 80 million total employees. This equals $.275 \times 80$ million $= 22$ million employees. The first figure exceeds the second by $28 - 22 = 6$ million (C).

16. **(D, E, F)** The question asks, when is $n^2 \geq 2n$. Since we are only considering positive values of n, we can divide both sides by n to obtain $n \geq 2$. Thus, the statement is satisfied for values of n greater than or equal to 2, (D), (E), and (F).

    *10^{-2} means $\dfrac{1}{10^2} = \dfrac{1}{100} = .01$. (A) and (B) are not correct because squaring 0.01 or 0.9 yields an even smaller value, certainly not "at least twice the number." (C) is not correct because $1^2 = 1$, whereas twice 1 equals 2. (D) is correct, because $2^2 = 4$, which is exactly twice 2, or 2×2, and a number is at least equal to itself. (E) and (F) are correct, because if $n > 2$, then $n^2 = n \times n > n \times 2$.

17. **(A, C, D)** (A) is sufficient because if the solid is a cube, the volume can be found by cubing the side length 8. That is, volume would equal 8^3. (B) is not sufficient because the face with area 64 might have dimensions of, say, 16×4 or 32×2, producing solids of varying volumes. (C) is sufficient because if $BC = CD = AB = 8$, the volume will equal $8 \times 8 \times 8 = 8^3$, *length times width times height.* (D) is sufficient, because in an isosceles right triangle (45-45-90 triangle), it is possible to determine all three side lengths from knowing just one. The leg lengths always equal the length of the hypotenuse divided

    by $\sqrt{2}$. Here, BC and CD would both equal $\dfrac{8\sqrt{2}}{\sqrt{2}} = 8$, and again we know the length,

    width, and height of the solid. (E) is not sufficient, because there is no way to determine the solid's height. The vertical length BC can be stretched to any height, producing varying volumes, but as long as $CD = 8$, AC will remain equal to BD as given. (See diagram.)

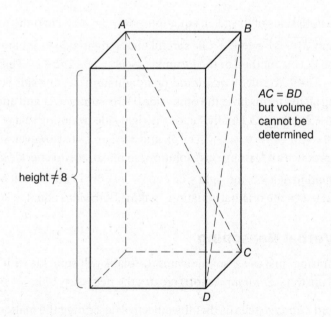

AC = BD
but volume
cannot be
determined

height ≠ 8

The answer is (A), (C), and (D).

18. **(B, D, E)** The numbers that make $g(x)$ undefined are numbers that make the denominator equal to 0, because division by 0 is not defined. The product $(x-1)(x+2)(x-3)$ will equal 0 when any of the individual factors equals 0, because zero times anything equals zero. Then either $x-1=0$, $x+2=0$, or $x-3=0$, and x could equal 1, –2, or 3, choices (B), (D), and (E).

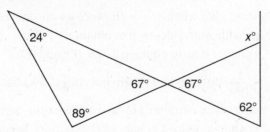

19. **(129)** First, compute the missing angle in the left-hand triangle, by subtracting the two known angles from 180°. $180 - 24 - 89$ yields 67°. Because "vertical angles" are congruent, the angle directly across from this one also measures 67°. Two angles are now known in the right-hand triangle, and we can compute its third angle as $180 - 67 - 62$, which equals 51°.

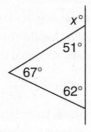

Finally, the two adjacent angles that make up a straight line add up to 180°, so $x = 180 - 51 = 129$.

20. **(6)** Square both sides of the given equation, $\sqrt{2x-3} = x-3$, in order to get rid of the square root: $\left(\sqrt{2x-3}\right)^2 = (x-3)^2$. Be careful on the right-side to square the binomial by using the F.O.I.L. method or the formula $(a-b)^2 = a^2 - 2ab + b^2$. This yields $2x-3 = x^2 - 6x + 9$. To solve a *quadratic*, or x^2, equation, set one side equal to zero first, by grouping all the terms onto the other side. Here, subtract $2x$ and add 3 to both sides to obtain: $0 = x^2 - 8x + 12$. Finally, factor the right side by noting that -6×-2 equals 12, while $-6 + -2 = -8$. So $0 = (x-2)(x-6)$, and $x = 2$ or $x = 6$. However, squaring both sides may produce an "extraneous" solution, so make sure to check each result in the original equation. If $x = 2$, the right side equals $\sqrt{4-3} = 1$, but the left equals $2 - 3 = -1$. Only $x = 6$ satisfies the original equation, making both sides equal to 3.

Section 4—Verbal Reasoning

1. **(B)** The phrasing "just as . . . so" indicates the blank will coincide with the professor's *curt* (brief) answers. *Summary* (short) creates the necessary link.

2. **(B)** The word *although* tells us that the adjective describing the matter will be different than the description in the second part of the sentence, which explains that the

disagreement is from a *fundamental* (foundational) schism, or split. Therefore, *nugatory* (trivial) makes sense.

3. **(C, F)** Start with the second blank. If the critics wanted the movie to be accessible to more people, then *forthright* (direct) would fit blank (ii). The word *but* signifies a shift, so *nicety* (understatement) works for blank (i).

4. **(C, D)** If critics once categorized Westerns as *patent* (obvious) escapism, then using *derided* (ridiculed) for blank (i) to describe that criticism would make sense. And, if those films are now *lauded* (praised), then only *exemplars* (ideal models) fits blank (ii).

5. **(A, F)** Looking at the relationship between the two blanks helps on this question. If the blank (i) was a word like "supported," blank (ii) would have to be a word like "similar." Or, if blank (i) was a word like "weakened," blank (ii) would be something like "different." Looking at the choices, only *bolstered* (supported) and *complementary* (shared in a helpful way) create a workable relationship.

6. **(A, D, G)** Blank (i) is explained by looking at the rest of the sentence after the blank. The word "and" implies continuation, so the right answer should go along with "naturalness," and should match "what natural intelligence might . . . do." *Plausibility* (believability) is a good match. Blank (ii) is clarified by looking at the next sentence, which says "these goals are . . . secondary and . . . undesirable." Therefore, they are not *optimal*, or ideal. Blank (iii) must be a negative word to go along with "detracts," and so *discomfits* (frustrates) is the only possible choice.

7. **(B)** If the students can now buy sodas for less money, it would explain why their soda consumption would increase.

8. **(A)** The author says that "a neutrino-dominated universe would have . . . caused a 'top-down' formation," and then follows by explaining that, in a top-down formation, larger structures would have formed, then broken apart, supporting the statement that the average distance between galaxies would grow as time passed.

9. **(E)** The mention of large galaxies is part of the author's description of a sequence of events in the "bottom-up" theory, which he claims to explain the universe and which he uses to argue against a model using neutrinos as the main source of dark matter.

10. **(B, C)** The author says that, in the novel, "tramps appear as professional parasites . . . (that) cadge money off of . . . well-meaning marks," which supports choice (B). Choice (C) is also supported by this depiction, as well as by the descriptions that follow, where tramps are "defined as drunkards" and as "immigrants with weak work habits"—all supporting the idea that tramping is done of one's own *volition* (will).

11. **(Sentence 8: This sometimes takes . . . companion.)** The "Thoreauvian" tramp explains that he "could tramp forever and forever, with Nature for a companion." In doing so, he personifies (gives human qualities to) Nature to explain his reason for being a tramp.

12. **(C)** The author says that there is "a direct relation between the size of the neocortex and cognitive abilities." Since the author also says that the size of a human neocortex is quadruple that of a chimpanzee's, the ability of a human neocortex is the biggest difference.

13. **(B, F)** The main clue for the blank is that the companies described after the blank "are not afraid to take risks," implying they are *aggressive* or *intrepid* (bold). The other clue is that the businesses that embrace the *status quo* (the way things are) will not compete well against the later-mentioned companies.

14. **(C, D)** If sunspots were, in the past, incorrectly thought to be planets, there must have been a *lack* or *scantness* (insufficient quantity) of knowledge at that time compared to the knowledge available now.

15. **(A, D)** The clues given for the blank are *deluged* (overwhelmed) and the implication that people should filter out certain information. This makes sense if people receive *copious* (large) or *profuse* (abundant) amounts of information.

16. **(D, E)** Since the governments are allowing the businesses to merely pay a *modicum* (small portion) of taxes, they must be continuing to *propitiate* (gain the favor of) or *coddle* (treat with excessive kindness) them.

17. **(D)** The argument is that drivers now use less gasoline than they did before the advent of hybrid vehicles. Knowing that the number of miles driven in a hybrid vehicle that was powered by electricity *exceeds* the number that could have been driven with the gasoline used to make the electricity strengthens the argument. It explains that more miles come from that electricity, proving that hybrid vehicles use less gas than conventional cars and trucks.

18. **(C)** In the second sentence of the passage, the author implies that the novel is not clearly outlined or logically structured and says that these qualities may frustrate readers. In the last sentence, the author claims that its lack of structure helps it "achieve(s) its authenticity," which indicates the author believes that the structure also adds to the novel's worth.

19. **(D)** The second sentence provides help to interpret the first, since in it, the author talks about *A Killing in This Town*'s lack of structure. The first sentence also implies that Vernon decided to improvise rather than plan the novel.

20. **(E)** Throughout the passage, the author talks about the novel's structure. Although the author complains about the "randomness" of its development, this is a comment on the nature of the narrative development rather than a comment on the lack of development.

Section 5—Quantitative Reasoning

*Indicates an alternative way to solve the problem.

1. **(C)** The *zero product property* states that when several numbers multiply to equal zero, one of the individual numbers must equal zero. From the first equation, one of the unknowns, *a, b,* or *c* must be 0. But *b* and *c* both appear in the second equation, which shows that *bcd* equals 12, a non-zero value. So neither *b*, nor *c*, nor *d* can equal zero, and therefore, in the first equation, *a* must have been the variable equal to zero. A similar analysis of the second and third equations reveals that *e* = 0. So *a* = 0 = *e*, and the quantities are equal, (C).

2. **(C)** In column A, work within the parentheses first. $\left(\sqrt{3}+\sqrt{3}+\sqrt{3}\right)^2 = \left(3\sqrt{3}\right)^2$, which equals 9×3, because $(ab)^2 = a^2b^2$. So Quantity (A) is 27. In column B, simplify under the radical first. $\frac{54}{2} = 27$, so Quantity (B) $= \left(\sqrt{27}\right)^2 = 27$, and the quantities are equal, (C).

Remember that squaring and taking a square root are inverse operations, so squaring a radical generally yields the value underneath the radical.

*Simplify column A to $\left(3\sqrt{3}\right)^2$ and column B to $\left(\sqrt{27}\right)^2$. In column B, $\sqrt{27} = \sqrt{9 \times 3} = 3\sqrt{3}$, so the quantities must be equal because the values inside the parentheses, before squaring, are both $3\sqrt{3}$.

3. **(D)** First, try to find a number which multiplied by itself four times equals 81. Observe that $81 = 9 \times 9$, and that $9 = 3 \times 3$, so that $81 = 3 \times 3 \times 3 \times 3 = 3^4$, so $x = 3$ satisfies the first equation. Next, solve for y by dividing both sides of the second equation by 8 to obtain $y^3 = 8$, and $y = 2$ (since $2 \times 2 \times 2 = 8$). It may seem that if $x = 3$ and $y = 2$, then (A) is greater, but recall that a negative number raised to an even power is positive. Here, $(-3)^4$ also equals 81, so x could equal 3 or -3. Since $3 > 2$, but $-3 < 2$, (D) is correct.

4. **(B)** Use the formula for the area of a circle, area $= \pi r^2$. Since the area is given as 36π, we know $\pi r^2 = 36\pi$. Now look for cancellation! Dividing both sides by π yields $r^2 = 36$ and $r = 6$. Because the radius is 6, two sides lengths of the triangle equal 6. If x were equal to 90, then the triangle would be a right triangle and its area, given by $\frac{1}{2} \times$ base $\times$ height, would equal $\frac{1}{2} \times 6 \times 6$, or 18.

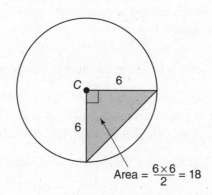

Area $= \frac{6 \times 6}{2} = 18$

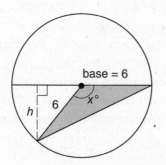

$x > 90$, so height $h < 6$.

Triangle Area $< \frac{6 \times 6}{2} = 18$

But we are given $x > 90$, which makes the height of the triangle less than 6 and the area less than 18, so (B) is greater. Notice that in an obtuse triangle, when the base is a side adjacent to the obtuse angle, then the altitude drawn for the purposes of computing area lies outside the triangle and is smaller than the side it intersects.

5. **(A)** It may be easier to think about this problem with smaller numbers. For example, if set S contained the multiples of 3—3, 6, 9, 12, 15, 18 . . .—and set T contained the multiples of 5—5, 10, 15, 20, 25 . . .—then the intersection, or overlap, of the two sets would be the set of all multiples of 15. This set—15, 30, 45, 60 . . .—continues indefinitely and is infinite. In general, if one set consists of all multiples of m and another set consists of all multiples of n, then the intersection of the two sets will contain all multiples of the integer, mn, which is an infinite set, as long as neither number is 0. Infinity is greater than 9, so (A) is correct.

6. **(B)** The easiest approach is to substitute the xy-coordinate values of points on the curve into the functions given in the answer choices, to see which choice produces the proper y-value for a given x-value. Begin with the vertex, an important point on a parabola, given here by the coordinates $(1, -2)$. If the equation of the parabola is $g(x)$, then $g(1)$ must equal -2. In choice (B), $g(1) = (1-1)^2 - 2 = 0 - 2 = -2$. No other choice contains a function such that $g(1) = -2$.

    *The function given in choice (B), $g(x) = (x-1)^2 - 2$, represents a transformation of the common function, $f(x) = x^2$, whose graph in the xy-plane is a parabola pointed upward with vertex at the origin $(0, 0)$. Replacing x with $(x-1)$ causes a horizontal translation 1 unit to the right, and subtracting 2 causes a vertical translation 2 units down. Since the graph depicted has been shifted 1 unit to the right and 2 units down from the origin, (B) is correct.

7. **(D)** $88 \frac{\text{points}}{\text{test}} \times \text{tests} = 704$ points that the student scored in total on all eight tests combined. When two scores are dropped, six remain, and the total points for six tests at the new average of 92 points per test is equal to $6 \times 92 = 552$. The sum of the points that were dropped must account for the difference $704 - 552$, or 152 points. Finally, the average of the two dropped tests is their sum, 152, divided by 2, or $\frac{152}{2} = 76$, (D).

8. **(D)** The sum of the first 80 positive integers means $1 + 2 + 3 \ldots + 79 + 80$. The sum of the first 100 positive integers is $1 + 2 + 3 \ldots + 79 + 80 + 81 \ldots 100$. There is much duplication on the two lists, and the second exceeds the first exactly by the sum $81 + 82 + 83 \ldots + 100$. One way to complete the problem would be to add those 20 numbers on your calculator to obtain 1,810, (D). Since this risks a typing error, it is helpful to know how to quickly add numbers in an *arithmetic series*, one in which all terms are separated by a constant difference, such as $5 + 8 + 11 + 14 + 17$, or $81 + 82 + 83 \ldots + 100$. Simply find the typical term by averaging the first and last terms, and multiply this by the number of terms. Here, $\frac{81+100}{2} \times 20 = \frac{181}{2} \times 20 = \frac{181}{1} \times 10 = 1,810$, answer (D) again, more quickly and efficiently.

9. **(18)**

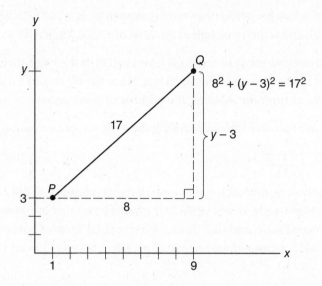

First, draw the picture. The horizontal distance between the two points is the difference of their x-coordinates, $9 - 1 = 8$. The diagonal distance between the points, given as 17, forms the hypotenuse of a right triangle, with one leg of length 8 and one of length $(y - 3)$. By the Pythagorean theorem, $(y - 3)^2 + 8^2 = 17^2$. Using the onscreen calculator, we find that $(y - 3)^2 = 289 - 64 = 225$. Now take the square root of each side, noting that only the positive solution need be considered, because $y > 0$. Then

$\sqrt{(y-3)^2} = \sqrt{225}$, and $y - 3 = 15$, so $y = 18$.

10. **(E)**

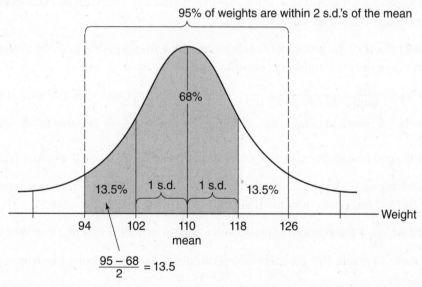

If 68% of pythons weigh within 1 standard deviation of the mean and 95% weigh within 2 standard deviations of the mean, then the difference 95% – 68% = 27% weigh between 1 and 2 standard deviations from the mean. Here, each standard deviation equals 8 kg, so 1 to 2 standard deviations correspond to 8 to 16 kg. Pythons weighing from 8 to 16 kg from the mean of 110, would have weights in either the interval 94 to 102, if they are below average, or in the interval 118 to 126, if they are above average.

The question asks what percentage weigh between 94 and 102 kg, which matches the lower interval, and is therefore half of the 27%, or 13.5%, choice (E).

11. **(84)** To find out how many of the small boxes will fit in the large, divide the volume of the large box by the volume of the small box. Since the volume of a rectangular solid is the product of its three dimensions, the number of boxes equals

$\frac{14 \times 16 \times 18}{2 \times 4 \times 6}$. We can save time by reducing the fractions before multiplying:

$\frac{14 \times 16 \times 18}{2 \times 4 \times 6} \rightarrow \frac{7 \times 4 \times 3}{1 \times 1 \times 1} = 7 \times 12 = 84$.

*Another equivalent approach is to reason that seven boxes that are 2 feet across will fit across a 14-foot-wide locker, while four rows of boxes that are 4 feet deep will fit in the 16-foot-deep locker, and that this 7×4 rectangular array of boxes can be stacked three levels high, because three boxes that are 6 feet tall will fit in an 18-foot-tall locker. $7 \times 4 \times 3 = 84$.

12. **(625)** The bar above the digits to the right of the decimal point means that those digits repeat forever. Begin to write the first sequence and look for a pattern: .135791357913579. . . . Notice that the 5th, 10th, and 15th digits are all 9, suggesting that any digit that is a multiple of 5 to the right of the decimal will equal 9. Then the 1,000th digit will be a 9, and the 1,003rd digit will be three digits after this, a 5. In the other number, .246824682468 . . . , the pattern contains four digits before repeating. Notice that the 4th, 8th, and 12th digits are all 8. We again see that any multiple of the pattern length will be the last digit of the pattern—that is, any digit a multiple of 4 to the right of the decimal point will be an 8. This means that the 76th digit is an 8, because 76 is a multiple of 4, since $76 = 19 \times 4$. Then the 78th digit will be two digits after this, a 4. Then m^n equals $5^4 = 625$.

13. **(240)** Think of the probability of choosing a blue marble as the number of blue marbles out of the total number of marbles. Initially we have

$P(\text{blue}) = \frac{\text{blue}}{\text{total}} = \frac{40}{30 + 40 + 50} = \frac{40}{120}$. If we add x blue marbles, this will add to the number of blue and to the total, so $P(\text{blue})$ becomes $\frac{40 + x}{120 + x}$. Set this result equal to the desired probability and then cross-multiply: $\frac{40 + x}{120 + x} = \frac{7}{9}$. So $9(40 + x) = 7(120 + x)$.

Distribute on both sides, and $360 + 9x = 840 + 7x$. Combine like terms by subtracting $7x$ and 360 from both sides to obtain $2x = 480$. Divide by 2, and $x = 240$.

14. **(.05 or $\frac{1}{20}$)** The number of male students at the school is 60% of 25, or $.60 \times 25 = 15$.

Of these 15 males, 40% are male transfer students. So there are $.4 \times 15 = 6$ male transfer students.

To find the probability that two randomly selected students will be in this group of six out of 25, we can reason, "The first student selected must be a male transfer AND the second student must be a male transfer." The AND requires you to multiply the two probabilities. The first probability is simply $\frac{6}{25}$, but if one male transfer student is selected, there will be only five such students remaining to choose from, out of 24 students in all. Then the second probability is $\frac{5}{24}$, and the probability of both students being in this group is $\frac{6}{25} \times \frac{5}{24}$. You can find the product on your calculator, or perhaps faster by hand by cross-canceling: reduce 6 with 24 and 5 with 25 to obtain $\frac{1}{5} \times \frac{1}{4} = \frac{1}{20}$ or .05.

15. **(A, D)** Recall that an integer is a positive or negative whole number with no fractional part: . . .–3, –2, –1, 0, 1, 2, 3. . . . When the quantity $4n^2$ is divided by 15, the result will be an integer whenever $4n^2$ contains as factors all prime number factors of 15, namely 3 and 5. Choices (A) and (D) satisfy this condition, because $75 = 3 \times 5^2$, and $135 = 3^3 \times 5$. Choice (B), $n = -9$, does not work; 9 is not divisible by 5, so $4n^2$ will not be divisible by 5 or by 15. (C) does not work; if $n = 4$, then 3 and 5 are not factors of n or of $4n^2$. So $4n^2$ will not be divisible by 15, and division will produce a non-integer value. You can also evaluate these quantities directly by using your calculator to plug in the numbers in the answer choices. For example, if $n = 4$, then $\frac{4n^2}{15} = \frac{64}{15} \approx 4.267$, is not an integer. Ignore the negative signs when entering your numbers; they are not relevant to this problem and will disappear when squaring.

16. **(A, D)** *Sum* implies addition, so this problem requires the three numbers in the circle to add up to the fourth. One possibility is $x = 6 + 17 + 28$, and $x = 51$. Another possibility is for 28, the largest given number, to equal the sum of the other three. Then $x + 6 + 17 = 28$. So $x = 28 - 23 = 5$. The answer is (A) and (D).

17. **(A, C)** Tuition is the bottom part of each bar, which grew each year, so (A) is correct. Rent is the middle part of each bar. In 2007, rent spans more than two horizontal lines and is thus greater than $2,000. In 2008, rent spans fewer than two horizontal lines, and is thus less than $2,000. So rent decreased from 2007 to 2008, and (B) is not correct. (C) is correct, because rent plus food plus tuition equals the height of the full bar, which clearly grew each year. The answer is (A) and (C).

18. **(B)** Compare the sizes of the top part of each bar, food, and notice that this is smallest in 2008. So in 2008, (B), food expenses were less than in the previous year.

19. **(D)** Tuition, the bottom part of each bar appeared to increase from $4,000 to $5,500 from 2007 to 2010. Find the percent change by computing the amount of change, the difference of the two numbers, and dividing this by the original or starting value. Here, we have $\frac{5,500 - 4,000}{4,000} = .375$. This is the answer in decimal form. Multiply by 100, or shift the decimal two places mentally to obtain 37.5%, approximately 38%, (D).

20. **(D)** The underlined words, *tuition* and *rent*, comprise the bottom two parts of the bar. The phrase "over the period shown" suggests that we should compare the heights of these bars in the first and last years depicted, 2007 and 2010. In 2007, the lower two parts of the bar measure just above $6,000, say $6,100, while in 2010 this height is just below $8000, say $7900. Then the overall increase in tuition plus rent is $7,900 - 6,100 = \$1,800$. The change occurs in a three-year span (2010 – 2007 = 3), so the per year average increase is $\frac{1,800 \text{ dollars}}{3 \text{ years}} = 600 \frac{\text{dollars}}{\text{year}}$, (D).

Practice Test 2

SECTION 1—ANALYTICAL WRITING

TIME: 60 MINUTES—2 WRITING TASKS

TASK 1: ISSUE EXPLORATION

TIME: 30 MINUTES

The topic is presented in a one- to two-sentence quotation commenting on an issue of general concern.

Your essay will be judged on the basis of your skill in the following areas:

- response to the specific task instructions
- consideration of the complexities of the issue
- organization, development, and expression of your ideas
- support of your position with relevant reasoning and examples
- control of the elements of standard written English

TOPIC

Technology causes more problems for modern societies than it solves.

DIRECTIONS: Write a response in which you discuss the extent to which you agree or disagree with the claim. In developing and supporting your position, be sure to address the most compelling reasons and/or examples that could be used to challenge the position.

TASK 2: ARGUMENT ANALYSIS

TIME: 30 MINUTES

Your essay will be judged on the basis of your skill in the following areas:

- identification and assessment of the argument's main elements
- organization and articulation of your thoughts
- use of relevant examples and arguments to support your case
- handling of the mechanics of standard written English

TOPIC

The following appeared as part of a letter to the editor of a scientific journal:

A new study of a colony of meerkats provides insights into the effects of dominance on a male meerkat's levels of testosterone. The study showed that the dominant male of the meerkat colony had blood levels of testosterone that were, on average, about double those of the colony's non-dominant males. Alpha, or dominant, male dogs also have higher levels of testosterone than non-dominant males. The study also found that the male offspring of dominant male meerkats were born with higher testosterone levels than male offspring of non-dominant males.

DIRECTIONS: Write a response in which you discuss one or more alternative explanations that could rival the proposed explanation and explain how your explanation(s) can plausibly account for the facts presented in the argument.

SECTION 2—VERBAL REASONING

TIME: 30 MINUTES—20 QUESTIONS

> **DIRECTIONS:** For Questions 1 to 6, select *one* entry for each blank from the corresponding column of choices. Fill all blanks in the way that best completes the text.

1. The anthropologist discovered that because direct insult in the society carried with it a high risk of physical conflict, most slights were _____ rather than spoken.

Ⓐ	averred
Ⓑ	allayed
Ⓒ	dispersed
Ⓓ	purported
Ⓔ	insinuated

2. In a world where technological impasses are hurdled with greater and greater rapidity, it comes as no surprise that any given _____ does not merit much concern.

Ⓐ	quagmire
Ⓑ	discernment
Ⓒ	fecundity
Ⓓ	misinterpretation
Ⓔ	imperilment

3. Despite the typical characterization of art forgery as the realm of the (i) _____, some recent papers have underscored the artistry present in counterfeit pieces and ignored or made light of the inherent criminality. Needless to say, many critics have (ii) _____ these papers, saying their authors lack the ethics and good sense to be taken seriously.

Blank (i)		Blank (ii)	
Ⓐ	craven	Ⓓ	lambasted
Ⓑ	reprobate	Ⓔ	extolled
Ⓒ	covetous	Ⓕ	eulogized

4. In assaying the quality of a high school's academic curriculum, it has become commonplace and even (i) _____ to discredit the people who argue in favor of more progressive subjects. Indeed, those who most (ii) _____ criticize "new-age" administrators are often the most heralded among their peers.

Blank (i)	Blank (ii)
Ⓐ fortuitous	Ⓓ incisively
Ⓑ outmoded	Ⓔ lamely
Ⓒ fashionable	Ⓕ jocosely

5. It is unsurprising that the recent (i) _____ of historical novels is due to the fragmenting of some of our traditional historical narratives. New documents have acted as amplifiers for heretofore unheard voices, and many authors have (ii) _____ the opportunity to turn a light toward some of the darker corners of the past.

Blank (i)	Blank (ii)
Ⓐ want	Ⓓ forsaken
Ⓑ rash	Ⓔ misapprehended
Ⓒ void	Ⓕ recognized

6. Improvement in the quality of basic demographic data and the care with which it is managed may yield more (i) _____ information as time moves forward, which will greatly enhance the ability to prove and disprove extreme age claims. Given human nature, however, and a number of the modern and historic sources of age misreporting, age validation will continue to need to be (ii) _____ part of valid exceptional longevity research. Even areas thought to have complete birth registration have seen problems with immigrant cases, unreported deaths, pension fraud, and the like. The older the alleged age of a longevity claim, the more (iii) _____ must be the validation procedure.

Blank (i)	Blank (ii)	Blank (iii)
Ⓐ veritable	Ⓓ an ineffable	Ⓖ consummate
Ⓑ incredulous	Ⓔ a requisite	Ⓗ cavalier
Ⓒ incredible	Ⓕ a dire	Ⓘ antiquated

Question 7 is based on the following reading passage:

Syndrome Z, a degenerative bone disease, is most commonly found in cows raised in Country A. Recently, it was theorized that the syndrome was caused by those cows' exposure to pesticides that are only used in Country A, since few of the cows in Country B tested positive for the syndrome. However, this fact does not indicate that the pesticides are responsible for the syndrome because _____.

7. Which of the following most logically completes the passage?

Ⓐ it was discovered that horses can also develop Syndrome Z

Ⓑ there was at least one case of Syndrome Z in an area in Country A where a lower amount of the pesticides was used

Ⓒ a few of the cows in Country A died due to massive pesticide poisoning after eating pesticide-tainted feed

Ⓓ Syndrome Z only shows signs after about 3 years, and most of the cows in Country B are slaughtered for meat within the first 3 years of their lives

Ⓔ the pesticides thought to be responsible for Syndrome Z are organic

Questions 8 to 11 are based on the following reading passage:

Creativity is a frequent element in the mythology, philosophy, or religion of many cultures, and it is fair to say that it is a malleable concept that has fascinated mankind for centuries. Among a manifold of definitions, creativity can be defined as a cognitive
Line process to generate novel or unconventional solutions. This cognitive process relies on
(5) two essential mechanisms: (i) divergent thinking, which generates original, new ideas and (ii) convergent thinking, which logically evaluates a variety of possible solutions to find the optimal one. For instance, philosophers such as Pythagoras and the Pythagoreans contemplated beauty as an objective principle that maintains harmony, order, and balance. From beauty, however, it is only a small step to creativity—people admire
(10) the beauty of artifacts of various kinds but very often these artifacts are the product of a creative process undertaken by an artist. And, creativity and beauty are not restricted to the liberal arts only. Many theories in science are considered to be the outcome of an equally creative process and people often mention the elegance or beauty of a theory. In the more recent mid-1980s, for instance, science encountered a discourse with
(15) beauty and the creative forces in nature through chaos theory, the inspirational field of science that captured, among many other things, the dynamic of natural systems in images, called fractals, of astonishing beauty.

Creativity has had strong ties to computing for some time. The goal of web design, for instance, is not to add to the functionality of an application but to make an applica-
(20) tion aesthetically pleasing and accessible to its users. This does not mean that the production of computer code is a mundane task: on the contrary, many regard good coding as a highly creative activity. As another example, take the field of humanoid robotics where the physical appearance of a robot, its gestures, or its tone of voice may have an

impact on user acceptance, e.g., in health care. Computational creativity, which is a
(25) relatively young field, relates to many of these issues. The field, which by its very nature is a multidisciplinary scientific endeavor, carries the vision to better understand
human creativity and to construct, via computers and intelligent algorithms, artifacts
demonstrating human-level creativity or tools that are able to support the creative processes of humans.

For Question 8, consider each of the choices separately and select *all* that apply.

8. The passage indicates that the philosopher Pythagoras would agree with which of the
following statements?

Indicate *all* that apply.

A Beauty and creativity are essentially the same concept.
B Beauty is a principle unaffected by interpretations of it that are conflicting.
C A person's well-being will be supported if he watches a beautiful sunset or
    witnesses an act of kindness.

9. In the first paragraph of the passage, the author is primarily concerned with

Ⓐ summarizing the views of an important historical figure
Ⓑ analyzing the contradictions inherent in a hypothesis
Ⓒ drawing a parallel between two concepts
Ⓓ discussing the applications of a concept
Ⓔ establishing a system of classification

10. The author implies that which of the following is a likely argument from a reader in
response to an assertion in the passage?

Ⓐ Web pages should be visually appealing as well as easy to use.
Ⓑ It is unlikely that robots, no matter how technologically advanced, will ever take
    the place of nurses.
Ⓒ Though remarkable for its beautiful images, chaos theory has few scientific
    applications.
Ⓓ Applying wisdom learned from ancient philosophers to modern computing is
    problematic.
Ⓔ Though computational creativity produces useful creative tools, working in the
    field can be monotonous.

11. It can be inferred from the passage that the author believes which of the following
could be a likely result of computational creativity?

Ⓐ A popular web page that has several new features added to it.
Ⓑ An automated cash machine that dispenses cash 50% faster than its predecessor.
Ⓒ A new mobile phone that becomes part of a work of modern art.
Ⓓ A robot that can dispense the appropriate medication to a hospital patient.
Ⓔ An algorithm that successfully models the frequency of ocean waves.

12. The king's advisor, though lately reviled for his fawning behavior, was, in the past, criticized for his _____ manner.

   A humble
   B imperious
   C servile
   D domineering
   E disinterested
   F subservient

13. The first advocates of electrically powered vehicles were so _____ in their praise that they failed to anticipate what were, in retrospect, obvious consequences of battery disposal.

   A stringent
   B diffident
   C retiring
   D immoderate
   E strict
   F effusive

14. Since the compound called ATP is essential in allowing cells to create energy, it follows that its production is _____ component to cellular function.

   A a prerequisite
   B a trivial
   C a negligible
   D a notorious
   E an indispensable
   F an infamous

15. The novel, once widely banned for what was thought of as _____ subject matter, is now accepted and even celebrated for the passages that contain salacious details about a love affair.

   A unwholesome
   B salutary
   C prurient
   D salubrious
   E macabre
   F nightmarish

Question 16 is based on the following reading passage:

The theoretical justification of the link between customer satisfaction and national consumption is quite obvious. Customer satisfaction is a driver of consumption expenditure because it measures the quality of economic output. When consumers are satisfied
Line with their previous purchases, their willingness to spend increases and vice versa. In
(5) this regard, customers' views on satisfaction are perhaps more reliable than consumer confidence indicators as the former are based on actual experience with products while the latter relies on perception. Similarly, actions taken by firms to improve satisfaction and policies that ensure that firms allocate sufficient resources to this action are more easily monitored compared to efforts to raise consumer sentiments. One produces
(10) direct results while the other is still dependent on the whims and fancies of the consumer.

16. Select the sentence that uses a previously stated assertion to support a further assertion.

Questions 17 to 19 are based on the following reading passage:

Ozone has potential negative impacts on human health and vegetation, and also acts as an important greenhouse gas. Background ozone levels in western Ireland have shown a steady increase over the past two decades. During the same period, the relative
Line contribution to these increasing ozone levels from air over the North Atlantic has also
(5) significantly grown. Deposition of ozone to surface ocean waters via physical uptake and chemical reactions in the surface layer likely constitute a significant, albeit highly variable "buffer" curtailing the rate of ozone increase in this region. Past tests have shown the ocean surface to be adept at absorbing ozone from the surrounding air. But researchers have recently completed studies that show that the ocean near the coast of
(10) western Ireland has surprisingly low levels of ozone at the surface.

17. Which of the following, if true, best reconciles the apparent discrepancy presented in the passage?

Ⓐ Certain corn plants have been shown to have a higher yield in areas with a greater ozone concentration than normal.

Ⓑ Historical ozone measurements in Ireland were made with an outdated, less accurate methodology.

Ⓒ Ozone levels in the North Atlantic, though higher than the world average, have been shown to have no harmful effects on birds native to that region.

Ⓓ Ozone, once absorbed by the surface of the ocean, can migrate to surrounding environments.

Ⓔ Once the ozone concentration in a region reaches a certain level, it is difficult for that region to retain more ozone.

18.   In the context in which it appears, "adept" (line 8) most nearly means

Ⓐ proficient
Ⓑ adaptable
Ⓒ inept
Ⓓ mundane
Ⓔ deficient

19.   The author of the passage mentions the background ozone levels in western Ireland primarily in order to

Ⓐ provide context in which to consider the findings of the recent studies
Ⓑ argue in favor of curtailing processes that add greenhouse gases to the environment
Ⓒ indicate that western Ireland is a unique region in that its ozone concentration has risen steadily over the years
Ⓓ assert that the buffering effect of the ocean in the region may be due to surface temperature
Ⓔ support the correlation between the ocean's buffering effect and the levels of background ozone in western Ireland

Question 20 is based on the following reading passage:

Component H, a crucial part of the motherboard in a popular new laptop computer, is thought to require an operating temperature of below 70 degrees Celsius to function optimally. Recent tests, however, have shown that Component H performs quite well at temperatures up to 80 degrees Celsius. Therefore, if **Component H is the most heat-sensitive component in the laptop**, it may be possible to lower the laptop's battery use by reducing its fan speed. **Users would then enjoy more battery life without damage to their laptops.** But further tests are necessary, since Component K, another part of the new laptop, has not been tested at temperatures above 70 degrees Celsius due to the previous restrictions for Component H.

20.   In the argument, the two **boldfaced** portions play which of the following roles?

Ⓐ The first is an assertion that the argument argues against; the second is the position supported by the argument.
Ⓑ The first supports the position that the argument argues against; the second is that position.
Ⓒ The first provides reasoning for the position the argument opposes; the second provides additional support for that position.
Ⓓ The first is the argument's position; the second is the position that the argument argues against.
Ⓔ The first is a rebuttal of the argument's position; the second is the argument's position.

SECTION 3—QUANTITATIVE REASONING

TIME: 35 MINUTES—20 QUESTIONS

DIRECTIONS: For Questions 1 to 5, compare Quantity A and Quantity B, using the additional information given, if any, and select *one* of the following four answer choices:

Ⓐ Quantity A is greater.

Ⓑ Quantity B is greater.

Ⓒ The two quantities are equal.

Ⓓ The relationship cannot be determined from the information given.

S is the set of all test scores in Ms. K's class.
T is the set of all test scores in Ms. K's class, after
Ms. K added 10 points to every test score in the class.

	Quantity A	Quantity B
1.	The standard deviation of set S	The standard deviation of set T.

Three-fourths of a cup of dry rice cooked with five-fourths of a cup of
water is sufficient to feed eight people one portion of rice each.

	Quantity A	Quantity B
2.	The number of people who can be fed one portion of rice with six cups of dry rice and an unlimited supply of water	65

---

p is the probability that a school's hockey team wins today.
s is the independent probability that the school's lacrosse team wins today.
p and s are not both equal to 0.

	Quantity A	Quantity B
3.	$p + s$	ps

$$0 < w < x < y < 100$$

	Quantity A	Quantity B
4.	$100 - y$	$y - w$

The cost of ten hot dogs and nine pretzels is $74.15.

The cost of nine hot dogs and ten pretzels is $74.05.

Quantity A	Quantity B
The cost of one hot dog	The cost of one pretzel

5.

DIRECTIONS: For Questions 6 to 20, select *one* answer choice unless otherwise instructed.

---

6. If $\dfrac{4-x}{x-2} = \dfrac{-3}{x}$, then x could equal which of the following?

   Ⓐ 10
   Ⓑ 9
   Ⓒ 8
   Ⓓ 7
   Ⓔ 6

7. In the xy-plane, the center of a circle is located at $(-8, -11)$. The point $(-8, -8)$ lies inside the circle, and the point $(-11, -7)$ lies outside the circle. If the circle's radius is an integer, what is its area?

   Ⓐ 4π
   Ⓑ 9π
   Ⓒ 16π
   Ⓓ 25π
   Ⓔ 36π

8. Rectangle A measures 12 m wide by x m long and has an area equal to the area of Rectangle B, which measures 30 m wide by 48 m long. What is the perimeter of Rectangle A?

   Ⓐ 120 m
   Ⓑ 156 m
   Ⓒ 248 m
   Ⓓ 264 m
   Ⓔ 1,440 m

9. At 12:00 noon, a pool is $\dfrac{3}{25}$ full. It is being filled at a constant rate of 2 gallons per minute. At 2:30 PM, the pool is 28% full. How many gallons does the full pool hold?

   Ⓐ 1,875
   Ⓑ 1,925
   Ⓒ 1,975
   Ⓓ 2,025
   Ⓔ 2,075

For Questions 10 to 12, enter your answer in the grid below the question. Equivalent forms of the correct answer, such as 2.5 and 2.50, are all correct. Fractions do not need to be reduced to lowest terms.

10. An inheritance is to be divided with Heir A receiving 35%, Heir B receiving 30%, Heir C receiving 25%, and Heir D receiving the remaining $840. How much money does Heir A receive?

$

11. If $x = 10^{-1}$, what is the value of $(3+x)(3-x)\left(\dfrac{1}{x}\right)$?

12. A four-sided die is labeled with the letters A, B, C, and D, one letter per side. When the die is rolled, each letter has an equal probability of landing face down. If the die is rolled three times, what is the probability that the letters landing face down spell out the word "B-A-D" in order? (Enter your answer as a fraction.)

Questions 13 to 16 are based on the following data, which shows the percentage of revenue earned from three different categories of product sold by four different grocery stores. Figures at left are percentages. Each store received revenue only from the three categories depicted: Beverages, Packaged Food, and Prepared Food.

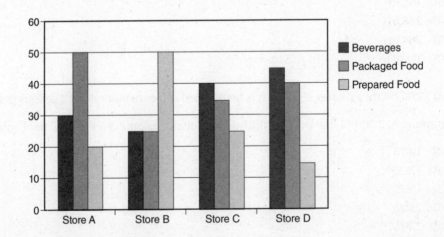

For Question 13, enter your answer in the grid below the question. Equivalent forms of the correct answer, such as 2.5 and 2.50, are all correct. Fractions do not need to be reduced to lowest terms.

13. The store with the highest percentage of revenue from packaged food earned $980 in revenue from packaged food. How much did it earn from beverages?

$ [   ]

14. What is the ratio of revenue from prepared food to revenue from packaged food for the store whose beverages accounted for the highest percentage of earned revenue?

Ⓐ 3:8
Ⓑ 8:3
Ⓒ 2:1
Ⓓ 1:2
Ⓔ 2:5

15. How many stores earned at least as much revenue from one category of product sold as from the other two categories of products combined?

Ⓐ 0
Ⓑ 1
Ⓒ 2
Ⓓ 3
Ⓔ 4

16. If all four stores earned exactly the same amount of total revenue, what percentage of the total revenue of the four stores combined came from beverages?

Ⓐ 27.5%
Ⓑ 30%
Ⓒ 35%
Ⓓ 37.5%
Ⓔ 40%

For Questions 17 and 18, consider each of the choices separately and select all that apply.

17. John bought one book and paid the price marked inside the book plus sales tax with a $20 bill. He received exact change, which was less than $5. The sales tax was 9% of the book's marked price. Which of the following must be true?

Indicate all that apply.

A The marked price of the book was more than $13.50.
B The marked price of the book was less than $18.50.
C The sales tax on the book was less than $1.50.

18. The set S is the set of all *odd* integers, and a and b are two elements of set S, with $b > 0$. Which of the following must also be an element of set S?

Indicate *all* that apply.

- A $a + b$
- B $a - b$
- C ab
- D $a \div b$
- E a^b

For Questions 19 and 20, enter your answer in the grid below the question. Equivalent forms of the correct answer, such as 2.5 and 2.50, are all correct. Fractions do not need to be reduced to lowest terms.

19. A man driving for 8 hours at 59 miles per hour travels how many miles farther than a woman driving for 6 hours at 49.5 miles per hour?

 miles

20. The function $f(x) = \left(x - \dfrac{1}{2}\right)^2$ is graphed in the xy-plane. The x-intercept of the graph is $(a, 0)$. The y-intercept of the graph is $(0, b)$. What is the value of ab?

SECTION 4—VERBAL REASONING

TIME: 30 MINUTES—20 QUESTIONS

> **DIRECTIONS:** For Questions 1 to 6, select *one* entry for each blank from the corresponding column of choices. Fill all blanks in the way that best completes the text.

1. As expected, the archaeological dig uncovered only _____ tools; the ancient tribe being studied had been known to have only primitive hunting and gathering skills.

Ⓐ callous
Ⓑ recalcitrant
Ⓒ intractable
Ⓓ intangible
Ⓔ rudimentary

2. After the board meeting, it became apparent that the union's opposition to more restrictive regulations had strengthened, making implementation of those regulations more _____.

Ⓐ transparent
Ⓑ challenging
Ⓒ fluid
Ⓓ intelligible
Ⓔ unnecessary

3. The (i) _____ manner by which the poet conducted his personal life lay in sharp contrast to his public persona: on a brightly lit stage, in front of an appreciative crowd, he displayed (ii) _____ that cheered even the gloomiest souls.

Blank (i)	Blank (ii)
Ⓐ methodical	Ⓓ a despondency
Ⓑ morose	Ⓔ an enormity
Ⓒ meagerness	Ⓕ a jocundity

4. In the current economic climate, it has become (i) _____ to posit that savvy job-seekers ought to establish at least a year's worth of experience at any given position, so as to demonstrate their (ii) _____ to future employers. Indeed, those who make this suggestion often quote each other in the media in what essentially amount to congratulatory, self-serving articles. Yet these so-called (iii) _____ often betray their lack of expertise by then suggesting the omission of jobs that do last less than one year from a job-seeker's resume.

Blank (i)	Blank (ii)	Blank (iii)
Ⓐ vital	Ⓓ steadfastness	Ⓖ dilettantes
Ⓑ problematic	Ⓔ peversity	Ⓗ pundits
Ⓒ popular	Ⓕ vigor	Ⓘ stalwarts

5. That the student's progress report highlighted his (i) _____ nature failed to draw much ire from his parents, for, despite his habitual lateness, his grade point average was (ii) _____.

Blank (i)	Blank (ii)
Ⓐ dilatory	Ⓓ middling
Ⓑ lackadaisical	Ⓔ exemplary
Ⓒ irreverent	Ⓕ profound

6. The (i) _____ of dissociative disorder sections in commonly used general psychiatric screening instruments has led to the (ii) _____ of dissociative disorders in large-scale epidemiological studies for many decades. Although studies using specific instruments have begun to correct this lack, the inclusion of testing for dissociative disorders in future general psychiatric screening studies is (iii) _____ for prevention of false negative diagnosis in future research, will facilitate better differential diagnosis between dissociative and other psychiatric disorders, and will also help to gather detailed information.

Blank (i)	Blank (ii)	Blank (iii)
Ⓐ dearth	Ⓓ acquittal	Ⓖ debatable
Ⓑ abundance	Ⓔ justification	Ⓗ fundamental
Ⓒ confounding	Ⓕ omission	Ⓘ incongruous

Questions 7 to 9 are based on the following reading passage:

Writing any history of the Revolutionary War and its effects on national identity requires entering into a conversation layered with some of the most powerful and enduring narratives and interpretative frameworks of the historical profession. It also
Line means acknowledging recent Native American histories and challenges from Atlantic
(5) World and African Diaspora studies that assert alternatives to the understanding of our national origins. Liam Riordan, in his work *Many Identities, One Nation: The Revolution and Its Legacy in the Mid-Atlantic*, acknowledges these challenges and his relationship to a third category of analysis: the parochial context of community studies that often is overlooked in favor of a more national scope. With these predominate narratives in
(10) mind, he argues that everyday life in three towns along the Delaware River from 1770 to 1830 reveals that the nation was composed of local struggles over power that held religion, popular sovereignty, ethnicity, and gender in uneasy tension. Overshadowing such local contests, however, were efforts of trans-regional political and religious organizations through which respectable, white, Protestantism came to present itself
(15) as normal, with special claims to being American by the 1820s. Riordan draws illustrative sources from personal correspondence, local newspapers, church bulletins, and census information. He uses several local personalities as examples of how individuals navigated local political and religious environments and he clearly demonstrates the religious culture in these towns. Choosing 1770–1830 allows Riordan a nuanced analy-
(20) sis of how colonial parochialism managed the urgency required by the Revolution as well as the nation-building and millennial movements that followed.

7. The author of the passage would probably consider which of the following to be most similar to the challenges in lines 3 through 6?

Ⓐ A group of laborers in a factory who go on strike in order to try to negotiate better working conditions.

Ⓑ A dissident who questions his church's doctrine about whether women should be allowed to be priests in the church.

Ⓒ A document found in a tomb giving a contradictory account to the established record of a battle in the Civil War.

Ⓓ A Native American who stages a protest in order to try to change restrictive reservation laws.

Ⓔ A scientist who, after careful experimentation, puts forward a paper that debunks current wisdom regarding Atlantic Ocean pollution concentrations.

8. Select the sentence in the passage in which the author puts forward an assertion that supersedes one of her previous assertions.

9. In the context in which it appears, "parochial" (line 8) most nearly means

    Ⓐ limited
    Ⓑ unclear
    Ⓒ religious
    Ⓓ historical
    Ⓔ partisan

Questions 10 and 11 are based on the following reading passage:

The public intellectual is one who has become elevated to a symbol, a person that stands for something far larger than the discipline from which he or she originated. Such an intellectual is often speaking about things beyond his or her area of expertise. *Line* Some people will refuse such an invitation, others will accept the opportunity that has (5) been given them. Such a person must be careful, he must be aware of the limitations of his knowledge, he must acknowledge his personal prejudices because he is being asked to speak for a whole realm of thought, and he must be aware of the huge possible consequences of what he says and writes and does. He has become, in a sense, public property because he represents something large to the public. He has become an idea (10) himself, a human striving. He has enormous power to influence and change, and he must wield that power with respect.

For Questions 10 and 11, consider each of the choices separately and select *all* that apply.

10. It can be inferred from the passage that the author would agree with which of the following statements?

    Indicate *all* that apply.

    A   Public intellectuals often speak about topics that they would better have avoided due to their lack of background knowledge in those subjects.
    B   Public intellectuals have a duty to share their expertise with the public.
    C   The words of public intellectuals are often accepted unquestioningly by their audiences.

11. The author uses the word "striving" (line 10) primarily in order to

    Ⓐ underscore the effort necessary for public intellectuals to adequately address their topics
    Ⓑ explain the belief held by the public that public intellectuals are infallible sources of knowledge
    Ⓒ emphasize the care that public intellectuals must use due to their stature
    Ⓓ convey the idea that public intellectuals represent the attempt of humanity to understand their world
    Ⓔ indicate that public intellectuals, despite their prominence, are subject to the same difficulties as the rest of humanity

Question 12 is based on the following reading passage:

In a certain journal covering radiation oncology, it was noted by a student that, in 2009, there were 50% fewer articles about gamma knife radiation machines than there were in 2008. Most major hospitals replaced their older gamma knife technology with a newer iteration of the technology in 2009, a process that required several months. Consequently, the student assumed the decline in articles was due to the equipment changeover.

12. Which of the following, if true, most seriously undermines the student's assumption?

Ⓐ Safety regulations regarding the operation of gamma knife equipment were recently relaxed, due to new research proving the technology was safer than previously thought.

Ⓑ All the articles about gamma knife technology that were submitted to the journal in 2009 were accepted and published.

Ⓒ In 2009, the journal implemented a new editorial policy that required new articles to undergo a time-consuming and rigorous peer-approval process before publication.

Ⓓ In 2008, the journal was published in 16 languages, while in 2009, it was published in 20 languages.

Ⓔ Gamma knife equipment, due to its delicate nature, can only support one research experiment per year.

> **DIRECTIONS:** For Questions 13 to 16, select the *two* answer choices that, when used to complete the sentence, fit the meaning of the sentence as a whole *and* produce completed sentences that are alike in meaning.

13. Never a master of political intrigue, the senator was often chastised for his heavy-handed approach, which sharply contrasted with his opponent's _____.

[A] craft
[B] ineptitude
[C] caginess
[D] ambivalence
[E] uncertainty
[F] clumsiness

14. When viewed by itself, the artist's sculpture held little meaning, but when it was placed in the garden in _____ with his other work, it gracefully added to the scope of the installation.

[A] isolation
[B] concert
[C] intransigence
[D] conjunction
[E] obsequy
[F] insularity

15. Never known for deigning to explain himself, the editor rejected any submissions that he deemed lacking in a certain quality, a quality that he refused to _____.

[A] explicate
[B] conflate
[C] concede
[D] amalgamate
[E] elucidate
[F] admit

16. Despite the servant's reputation for what bordered on slavish devotion to the nobleman, he was not immune to occasional bouts of _____ regarding his master's needs.

[A] immaturity
[B] prevarication
[C] puerility
[D] nonchalance
[E] insouciance
[F] deception

DIRECTIONS: For Questions 17 to 20, select *one* answer choice unless otherwise instructed.

Questions 17 and 18 are based on the following reading passage:

The impact of triclosan, an antibacterial agent commonly added to consumer products, on microbial populations in soil irrigated with waste water from households was examined. It was found that irrigation of soil with triclosan-containing waste water results
Line in both an increase in resistant bacteria and a concomitant decrease in overall micro-
(5) bial community diversity. These changes in the soil microbiota raise public health and environmental concerns about the release of untreated household waste streams into terrestrial ecosystems. Before irrigation with waste water can become a useful water reuse alternative, additional research focusing on the long-term impacts of triclosan and other pharmaceuticals and personal care products is needed.

For Question 17, consider each of the choices separately and select *all* that apply.

17. Which of the following statements is supported by the passage?

Indicate *all* that apply.

[A] In soil irrigated with triclosan-containing waste water, the overall number of bacteria decreased.
[B] The use of triclosan should be curtailed whenever possible due to its environmental impact.
[C] Bacteria that develop a resistance to anti-bacterial drugs are of more concern than bacteria that have not developed such a resistance.

18. The passage provides information on each of the following except

(A) whether soil irrigation with triclosan-containing waste water affects how many different types of bacteria will be found in that soil

(B) the origin of the triclosan detected in the soil samples studied

(C) whether irrigation with waste water is a viable idea

(D) what changes soil microbiota undergo when exposed to triclosan

(E) the reasoning for introducing waste water into the ecosystem studied

Questions 19 and 20 are based on the following reading passage:

In general, current practice for inspecting cargo shipments of fruits and vegetables at United States ports is based on inspecting 2% of the items in a container for the presence of pests, with some allowances for the size, contents, and origin of the container.
Line Although simple to apply, this inspection rule appears not to have any economic con-
(5) tent. That is, it does not consider the costs of inspections or the losses of failing to prevent an invasive species from entering the country, nor does it account for the severe uncertainty associated with finding infestations in shipping containers—which are often no better than guesswork—and the potential losses from introductions of poorly understood or surreptitiously introduced invasive species. Our recommendation is to
(10) choose an inspection strategy that is robust in the sense that it maximizes the set of possible outcomes under which a performance criterion is met.

19. In the context in which it appears, "severe" (line 6) most nearly means

(A) austere
(B) strict
(C) plain
(D) momentous
(E) trivial

20. Which of the following best characterizes the function of the following portion of the passage? (" . . . appears not to have any economic content.")

(A) It reiterates an assertion previously stated in the passage.
(B) It provides concrete evidence that supports the passage's position.
(C) It provides a specific instance illustrating a broader principle.
(D) It suggests that a particular strategy is unsound.
(E) It summarizes a justification for a policy with which the author disagrees.

SECTION 5—QUANTITATIVE REASONING

TIME: 35 MINUTES—20 QUESTIONS

DIRECTIONS: For Questions 1 to 5, consider each of the choices separately and select *all* that apply.

---

1. There are at least three times as many boys as girls in a class. On a test, the boys' average score is 78, and the girls' average score is 94. Which of the following *could be* the average test score for the entire class?

    Indicate *all* such values.

    A   88
    B   86
    C   84
    D   82
    E   80

2. The function f is defined by $f(x) = \sqrt{x^2}$. For which of the following values of x is $f(x) = x$?

    Indicate *all* such values.

    A   −10,000
    B   −1
    C   −.00001
    D   0
    E   .00001
    F   10,000

3. The positive integers k, m, and n have the property that k is a factor of m, and m is a factor of n. Which of the following must be true?

    Indicate *all* that apply.

    A k is a factor of n.
    B m is a factor of kn.
    C n is a factor of km.
    D $\dfrac{n}{k}$ and $\dfrac{n}{m}$ are both integers.

PRACTICE TEST 2

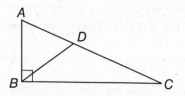

4.   In right triangle *ABC* above, *BC* = 12, and *AD* = 9. Which of the following statements, considered individually, is sufficient to determine the triangle's area?

Indicate *all* that apply.

- [A] Triangle *ABD* is equilateral
- [B] $DC = 6$
- [C] $\overline{BD}$ is not perpendicular to $\overline{AC}$
- [D] $AB = \dfrac{3}{4} BC$
- [E] $AB \neq AD$

5.   For which of the following integers, *n*, is the number 60*n* equal to the square of another integer?

Indicate *all* such values of *n*.

- [A] 2^{28}
- [B] $2^9 \times 3^5$
- [C] $3^3 \times 5^5$
- [D] $2^{10} \times 3^9 \times 5^8$
- [E] $3 \times 5 \times 7^{28}$

Questions 6 to 8 are based on the following data, which shows the high and low dollar values of five tech company's stocks in the year 2012.

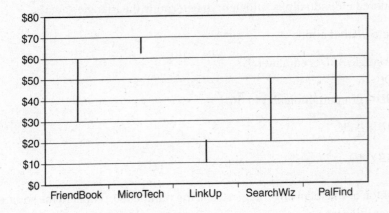

6. If Joe bought 800 shares of PalFind at the stock's lowest value during the year and sold the shares at the stock's highest value during the year, what was Joe's profit?

    Ⓐ $1,600
    Ⓑ $8,000
    Ⓒ $16,000
    Ⓓ $32,000
    Ⓔ $46,400

7. For the company whose stock value changed by the highest percentage during the year, what percent of the stock's maximum value was its minimum value?

    Ⓐ 30%
    Ⓑ 35%
    Ⓒ 40%
    Ⓓ 45%
    Ⓔ 50%

For Question 8, enter your answer in the grid below the question. Equivalent forms of the correct answer, such as 2.5 and 2.50, are all correct. Fractions do not need to be reduced to lowest terms.

8. Ann held 90 shares of the company whose stock value changed by the least amount during the year. If she sold these shares at their maximum value and used the money to buy shares of the least expensive stock at its lowest value of the year, how many shares was she able to buy?

9. A vintage clothing dealer bought x shirts at c dollars each and sold them at r dollars each. Which of the following expressions represents the profit the dealer made?

    Ⓐ $x(c-r)$
    Ⓑ $x(r-c)$
    Ⓒ $c(x-r)$
    Ⓓ $r(x-c)$
    Ⓔ $x(c+r)$

10. What is the ratio of $\frac{3}{5}$ to $\frac{6}{11}$?

    Ⓐ $\frac{10}{11}$

    Ⓑ $\frac{11}{10}$

    Ⓒ $\frac{18}{55}$

    Ⓓ $\frac{63}{55}$

    Ⓔ $\frac{55}{18}$

11. To earn a joint degree, a student must take any two math classes from the eight math classes that are offered and any two physics classes from the nine physics classes that are offered. How many different combinations of classes can a student take if he or she wishes to earn a joint degree?

    Ⓐ 68
    Ⓑ 288
    Ⓒ 988
    Ⓓ 1,008
    Ⓔ 4,032

12. If $5b = 6c = 7d = 120$, then what is the value of $\frac{7bd}{c}$?

    Ⓐ 100
    Ⓑ 120
    Ⓒ 144
    Ⓓ 148
    Ⓔ 196

For Question 13, enter your answer in the grid below the question. Equivalent forms of the correct answer, such as 2.5 and 2.50, are all correct. Fractions do not need to be reduced to lowest terms.

13. The diagonal length of a rectangular TV screen measuring 70×240 is how much greater than the diagonal length of a rectangular TV screen measuring 80×150?

Questions 14 and 15 are based on the following table:

Country	Currency	Amount of currency that can be bought for 1 U.S. Dollar
China	Yuan	6.5 Yuan
Thailand	Baht	30 Baht
India	Rupee	44.5 Rupees
Switzerland	Swiss Franc	0.8 Swiss Francs

14. One Chinese Yuan is worth approximately how many Thai Baht?

Ⓐ 0.2
Ⓑ 0.3
Ⓒ 4.4
Ⓓ 4.6
Ⓔ 5.0

15. Which of the following is worth the most?

Ⓐ One U.S. Dollar
Ⓑ One Baht
Ⓒ One Yuan
Ⓓ One Rupee
Ⓔ One Swiss Franc

DIRECTIONS: For Questions 16 to 20, compare Quantity A and Quantity B, using the additional information given, if any, and select *one* of the following four answer choices:

Ⓐ Quantity A is greater.

Ⓑ Quantity B is greater.

Ⓒ The two quantities are equal.

Ⓓ The relationship cannot be determined from the information given.

Line L in the xy-plane is given
by the equation $6x + 8y = 72$.

Quantity A	Quantity B
16. The x-coordinate of the x-intercept of line L	The y-coordinate of the y-intercept of line L

On a list of 19 real numbers,
ten numbers are greater than 60,
and nine numbers are less than 60.

Quantity A	Quantity B
17. The median of the list	60.1

$d \neq 0$

Quantity A	Quantity B
18. The average speed when d miles is driven in h hours	The average speed when $9d$ miles is driven in $8h$ hours

$n = 3^3$

Quantity A	Quantity B
19. n^n	3^{81}

$10 < |k| < 20$

Quantity A	Quantity B
20. The greatest negative integer, k, that makes the above statement true	The greatest negative integer, k, that makes the above statement false

ANSWER KEY
Practice Test 2

Section 2: Verbal Reasoning

1. **E**
2. **A**
3. **B, D**
4. **C, D**
5. **B, F**
6. **A, E, G**
7. **D**
8. **B, C**
9. **D**
10. **C**
11. **C**
12. **B, D**
13. **D, F**
14. **A, E**
15. **A, C**
16. **Sentence 5**
17. **D**
18. **A**
19. **A**
20. **C**

Section 3: Quantitative Reasoning

1. **C**
2. **B**
3. **A**
4. **D**
5. **A**
6. **E**
7. **C**
8. **D**
9. **A**
10. **$2,940**
11. **89.9**
12. $\left(\dfrac{1}{64}\right)$
13. **$588**
14. **A**
15. **C**
16. **C**
17. **A, B**
18. **C, E**
19. **175**
20. **.125**

Section 4: Verbal Reasoning

1. **E**
2. **B**
3. **B, F**
4. **C, D, H**
5. **A, E**
6. **A, F, H**
7. **C**
8. **Sentence 5**
9. **A**
10. **C**
11. **D**
12. **C**
13. **A, C**
14. **B, D**
15. **A, E**
16. **D, E**
17. **C**
18. **C**
19. **D**
20. **D**

Section 5: Quantitative Reasoning

1. **D, E**
2. **D, E, F**
3. **A, B, D**
4. **A, B, D**
5. **C, E**
6. **C**
7. **C**
8. **630**
9. **B**
10. **B**
11. **D**
12. **C**
13. **80**
14. **D**
15. **E**
16. **A**
17. **D**
18. **B**
19. **C**
20. **B**

ANSWER EXPLANATIONS

Section 2—Verbal Reasoning

1. **(E)** If direct insults are dangerous, it makes sense that *slights* (insults) are *insinuated* (hinted at) instead of declared.

2. **(A)** If *impasses* (obstacles with no obvious solution) are *hurdled* (overcome) with rapidity (*speed*), then it would *not* be surprising that a *quagmire* (difficult position) would not be worrisome.

3. **(B, D)** The word *despite* signifies a shift, and so blank (i) must be a word like *reprobate* (evil) because the papers have ignored the criminality of forgery. The most helpful clue for blank (ii) is that the critics say the papers' authors "lack the ethics and good sense," so it makes sense that they *lambasted* (vigorously attacked) the papers.

4. **(C, D)** The clue for blank (i) is found in the second sentence, since those who criticize new-age administrators are heralded, making *fashionable* a good fit. Since there is a logical connection between criticizing and being heralded, *incisively* (sharply) is a good fit for the second blank.

5. **(B, F)** The use of "many" authors provides a clue for blank (i), so *rash* (large number) is supported. For blank (ii), logically, if the new documents have amplified voices that were previously unheard, it makes sense that the authors have *recognized* the opportunity to write about these voices.

6. **(A, E, G)** Blank (i) is explained by the part of the sentence after it, specifically, "which will greatly enhance the ability. . . . " So, *veritable* (true; correct) information makes the rest of the sentence logical. Blank (ii) is explained by the preceding portion of the next sentence "Given human nature, however, . . . age misreporting," which implies that there is a problem that can be solved with age validation, which is therefore *a requisite* (necessary) process. Blank (iii) is explained by the sentence containing blank (ii), which mentions "exceptional longevity research." Therefore, it is logical that these claims need a significant validation procedure, making *consummate* (complete) a good choice, and the only choice that could work (*cavalier* means dismissive and *antiquated* means old-fashioned).

7. **(D)** It would seem that pesticide exposure would be a good explanation for the syndrome, since the cows in Country B were not exposed to the pesticides and now have the syndrome. However, if choice (D) is true—that the cows in Country B are slaughtered before they are old enough to develop signs—then it's possible that those cows would have developed the syndrome as much as those in Country A.

8. **(B, C)** The author says that Pythagoras thought of beauty as an *objective* (based on fact) principle, or one that is not affected by differing opinions. The author also says that Pythagoras believed beauty "maintains harmony, order, and balance," which supports the notion that a person's well-being will be supported by watching something beautiful (like a sunset or an act of kindness).

9. **(D)** In much of the first paragraph, the author introduces the concept of creativity, then proceeds to explain how creativity applies to philosophy and science, linking beauty and creativity as well as showing how creativity is applied to science.

10. **(C)** The author of the passage begins by defining creativity, then quickly connects the concept to beauty, saying that there is only a "small step" between the two. He then provides examples—like the example about chaos theory—that further demonstrate the relation, or parallel, between the concepts.

11. **(C)** In the final sentence of the passage, the author explains that the field of computational creativity helps "construct . . . tools that are able to support the creative processes of humans." If a new mobile phone becomes part of a work of art, then its creation certainly has supported a human creative process.

12. **(B, D)** The word *though* creates a shift from the fact that the advisor was recently *reviled* (hated) for his *fawning* (trying to gain favor through flattery) behavior. *Imperious* (commanding) and *domineering* (controlling) create the necessary shift.

13. **(D, F)** If the advocates did not anticipate "obvious consequences," then their praise must have been excessive, so *immoderate* (without moderation) and *effusive* (gushing) are appropriate choices.

14. **(A, E)** Since ATP is essential for cellular energy, it makes sense that its production is *a prerequisite* (required) or *an indispensable* (necessary) component.

15. **(A, C)** If the novel was previously banned for the *salacious* (sexually appealing) details, then it would be logical to say those passages were thought of as *unwholesome* or *prurient* (arousing unwholesome desire).

16. **(Sentence 5: Similarly, actions . . . sentiments.)** This sentence, by the use of the word "similarly," compares the relative ease by which firms can measure customer satisfaction to the previous sentence's assertion that customer satisfaction is a more reliable indicator than customer confidence, and then uses this comparison to extend its assertion (that measuring satisfaction is easier).

17. **(D)** The word "but" hints at a shift, or conflict. The discrepancy, that there are surprisingly low levels of ozone at the ocean's surface despite its absorption ability, can be explained if the absorbed ozone can leave the ocean and migrate to the surrounding area.

18. **(A)** If the ocean water tested had surprisingly low levels of ozone, it makes sense that the ocean is usually *adept* (skilled) at absorbing ozone. *Proficient* (expert) is a good replacement.

19. **(A)** The author most likely provides the information about ozone levels in western Ireland to point out that there are increased ozone levels over land as well as over the ocean, where the study took place, thereby providing more background information for his readers.

20. **(C)** The position of the argument is that further testing is needed before the laptop's fan speed is reduced. Therefore, it is arguing against the position to lower the fan speed. The first boldfaced portion gives reasoning that this may be done by saying that if Component H is the most heat-sensitive, then its viability is the crucial factor. The second boldfaced portion provides additional reasoning for the argument's position by outlining a benefit of adopting the position.

Section 3—Quantitative Reasoning

*Indicates an alternative way to solve the problem.

1. **(C)** Standard deviation is a measure of the dispersion of the numbers on a list from the list's mean, or average. When the teacher adds 10 points to every score, the scores and their average are all shifted upward by 10, but the spread of the test scores from their mean remains unchanged. Therefore, the standard deviation of the new set is the same as that of the original set, and (C) is correct. To compute an actual standard deviation will not be required on the GRE. The complicated formula involves subtracting every number on the list from the mean, then averaging the squares of these differences, and finally taking the square root.

2. **(B)** Because there is an unlimited supply of water in Column (A), only the amount of rice and the number of people matter. Set up a ratio to compare these quantities, using x to represent the unknown number of people: $\dfrac{\text{rice}}{\text{people}} = \dfrac{\frac{3}{4}}{8} = \dfrac{6}{x}$. Cross-multiply to obtain $\frac{3}{4}x = 48$. Isolate x by multiplying both sides by $\frac{4}{3}$, the reciprocal of $\frac{3}{4}$. Then $1x = 48 \times \frac{4}{3} = 64$. Since 64 is less than 65, (B) is greater.

3. **(A)** The probability of any event is always between zero and one, inclusive, which means that $0 \le p \le 1$, and $0 \le s \le 1$. Recall that the product of two decimals between 0 and 1 is smaller than either one of them ("fraction of a fraction") and that the sum of *any* two positive numbers is greater than either one of them. This suggests that Quantity (A), $p + s$, is greater than Quantity (B), ps. Choice (A) is correct, but don't forget to check the boundary cases, because p or s could equal 0 or 1, when some of these general rules do not apply. If p equals 1, then $p + s$ equals $1 + s$, while ps equals $1s$. Since $1 + s > s$, (A) is greater. If $p = 0$, then $p + s = s$, while $ps = 0$, and again (A) is greater.

   *Pick plausible values for p and s, consistent with the fact that p and s represent probabilities, and test each pair. For example, if $p = \frac{1}{4}$ and $s = \frac{3}{4}$, then $p + s$ equals 1, while ps equals $\frac{3}{16}$, and (A) is greater. If $p = .1$ and $s = .1$, then $p + s$ equals .2, which is much greater than ps, or .01. Finally, if $p = s = .9$ or .8, then $p + s > 1$, while $ps < 1$, confirming that Quantity (A) is greater. By testing a wide range of possible values for p and s, we are fairly certain that (A) will *always* be greater.

4. **(D)** We know that $0 < w < x < y < 100$, but we don't know how far apart the variables w, x, and y are spread between 0 and 100. For example, if $w = 1$, $x = 2$, and $y = 3$, then Quantity (A), $100 - y$, equals 97, while Quantity (B), $y - w$, equals only 2. But if $w = 10$, $x = 20$, and $y = 99$, then Quantity (A) equals only 1, while Quantity (B) equals 89. Therefore, there is not enough information to determine, and (D) is correct.

5. **(A)** In the second sentence given, there is one fewer hot dog but one more pretzel. Replacing one hot dog with one pretzel decreases the total cost, so the pretzel must be cheaper. Then the cost of the hot dog, Quantity (A), is greater.

*Represent the information with a linear system. If x is the price of one hot dog and y is the price of one pretzel, then $10x + 9y = 74.15$, and $9x + 10y = 74.05$. Try lining up the equations vertically and subtracting to find some type of cancellation.

$$
\begin{array}{r}
10x + 9y = 74.15 \\
-(9x + 10y = 74.05) \\
\hline
1x - 1y = .10
\end{array}
$$

Adding y to each side reveals that $x = y + .10$, so the cost of the hot dog is $.10 more than the cost of the pretzel, and (A) is greater.

*The on-screen calculator makes the traditional elimination method possible, but since this approach is much longer, try to spot one of the easier ways first. Set up a linear system, as in (*) above. Then multiply the first equation by 9 and the second equation by -10, so that the x coefficients become equal but opposite in sign. Some number crunching shows that

$$
90x + 81y = \$667.35
$$
$$
-90x - 100y = -\$740.50
$$

Add the two whole equations together to obtain $-19y = -73.15$. Dividing both sides by -19 shows that $y = \$3.85$. Finally, substitute this value back into one of the original equations and solve for x, to obtain $x = \$3.95$, and (A) is greater.

6. **(E)** If $\dfrac{4-x}{x-2} = \dfrac{-3}{x}$ then we can cross-multiply to obtain $x(4 - x) = -3(x - 2)$. Distribute on both sides to obtain $4x - x^2 = -3x + 6$. Now subtract $4x$ from each side, and add x^2 to each side, in order to combine like terms and to get one side equal to zero. Then $0 = x^2 - 7x + 6$. Factor the right side by noting that $(x - 6)(x - 1) = x^2 - 1x - 6x + 6 = x^2 - 7x + 6$. So $(x - 6)(x - 1) = 0$ and x could equal 6 or 1, the values that make either expression in parentheses equal to 0. Both values check in the original equation, but only $x = 6$, (E) is listed as an answer choice.

7. **(C)**

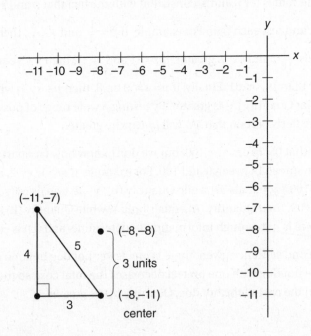

Make sure to draw the picture. The interior point (–8, –8), is located 3 units directly above the circle's center (–8, –11), so its distance from the center is 3 units. The exterior point (–11, –7) is located 3 units to the left and 4 units above the circle's center. Its distance from the center is given by the Pythagorean theorem as $\sqrt{3^2 + 4^2} = \sqrt{25} = 5$ units. If a point 3 units from the center lies inside the circle, while a point 5 units from the center lies outside the circle, then the radius of the circle is between 3 and 5 and must equal 4, since the radius is given as an integer. Then the area, given by πr^2, equals $\pi 4^2 = 16\pi$, (C).

8. **(D)** Compute the area of Rectangle B, by finding *length times width*, which equals 30×48, or 1,440. Similarly, the area of Rectangle A equals $12x$. These areas are given as equal, so $12x = 1{,}440$, and dividing by 12 yields $x = 120$. But be careful. The question asks for the perimeter of Rectangle A, not its length. Perimeter equals $2 \times (\text{length} + \text{width})$, which is $2 \times (120 + 12)$, or $2(132) = 264$, (D).

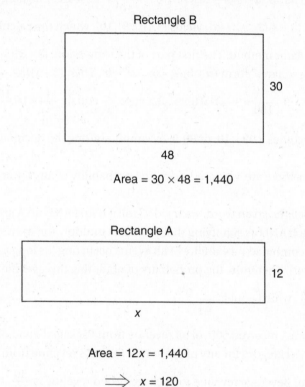

Rectangle B

30

48

Area = 30 × 48 = 1,440

Rectangle A

12

x

Area = 12x = 1,440

$\implies$ $x = 120$

Perimeter = 2 × 12 + 2 × 120 = 264

9. **(A)** First, change $\dfrac{3}{25}$ to a percent by setting it equal to $\dfrac{x}{100}$: $\dfrac{3}{25} = \dfrac{x}{100}$.

Multiply the top and bottom of the left fraction by 4, to get $x = 12$, i.e., 12%, which can also be obtained by cross-multiplying or by simply typing $3 \div 25$ on the calculator and converting .12 to 12%. Then the pool went from 12% full at 12:00 to 28% full at 2:30. The increase is $28\% - 12\% = 16\%$ of the pool's full volume in 2.5 hours.

During this time, the pool was filled at a rate of 2 gallons per *minute*. We must convert 2.5 hours into $2.5 \times 60 = 150$ minutes, in order to find that $2\frac{\text{gallons}}{\text{minute}} \times 150 \text{ minutes} = 300$ gallons. This means that 300 gallons were added and that 300 gallons represents 16% of the pool's total volume, say T. Then $300 = .16T$. Divide both sides by .16, and T equals $300 \div .16 = 1,875$, (A).

10. **($2,940)** Since the four shares together constitute 100% of the total, Heir D inherits 100% minus the sum of the other three heirs' percentages. Then his share is 10% of the total inheritance, because $100 - (35 + 30 + 25) = 100 - 90 = 10$. If Heir D's $840 inheritance is 10% of the total, then the total is $10 \times 840 = \$8,400$. Heir A received 35% of the total, which is $.35 \times 8400 = \$2,940$.

11. **(89.9)** Think of a negative exponent as "one over" the expression if it had a positive exponent. That is, $x^{-n} = \frac{1}{x^n}$. Here, $10^{-1} = \frac{1}{10^1} = \frac{1}{10} = 0.1$. Plugging this value into the expression $(3 + x)(3 - x)(1/x)$, yields $(3.1)(2.9)(10)$, which the calculator shows is 89.9.

*Non-calculator method: The first part of the expression, $(3 + x)(3 - x)$, fits the "difference of two squares" form $(a + b)(a - b) = a^2 - b^2$. Then $(3 + x)(3 - x) = 9 - x^2$, or $9 - \left(\frac{1}{10}\right)^2 = 9 - \frac{1}{100} = 9 - .01 = 8.99$. Because $\frac{1}{x}$ equals $\frac{1}{\frac{1}{10}} = 1 \times \frac{10}{1} = 10$, the final product becomes 8.99×10, or **89.9,** by simply shifting the decimal one place.

12. $\left(\dfrac{1}{64}\right)$ Since there are 4 lettered sides, the probability of any letter landing face down is $\frac{1}{4}$. To spell the given word, we need to roll a B first AND an A second AND a D third. Think of each AND as signifying that you must multiply the individual probabilities to find the combined probability of all events occurring (as long as the events are independent). Therefore, the probability of obtaining this specific sequence is $\frac{1}{4} \times \frac{1}{4} \times \frac{1}{4}$, which equals $\frac{1}{64}$.

13. **($588)** Store A received 50% of all revenue from Packaged Food, the highest percentage from this category for any of the stores. Store A's revenue from Beverages is 30%, so its ratio of Beverage revenue to Packaged Food revenue is $\frac{30}{50}$, or $\frac{3}{5}$. If it earned $980 from Packaged Food, then it earned $\frac{3}{5} \times 980 = \$588$ from beverages. You can also set up the ratio: $\dfrac{\text{beverages}}{\text{packaged food}} = \dfrac{30\%}{50\%} = \dfrac{.3}{.5} = \dfrac{x}{980}$. Cross-multiply to obtain $.5x = 294$, and $x = \dfrac{294}{.5} = \$588$.

14. **(A)** At Store D, the left-hand column, Beverages, is higher than for any other store. For Store D, the ratio of Prepared Food to Packaged Food is 15% to 40%, or 15:40. Divide both numbers in the ratio by 5, the greatest common factor of 15 and 40, to obtain the reduced ratio 3:8, choice (A).

15. **(C)** In order for one category to account for at least as much revenue as the other two categories combined, the one category must comprise at least half, or 50%, of the total

revenue. Only Stores A and B have a column that reaches the 50% level, so these two stores meet the condition described, choice (C).

16. **(C)** If each of the four stores earned exactly the same amount of total revenue, we might as well suppose that this number was $100—an unrealistic figure—but one that makes computing percents easy. Then the percentage of revenue from beverages for the four stores—30%, 25%, 40%, and 45%—would correspond precisely to the dollar figures $30, $25, $40, and $45. So the revenue from beverages would be $30 + 25 + 40 + 45 = \$140$ out of $4 \times 100 = \$400$ total revenue. Therefore, beverages would account for $\frac{140}{400} = .35 = 35\%$ of total revenue, choice (C).

17. **(A, B)** Let $b =$ the marked price of the book. The sales tax is 9% of the book's marked price, so tax $= .09b$. Then the cost of the book plus tax is given by $1b + .09b$, which equals $1.09b$. Since John received change for his $20 bill, and since the change was less than $5, he must have spent between $15 and $20. Then $\$15 < 1.09b < \$20$. Divide all three parts of this inequality by 1.09 to obtain $\$13.76 < b < \$18.35$. This result implies both (A) and (B), because b is certainly greater than $13.50 but less than $18.50. Choice (C) is not true, because if the marked price were $18, for example, then the sales tax would have been $.09 \times \$18 = \$1.62$, which is greater than $1.50, while the total price remains low enough, $19.62, to leave John change, as required.

18. **(C, E)** Set S is the infinite set of all odd integers: $\{\ldots -7, -5, -3, -1, 1, 3, 5, 7 \ldots\}$. Adding two odd integers yields an even integer, so (A) is not correct. For example, $5 + 3 = 8$. Subtracting two odd integers yields an even integer, so (B) is not correct. For example, $5 - 3 = 2$. (C) is correct because multiplying any two odd integers always results in another odd integer—for example, $3 \times -9 = -27$, and $7 \times 11 = 77$. This is because when neither number has 2 as a factor, the product will not have 2 as a factor (since 2 is a prime number). (D) is not correct, because dividing two elements from Set S will often produce a non-integer value. For example, $5 \div 3 \approx 1.67$. Finally, (E) is correct, because raising an odd number to *any* power will yield an odd result for basically the same reasons as (C) above. Repeated multiplication by the same odd number continues to yield products that lack 2 as a factor and are thus, by definition, odd. For example, $3^1 = 3$, $3^2 = 9$, $3^3 = 27$, $3^4 = 81$. The answer is (C) and (E).

19. **(175)** Use the formula $D = r \times t$, that is, distance = rate × time.

$59 \dfrac{\text{miles}}{\text{hour}} \times 8 \text{ hours} = 472$ miles that the man drove, and $49.5 \dfrac{\text{miles}}{\text{hour}} \times 6 \text{ hours} = 297$

miles that the woman drove. Then he drove $472 - 297 = 175$ miles farther.

20. **(.125)** Find the y-intercept by setting x equal to 0. $y = \left(0 - \dfrac{1}{2}\right)^2 = \left(-\dfrac{1}{2}\right)^2 = \dfrac{1}{4}$, which is b

in the problem. Find the x-intercept by setting y equal to 0. Then $0 = \left(x - \dfrac{1}{2}\right)^2$. Take

the square root of each side, and $x - \dfrac{1}{2} = 0$, so $x = \dfrac{1}{2}$. This is a in the problem. Then

$ab = \dfrac{1}{2} \times \dfrac{1}{4} = \dfrac{1}{8}$, or .125.

Section 4—Verbal Reasoning

1. **(E)** If the tribe had been known to only have "primitive" skills, then it makes sense that only *rudimentary* (crude) tools were discovered.

2. **(B)** If the union's opposition to the regulations grew stronger, then *implementing* (carrying out) those regulations would have become more *challenging*.

3. **(B, F)** Start with blank (ii). The clue for that blank is "cheered even the gloomiest souls," so *a jocundity* (a joking, mirthful manner) fits. Since the poet's personal life is in sharp contrast to his public *persona* (image), the word for the blank must be the opposite of the second blank. Therefore, a word like *morose* (gloomy) makes sense.

4. **(C, D, H)** The clue for blank (i) is found in the second sentence—if those who make the suggestion to establish a year of experience often write congratulatory articles about others who do the same, then *popular* is a logical fit. For blank (ii), having a year's worth of experience would demonstrate *steadfastness* (loyalty). For blank (iii), the author's use of "so-called" supports *pundits* (experts) because he continues to criticize them, and implies that only they think they are experts.

5. **(A, E)** The clue for blank (i) is given by the phrase "habitual lateness," so *dilatory* (characterized by being late) works. Blank (ii) is supported by the lack of *ire* (anger) from the parents, so *exemplary* (excellent) grades would be a good reason to not be upset at his lateness.

6. **(A, F, H)** Filling in blank (i) and (ii) is easier if the second sentence is used to help. Since there is a "lack," *dearth* (lack) works for blank (i), and *omission* (something left out) fits blank (ii). The author implies that good things will result from the inclusion of the testing, so *fundamental* (crucial) works for blank (iii).

7. **(C)** The challenges described in the passage are the Native American histories and the African Diaspora: narratives that, as the author says, "assert alternatives to the understanding of our national origins." Therefore, a document from a tomb that provides an alternate history for a battle would be analogous to these challenges.

8. **(Sentence 5: Overshadowing such . . . 1820s.)** The author, in the preceding sentence, asserts that Riordan argues "that the nation was composed of local struggles over power . . . ," but then, in the next sentence, claims that trans-regional organizations were "overshadowing such local contests." In other words, the preceding sentence is *superseded* (displaced in favor of something else) by the sentence beginning with "overshadowing."

9. **(A)** There is a context clue for the definition of *parochial* (limited in scope) that comes shortly after the word: "context of community studies that often is overlooked in favor of a more national scope." In other words, the parochial, or limited scope, is passed over for the larger, national one.

10. **(C)** The author implies that the audience of a public intellectual often believes that person's words without questioning, because the author says, among other things, that such an intellectual "has enormous power to influence and change."

11. **(D)** *Striving* (putting effort toward) is used by the author to convey people's attempt to understand. He implies this by emphasizing the powerful influence that a public intellectual has on his audience. Since the intellectual is imparting knowledge on the public, it makes sense that the public views the figure as their attempt or striving, to understand.

12. **(C)** The new editorial policy, implemented in 2009, entails undergoing a "time-consuming" and *rigorous* (thorough) process, which would adequately explain the drop in articles in that year, since it would take longer for those articles to be approved to be published.

13. **(A, C)** The senator's *heavy-handed* (clumsy) approach contrasts with his opponents', so his opponent must have *craft* (skill) or *caginess* (cleverness).

14. **(B, D)** Using the word *but* as a clue to the sentence's shift, the blank needs a word that means the opposite of "viewed by itself." *Concert* (simultaneous agreement) or *conjunction* (combination) create the necessary opposition.

15. **(A, E)** If the editor is not known for *deigning* (stooping) to explain himself, it would make sense that he would refuse to *explicate* (explain) or *elucidate* (clarify).

16. **(D, E)** The word *despite* indicates a shift, so if the servant has a reputation for *slavish* (excessive) devotion, then it is logical to use *nonchalance* (indifference) or *insouciance* (unconcern).

17. **(C)** The author explains that the "changes in the soil microbiota"—that he previously asserted to be caused by the triclosan-tainted water—raise "concerns" about public health. Since he claims that these changes include an increase in resistant bacteria, one can conclude that the passage supports the assertion that the resistant bacteria are of more concern than the non-resistant bacteria.

18. **(C)** The author, at the end of the passage, makes it clear that more research is needed before irrigation with waste water becomes a *viable* (workable) idea, so he stops short of providing information on whether it is a viable idea or not.

19. **(D)** In this context, the author is emphasizing that the uncertainty is significant, and claims that finding the infestations is no better than guesswork. Therefore, the uncertainty must be *momentous* (extremely significant).

20. **(D)** The author explains what he means by lack of "economic content" in the next sentence, saying that the current policy does not account for either costs or uncertainty. In other words, he is claiming that the current strategy is *unsound* (not well made).

Section 5—Quantitative Reasoning

*Indicates an alternative way to solve the problem.

1. **(D, E)** If there were an equal number of boys and girls, then the class average would equal the average of 78 and 94, which is $\frac{78+94}{2} = \frac{172}{2} = 86$. But since there are more boys in the class, the average is weighted toward their number, 78, and will be less than 86. So choices (A) and (B) may be eliminated. If there are at least 3 times as many

boys, then the class average will be at least 3 times as close numerically to their average as to the girls' average. To find this value, which will be the maximum average for the class, we find the number $\frac{1}{4}$ of the way from the boys' average to the girls' in order to obtain a 1:3 ratio of lengths. First, find the difference in the two averages, $94 - 78 = 16$, and then divide this by 4 to obtain $16 \div 4 = 4$. This number, 4, is added to 78, to obtain 82, the value 4 units from the boys' average and $94 - 82 = 12$ units from the girls' average, which creates a 4:12 or 1:3 ratio of distances on the number line.

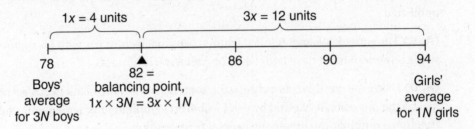

This means that "at least three times as many boys" implies that the class average is at most 82, and (D) and (E) are correct. (This is sometimes thought of as the leverage or "see-saw" principle. On a see-saw, a 100-pound boy must sit 3 feet from the fulcrum to balance a 150-pound boy sitting 2 feet from the fulcrum, because $100 \times 3 = 150 \times 2$.)

2. **(D, E, F)** When x is a negative number, squaring x will yield a positive number, whose square root in turn, is positive. So $\sqrt{x^2}$ will not equal x, but will equal $-x$. For example, say $x = -3$. Then $x^2 = 9$ and $\sqrt{x^2} = \sqrt{9} = 3$, the opposite of x. So (A), (B), and (C) may be eliminated. When $x \geq 0$, then taking the square root will cancel with squaring, its inverse operation, and (D), (E), and (F) are all correct. Note that $\sqrt{x^2} = |x|$, which equals x if and only if $x \geq 0$.

3. **(A, B, D)** The easiest way to solve this problem is to pick numbers for k, m, and n, and to assume our observations will hold in general, unless we have reason to think otherwise, in which case we would test other values too. We need k to be a factor of m, and m to be a factor of n, so say $k = 5$, $m = 10$, and $n = 20$. (A) is true, because 5 is a factor of 20. (B) is true because 10 is a factor of $20 \times 5 = 100$. (C) is not true, because 20 is not a factor of 50. (D) is true, because $\frac{20}{5} = 4$, and $\frac{20}{10} = 2$, and both 4 and 2 are integers.

The answer is (A), (B), and (D).

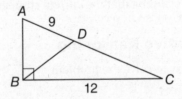

4. **(A, B, D)** If *ABD* is equilateral, then *AB*, the height in larger triangle *ABC* is 9, and since we also know base *BC*, we can compute the area, making (A) sufficient. (B) is correct, because if *DC* = 6, then *AC*, the hypotenuse of the right triangle, equals 9 + 6, or 15. This would allow us to compute *AB* from the Pythagorean theorem and the area as $\frac{\text{base} \times \text{height}}{2}$. (D) is correct because if $AB = \frac{3}{4}BC$, then $AB = \frac{3}{4} \times 12 = 9$, and we again know the base and height of the triangle. (C) and (E) are not correct. These choices present us with only negative information, that *BD* is *not* perpendicular to *AC*, or that $AB \neq AD$. These facts tell us very little, because they present no positive information that would allow us to determine an angle or side length in the figure. The answer is (A), (B), and (D).

5. **(C, E)** First factor the number 60 into its prime factors. Since $60 = 4 \times 15$, we have $60 = 2^2 \times 3 \times 5$. Notice that 2 appears squared in this expression, but that 3 and 5 appear to the first power. For a number to be the square of another integer, each prime in the prime factorization of the number must be raised to an even power. (A) is not correct, because $2^{28} \times 60$ will equal $2^{30} \times 3 \times 5$, which cannot be the square of an integer, because 3 and 5 are still to the first power. (B) is not correct, because multiplying 60 by $2^9 \times 3^5$ leaves an expression with 5^1. (C) is correct, because $(2^2 \times 3 \times 5) \times (3^3 \times 5^5) = 2^2 \times 3^4 \times 5^6$, which is the square of an integer, because all prime factors appear to even powers. Explicitly $2^2 \times 3^4 \times 5^6$ is equal to the square of $(2^1 \times 3^2 \times 5^3)$. (D) is not correct because of the 5^8 part, which multiplied by the 5 in $2^2 \times 3 \times 5$ yields 5^9, which will not be the square of an integer, because the exponent is odd. In (E), the product of $3 \times 5 \times 7^{28}$ and $2^2 \times 3 \times 5$ is $2^{30} \times 3^2 \times 5^2 \times 7^{28}$, which equals $(2^{15} \times 3^1 \times 5^1 \times 7^{14})^2$, so (E) is correct. The answer is (C) and (E).

6. **(C)** Joe bought the stock at just under $40, and sold it at just under $60. His profit is $60 - 40 = \$20$ per share. If he bought 800 shares, his profit was $800 \times 20 = \$16,000$, (C).

7. **(C)** FriendBook changed from $30 to $60 during the year. SearchWiz varied from $20 to $50 during the year. Both differences are $30, but for SearchWiz, $30 represents a higher percentage of the stock's value, because its stocks have a lower value. At SearchWiz, the stock's minimum value, $20, is 40% of its maximum value, $50, because 40% of $50 = .40 \times 50 = 20$, or because $\frac{20}{50} = \frac{2}{5} \times 0.4 = 40\%$. (C) is correct.

8. **(630)** MicroTech, whose stock values spanned less than one horizontal line on the graph, saw the least change in value. The highest value of the year for MicroTech stocks was $70. The least expensive stock, LinkUp, had a value of $10 at its lowest price of the year. This means that Ann could purchase seven stocks of the latter for every one stock sold of the former. Then if she sold 90 shares of MicroTech, she could purchase $90 \times 7 = 630$ shares of LinkUp.

9. **(B)** The profit per shirt is given by the price at which a shirt is sold minus the price at which it was bought. Here, this quantity is $r - c$. The total profit will equal the number of shirts sold $\times$ the profit per shirt, which is simply $x(r - c)$, choice (B).

10. **(B)** You are being asked to divide two fractions: $\dfrac{\frac{3}{5}}{\frac{6}{11}}$. Recall that to divide two fractions, multiply the fraction in the numerator by the reciprocal of the fraction in the denominator: $\dfrac{3}{5} \times \dfrac{11}{6}$. Cross cancel the 3 over 6, which reduces to $\dfrac{1}{2}$ to yield $\dfrac{\cancel{3}}{5} \times \dfrac{11}{\cancel{6}} = \dfrac{1}{5} \times \dfrac{11}{2} = \dfrac{11}{10}$, (B).

11. **(D)** We need to choose two math classes from eight offered and two physics classes from nine offered. These can be found with the "choose" function, written as $_nC_k$ or $\binom{n}{k}$ and defined for positive integers by the formula

$$\binom{n}{k} = \frac{n!}{k!(n-k)!} \text{ for } 0 \le k \le n$$

Recall that $n!$ means the product of all positive integers from 1 through n, inclusive. For math classes, we need $_8C_2$, so $n=8$ and $k=2$ in the formula above: $\dfrac{8!}{2! \times 6!}$. Most of the factors in the 8! expression cancel with all of the factors in 6!, and we are left with $\dfrac{8 \times 7}{2 \times 1} = 28$ choices for math. Similarly, the number of combinations of physics classes equals $_9C_2 = \dfrac{9!}{2! \times 7!} = \dfrac{9 \times 8}{2 \times 1} = 36$. The total combinations for math *and* physics classes equals $28 \times 36 = 1,008$, (D).

12. **(C)** If the four parts of the equation $5b = 6c = 7d = 120$ are all equal, then any two parts are equal, so $5b = 120$ and $6c = 120$. Then division shows that $b = 24$ and $c = 20$. We are asked for $\dfrac{7bd}{c}$, which equals $\dfrac{7db}{c} = \dfrac{7d(24)}{20}$, by substitution. Finally, substitute 120 for the entire $7d$, and the last expression becomes $\dfrac{(120)(24)}{20} = \dfrac{6}{1} \times 24 = 144$, (C).

13. **(80)**

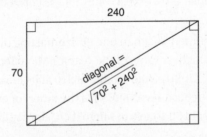 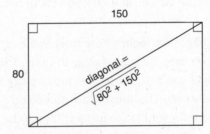

The diagonal of a rectangle divides the rectangle into two right triangles, and so the diagonal's length can be thought of as c, the hypotenuse, in the Pythagorean theorem: $a^2 + b^2 = c^2$. For the first TV, $70^2 + 240^2 = c^2$, and $c = \sqrt{70^2 + 240^2} = 250$. For the second TV, $80^2 + 150^2 = c^2$, and $c = \sqrt{80^2 + 150^2} = 170$. If you remember some common "Pythagorean Triples," such as 3-4-5, 5-12-13, 8-15-17, and 7-24-25, you can obtain these values more quickly, because the side lengths of both triangles in the problem are 10 times one of these common triples. Finally, the one TV screen is $250 - 170 = 80$ units longer.

14. **(D)** Since 6.5 Yuan = \$1 U.S. = 30 Baht, then 6.5 Yuan = 30 Baht. Divide both sides by 6.5 to obtain 1 Yuan $\approx$ 4.6 Baht, (D).

15. **(E)** One U.S. Dollar buys more than one Yuan, Baht, or Rupee, so those currencies are worth less than \$1. The U.S. Dollar buys fewer than one Swiss Franc, so the Franc is worth more than \$1, the only such currency, making the Swiss Franc, (E), greatest in value.

16. **(A)** Find the x-intercept of a graph by setting y equal to 0. Then $6x = 72$, and $x = 12$. Find the y-intercept of a graph by setting x equal to 0. Then $8y = 72$, and $y = 9$. Quantity (A) is greater.

17. **(D)** The median of a list of numbers is the middle value. If there are 19 numbers, the median will be the 10th smallest and the 10th largest. In other words, there will be nine values greater than the median, and nine values less than the median. Since there are also exactly nine numbers given as less than 60, these must be the nine smallest values, so the median will be the least of the numbers greater than 60. This number could be just barely greater than 60, say 60.0001, which is less than (B), or much greater than 60, say 1,000, which is greater than (B). Therefore, (D) is correct.

18. **(B)** The average rate or speed of a moving object equals the distance it travels divided by the time it takes to travel that distance. That is $r = \dfrac{d}{t}$ or $d = r \times t$. In Column (A), the rate is $\dfrac{d}{h}$. In Column (B), the rate is $\dfrac{9d}{8h}$, which equals $\dfrac{9}{8} \times \dfrac{d}{h}$, which is greater than $1 \times \dfrac{d}{h}$ (as long as the variables are positive), so (B) is greater.

    *Pick numbers. Let $d = 10$ and $h = 10$. Then Quantity (A) equals 1 mph, while Quantity (B) equals $\dfrac{90}{80} = 1.1$ mph, so (B) is greater.

19. **(C)** Since n equals 3^3, it equals, by definition, $3 \times 3 \times 3 = 27$. Then Quantity (A) can be written as n^{27}, or as $(3^3)^{27}$. The "power to a power" rule dictates that the exponents here are multiplied, and that in general $(x^m)^n = x^{mn}$. Then (A) equals $3^{3 \times 27} = 3^{81}$, matching Quantity (B), so the quantities are equal, (C).

20. **(B)** Recall that the absolute value of a number equals the distance from 0 to that number on a number line. The integers that satisfy $10 < |k| < 20$ are as follows: 11, 12, 13, 14, 15, 16, 17, 18, 19, -11, -12, -13, -14, -15, -16, -17, -18, -19. Of the negative integers on this list, the greatest is -11, so Quantity (A) is -11. The greatest of all negative integers, -1, makes the absolute value inequality false because $|-1|$ equals 1, which is not between 10 and 20. So Quantity (B) is -1. Since $-1 > -11$, (B) is correct.

Practice Test 3

SECTION 1—ANALYTICAL WRITING

TIME: 60 MINUTES—2 WRITING TASKS

TASK 1: ISSUE EXPLORATION

TIME: 30 MINUTES

The topic is presented in a one- to two-sentence quotation commenting on an issue of general concern.

Your essay will be judged on the basis of your skill in the following areas:

- response to the specific task instructions
- consideration of the complexities of the issue
- organization, development, and expression of your ideas
- support of your position with relevant reasoning and examples
- control of the elements of standard written English

TOPIC

Claim: Scholastic art and music programs are so important that the government should fund those programs in schools that cannot afford them.

Reason: Students who study art and music are more likely to succeed than those who do not.

DIRECTIONS: Write a response in which you discuss the extent to which you agree or disagree with the claim and the reason on which that claim is based.

TASK 2: ARGUMENT ANALYSIS

TIME: 30 MINUTES

Your essay will be judged on the basis of your skill in the following areas:

- identification and assessment of the argument's main elements
- organization and articulation of your thoughts
- use of relevant examples and arguments to support your case
- handling of the mechanics of standard written English

> **TOPIC**
>
> A recent study rating 100 college football players showed a strong relationship between their average number of colds caught per year and their teams' records. Of the players studied, those who had the fewest colds had teams with win/loss ratios that were, on average, 50% higher than teams with players that caught more colds. These results suggest that if a college football team wants to win, it should recruit players that catch a lower number of colds per year than their peers.

DIRECTIONS: Write a response in which you discuss what questions would need to be answered in order to decide whether the recommendation and the argument on which it is based are reasonable. Be sure to explain how the answers to the questions would help to evaluate the recommendation.

SECTION 2—VERBAL REASONING

TIME: 30 MINUTES—20 QUESTIONS

> **DIRECTIONS:** For Questions 1 to 6, select *one* entry for each blank from the corresponding column of choices. Fill all blanks in the way that best completes the text.

1. Often, the fame of a certain artist seems to have come out of nowhere when in fact his renown is the product of _____.

Ⓐ polarization
Ⓑ accolade
Ⓒ accretion
Ⓓ hedonism
Ⓔ hubris

2. Since the results of his experiments matched those from laboratories with the most stringent quality standards, the scientist was flabbergasted to discover that one of his suppliers had been _____ its chemicals all along.

Ⓐ adulterating
Ⓑ pirating
Ⓒ refining
Ⓓ pervading
Ⓔ mincing

3. If one considers that most lenders were (i) _____ of the tenuousness of the real estate market last year, it becomes all the more reprehensible that they proffered loans they knew consumers could not afford. Today, when most experts agree that property values are sliding rapidly, the fact that most lenders are still loaning money demands (ii) _____ from regulators.

Blank (i)	Blank (ii)
Ⓐ unaware	Ⓓ censure
Ⓑ cognizant	Ⓔ endorsement
Ⓒ enamored	Ⓕ uncertainty

4. Most studies of academic preparedness rank U.S. students far below their peers in math and science. Ever the contrarian, Phillips, in his new book, suggests that the studies' metrics are misguided. His (i) _____ of the studies has perhaps founded a school of thought that uses a new measure of success, but unsurprisingly, traditionalists have usually (ii) _____ his viewpoints.

Blank (i)	Blank (ii)
Ⓐ touting	Ⓓ reprehended
Ⓑ unnerving	Ⓔ comprehended
Ⓒ disparagement	Ⓕ eulogized

5. During the Cold War, amidst the threat of a nuclear attack, both the U.S. and the U.S.S.R. endeavored to prepare their populaces for the worst by offering survival tips. In order to give (i) _____ to the efficacy of these strategies, the countries often downplayed the severity of a post-nuclear war scenario, not wanting a potential panic on their hands. It was therefore necessary for the countries to hire physicists who were (ii) _____ in this deception to write informational pamphlets about nuclear fallout.

Blank (i)	Blank (ii)
Ⓐ credence	Ⓓ spurious
Ⓑ gravity	Ⓔ particulate
Ⓒ benignity	Ⓕ complicit

6. The (i) _____ of online marketplaces has facilitated the "flipping," or quickly reselling at a profit, of original artwork. Though this practice is (ii) _____ by artists and critics who seem to think art should be kept from the hands of the (iii) _____, is it surprising that goods in the private sector find their way to the highest bidder?

Blank (i)	Blank (ii)	Blank (iii)
Ⓐ proliferation	Ⓓ ignored	Ⓖ mercenary
Ⓑ stagnation	Ⓔ reviled	Ⓗ orthodox
Ⓒ sanctimony	Ⓕ regaled	Ⓘ hackneyed

7. Of the cars in City X, those built before 1980 have been built more skillfully than those built in the past year. Therefore, the way that automobile manufacturers built cars before 1980 is superior to the way manufacturers build cars today.

    Which of the following, if true, most seriously undermines the argument?

    Ⓐ Cars are generally built more skillfully than other vehicles, since more are produced.
    Ⓑ Cars built today generally weigh more than cars built before 1980.
    Ⓒ The parts used to make cars today are not appreciably different in quality from parts used in 1980.
    Ⓓ The more skillfully a car has been built, the less likely it is to be discarded and junked.
    Ⓔ The average number of training hours for those who manufacture cars is now half of what it was in 1975.

Questions 8 to 11 are based on the following reading passage:

Use of ecological theory for management of nature needs to follow different rules than use of physical theory to build skyscrapers or rockets. Whereas an engineer has a firm concept of stresses in constructing a structure of steel girders or thrust required to carry
Line a rocket payload, an ecologist has nothing comparable. In such cases, the theory can
(5) guide insight, but the insight must be tempered by local understanding of how well the organisms in question fit assumptions of relevant models. A manager must also realize that even if a population could in theory be managed for sustainable yield or maintained in habitat fragments of different size, populations might usually be so small that firm estimates and therefore predictions of persistence, extinction, or colonization are
(10) infeasible. If a Himalayan valley hosts three snow leopards, a manager of the cats and their prey may benefit from understanding that the local population may disappear and be replaced by other individuals or that the cats may simply trade individuals with other valleys. The capacity to actually estimate turnover on a quantitative basis is quite likely out of reach.

(15)   The quest for developing models that are based on larger, rigorous conceptual framework and that can be tested with appropriately sophisticated methodology should be pursued in ecology. We may profit, however, by acknowledging the shortcomings of ecological predictions, and frankly admitting when prediction is inappropriate because theories are insufficient or not appropriate for the targeted conservation
(20) practices. Development of predictive capabilities may take time but, as latest fishery science indicates, we are rapidly advancing toward our destinations. For reasons inherent in the field and the nature of nature, resource managers should avoid the pretense of predicting precise population changes. The concept of building resilience into policy to accommodate contingency, error, and chance is an operational approach to using

(25) theory for guidance rather than certainty. So, for instance, a general prediction that abundance of edible fish will change the fortunes of whatever game animals are common as indigenous people deplete in the Amazon may be warranted, but a pretense of predicting what each game or fish population will be given exploitation of it by indigenous people is not. Regarding reserve size, a prediction of persistence of animals and
(30) plants as a function of size of habitat patches may work well in uninhabited areas, but proximity of human settlements may overshadow it in many places. Contingencies that are not present in armchair models affect both examples.

The gist is not that ecological paradigms are failing, but that expectations of ecology as a science are not realistic in the real world in the same way that physics informs engi-
(35) neering or molecular biology informs medicine. Theory premised on predictions from large numbers is not much used in local situations where numbers of most organisms are low and where contingent effects may be overriding.

8. According to the passage, which of the following would be true if the described snow leopards were being studied?

    (A) Predictions of the leopards' persistence would have to be made on a quantitative basis due to the animals' small numbers.
    (B) The ecological paradigm used to make predictions about the leopards would be invalid.
    (C) Insight about the leopards' behavior would be more important than selecting a model that emulated their behavior.
    (D) Individual humans living in the valley would have to be closely monitored.
    (E) Care would have to be taken so as to avoid disturbing the leopards' habitat.

9. In the passage's final paragraph, the author is primarily concerned with

    (A) describing the limitations of a method
    (B) advocating a new ecological model
    (C) postulating that certain fields of study are supported by related fields
    (D) arguing that endangered animals are a bigger problem than previously thought
    (E) dismissing ecology as a science due to its lack of methodological rigor

10. According to the passage, which of the following circumstances would have the greatest chance of undermining a typical ecological model?

    (A) The organism being studied populates an area more quickly than anticipated.
    (B) Humans native to a studied organism's habitat hunt it more extensively due to poor crop yields.
    (C) Experimental data is lost due to faulty data storage.
    (D) Humans native to a studied organism's habitat migrate to another area.
    (E) The experimental data gathered from a large fishery is found to be based on faulty methodology.

11. It can be inferred from the passage that compared to the effect of humans consuming a species, the effect of native animals consuming that species is

Ⓐ less likely to influence ecological theorists
Ⓑ more applicable to the eventual survival of the species
Ⓒ necessary to quantify in order to establish a precise model for the species' population
Ⓓ more important in establishing a workable ecological model for that species
Ⓔ less likely to skew more traditional ecological models

DIRECTIONS: For Questions 12 to 15, select the *two* answer choices that, when used to complete the sentence, fit the meaning of the sentence as a whole *and* produce completed sentences that are alike in meaning.

---

12. Those who knew Alvarez were immune to his portrayal in the press as a boor, knowing that his veneer of churlishness hid a _____ human being.

A genial
B surpassing
C irascible
D affable
E choleric
F meek

13. Exceedingly _____ and only reliably produced by one mine in Australia, red diamonds are second only to jadeite in terms of their rarity.

A diaphanous
B brittle
C singular
D translucent
E valuable
F anomalous

14. Instead of the conventional advice to choose friends with personalities that contrast yours—for instance, befriending someone histrionic if you're _____—you may be happier if you find someone who has a more similar temperament to your own.

A fervid
B stolid
C phlegmatic
D demonstrative
E vehement
F saccharine

15. The situation was so fraught with uncertainty, the potential of discomfiture, and the threat of violence that even the most worldlywise traveler would have considered it a(n) _____.

- [A] embroilment
- [B] encomium
- [C] panegyric
- [D] hermitage
- [E] imbroglio
- [F] panacea

DIRECTIONS: For Questions 16 to 20, select *one* answer choice unless otherwise instructed.

Question 16 is based on the following reading passage:

The 30 or 40 mounds discovered up to this time in this region of the Takawgamis have, so far as examined, a uniform structure. Where stone could be obtained, there is found below the surface of the ground a triple layer of flat limestone blocks, placed over the
Line remains interred. In one mound, at the point where the Rainy Lake enters the Rainy
(5) River, there is a mound situated in which there was found on excavation, a structure of logs some ten feet square, and from six to eight feet high. In all the others yet opened, the structure has been simply of earth of various kinds heaped together. It is possible that the mound containing the log structure may have been for sacrifice, for the logs are found to have been charred. One purpose of all the mounds of the Takawgamis was evi-
(10) dently burial, and in them all, charcoal lumps, calcined bones, and other evidences of fire are found. Would this conclusion antagonize the theory that the mounds were used for observation? Perhaps with a limited amount of land, the Takawgamis, by necessity, built structures with a dual purpose. Studies of tribes with more territory often show that reconnaissance and sepulchering had separate domains.

16. Select the sentence that supports a theory put forward by the passage.

Questions 17 to 19 are based on the following reading passage:

In a cyclotron, charged particles, or ions, are accelerated inside an evacuated tank, to prevent them from colliding with air molecules and being scattered. The vacuum tank is placed between the poles of an electromagnet, which creates a field that bends the
Line ion beam into a circular orbit between two accelerating electrodes, or "dees." Because
(5) the ions carry a positive electric charge, they are attracted toward the dee, which is electrically negative at the moment. Were it not for the magnetic field, the ions would be accelerated in a straight line; instead, they are deflected into a circular path back toward the dee gap. By the time the ions again reach the dee gap, the sign of the electric potential on the dees is reversed, so that now the ions are attracted toward the oppo-
(10) site dee. As this process of alternating the electric potential is repeated, the ions gain speed and energy with each revolution. This causes them to spiral outward in a regular manner. Finally, they strike a target inserted into their path or are extracted from the cyclotron for use as an external beam.

17. Based on the information presented in the passage, which of the following most closely represents the sequence of events describing the path of an ion in a cyclotron?

Ⓐ A positively charged ion is repelled from a negative dee, then attracted to a positive dee.

Ⓑ A negatively charged ion is attracted to a positive dee, then repelled by a negative dee.

Ⓒ A positively charged ion is attracted to a negative dee, then attracted by a magnetic field.

Ⓓ A positively charged ion is attracted to a negative dee, then attracted to a negative dee.

Ⓔ A positively charged ion is attracted to a negative dee, which reverses the ion's electric potential.

18. In the context in which it appears, "regular" most nearly means

Ⓐ normal

Ⓑ agreeable

Ⓒ average

Ⓓ predictable

Ⓔ useful

19. The author of the passage mentions the magnetic field primarily in order to

Ⓐ argue that the magnetic field is less important than the dee gap in cycling the ions

Ⓑ suggest that ions would accelerate to dangerous speeds without a magnetic field

Ⓒ provide support for the notion that, in nature, ions tend to travel in straight lines

Ⓓ cast doubt on the hypothesis that ions tend to travel elliptically once deflected

Ⓔ indicate the necessity of deflecting the ions back toward the dee gap

Question 20 is based on the following reading passage:

Last year, a certain orchard produced a record number of oranges. Will this year set another record? Consider that each orange is either produced by a current tree or by the growth of a new tree. For existing trees this year, oranges have been growing at a
Line rate much lower than for those same trees last year. And, there is no evidence that the
(5) number of new orange trees this year will be higher than the number of new trees last year. **It is likely that the new trees this year will not produce more oranges than last year's new trees.** The conclusion is obvious. **The number of oranges produced this year will not surpass last year's record.**

20. In the argument given, the two portions in **boldface** play which of the following roles?

Ⓐ The first is an objection that the argument refutes; the second is the primary conclusion of the argument.

Ⓑ The first is a hypothesis that is used to support the position that the argument opposes; the second is a claim used to support the argument's main conclusion.

Ⓒ The first is a hypothesis that, if true, would support the argument's primary conclusion; the second is that primary conclusion.

Ⓓ The first is a hypothesis that, if true, would support the argument's primary conclusion; the second is a conclusion drawn to support that primary conclusion.

Ⓔ The first is an objection that the argument refutes; the second is the main conclusion of the argument.

SECTION 3—QUANTITATIVE REASONING

TIME: 35 MINUTES—20 QUESTIONS

> **DIRECTIONS:** For Questions 1 to 3, enter your answer in the grid below the question. Equivalent forms of the correct answer, such as 2.5 and 2.50, are all correct. Fractions do not need to be reduced to lowest terms.

1. A list contains n consecutive integers. The least integer on the list is –8, and the sum of the integers is 0. What is the value of n?

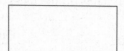

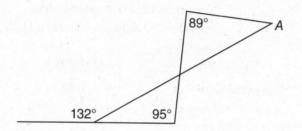

2. In the figure above, what is the degree measure of angle A?

3. One of the roots of the equation $2x^2 - 9x - 18 = 0$ is 6. What is the other root?

DIRECTIONS: For Questions 4 to 6, compare Quantity A and Quantity B, using the additional information given, if any, and select *one* of the following four answer choices:

(A) Quantity A is greater.

(B) Quantity B is greater.

(C) The two quantities are equal.

(D) The relationship cannot be determined from the information given.

x is a real number greater than 30.

y is a real number less than −40

	Quantity A	Quantity B
4.	$y - x$	$x - y$

The probability that independent events C and D will both occur is 0.11.

	Quantity A	Quantity B
5.	The probability that event C will occur	0.09

Mary paid $201 for a stereo that was marked at 25% off the original list price.

	Quantity A	Quantity B
6.	The amount Nan paid for the same stereo marked at 15% off the original list price	$227

DIRECTIONS: For Questions 7 to 20, select *one* answer choice unless otherwise instructed.

For Questions 7 to 9, consider each of the choices separately and select *all* that apply.

7. If p and m are odd integers, then which of the following must be an even integer?

   Indicate *all* that apply.

   A $p \times m$

   B $3p - 2m$

   C $2(p + 2m)$

   D $p + m$

   E $3(3p + 5m)$

8. The lengths of three sides of a triangle are 12, 17, and *x*. The *perimeter* of the triangle could be which of the following?

    Indicate *all* that apply.

    A 28
    B 34
    C 40
    D 57
    E 60

9. In a given month, a restaurant spends between 55% and 70% of its revenue on food and supplies, and between 23% and 28% of its revenue on staff salaries. The remaining revenue is the restaurant's net profit. If the restaurant earned $80,000 in revenue one month, which of the following could have been its net profit?

    Indicate *all* that apply.

    A $1,000
    B $1,700
    C $10,000
    D $17,000
    E $18,000

Questions 10 and 11 are based on the following chart, which shows how Ann spent her income of $4,080 one month.

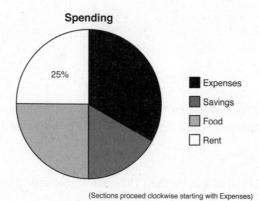

Spending

25%

■ Expenses
■ Savings
■ Food
□ Rent

(Sections proceed clockwise starting with Expenses)

For Question 10, enter your answer in the grid below the question. Equivalent forms of the correct answer, such as 2.5 and 2.50, are all correct. Fractions do not need to be reduced to lowest terms.

10. Ann spent twice as much on expenses as on savings. If she spent an equal amount on food plus rent as on expenses plus savings, how much did she spend on expenses?

    $ _____

11. Ann's rent represents 25% of her total spending. If her rent decreases by $244.80, and she uses this money to add to her savings, what percent of her total spending will then be used for rent?

Ⓐ 17%
Ⓑ 18%
Ⓒ 19%
Ⓓ 20%
Ⓔ 21%

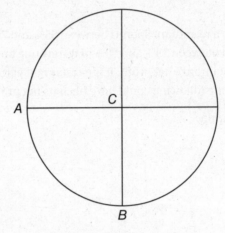

12. The circle above, with center C, has been divided into four congruent regions, each with area equal to 9π. What is the length of segment $\overline{AB}$ (not shown)?

Ⓐ 6
Ⓑ $6\sqrt{2}$
Ⓒ $6\sqrt{3}$
Ⓓ 6π
Ⓔ $9\sqrt{2}$

For Questions 13 to 15, enter your answer in the grid below the question. Equivalent forms of the correct answer, such as 2.5 and 2.50, are all correct. Fractions do not need to be reduced to lowest terms.

13. If six books cost a total of $29.10, then 16 books at the same price per book would cost how much?

$

14. If $69 - 11x = 3x - 99$, then what is the value of x?

15. A special language is invented with 12 consonants and five vowels. All words in the language contain exactly four letters. All words begin and end with a consonant and have two vowels in between. How many possible words in the language contain four *different* letters?

Questions 16 to 18 are based on the following table, which shows trends in sales at four companies over a 2-year period.

Company	Percent Changes in Total Sales	
	From 2009 to 2010	From 2010 to 2011
A	+10	−10
B	+12	+13
C	+17	−5
D	−3	+22

16. If the total sales for Company D in the year 2009 were $66,000, what were the sales at Company D in the year 2011, *rounded to the nearest dollar?*

$ [   ]

17. Which company's total sales increased by the most dollars over the 2-year period?

Ⓐ Company A
Ⓑ Company B
Ⓒ Company C
Ⓓ Company D
Ⓔ There is not enough information to determine.

For Question 18, consider each of the choices separately and select *all* that apply.

18. Which of the following statements must be true?

Indicate *all* that apply.

A Company A's total sales decreased over the 2-year period from 2009 to 2011.
B Company B's total sales increased by a higher percentage over the 2-year period than any of the other company's.
C At Company C, the ratio of total sales in 2011 to total sales in 2009 was 112:100, or 28:25.

For Questions 19 and 20, enter your answer in the grid below the question. Equivalent forms of the correct answer, such as 2.5 and 2.50, are all correct. Fractions do not need to be reduced to lowest terms.

19. A company manufactures nails that are meant to be precisely 10 cm long. The company devalues nails that differ in length from 10 cm. The amount a nail is devalued, in cents, is given by the function $D(x) = 6\sqrt{|x - 10|}$, where x represents the nail's length in centimeters and D represents the amount of the devaluation in cents. How much is a nail measuring 9.91 cm devalued?

 cents

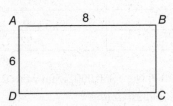 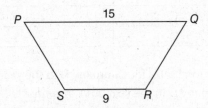

20. The area of rectangular region $ABCD$ above is equal to the area of the isosceles trapezoid $PQRS$, with PS equal to QR. What is the length of segment $\overline{QR}$?

SECTION 4—VERBAL REASONING

TIME: 30 MINUTES—20 QUESTIONS

> **DIRECTIONS:** For Questions 1 to 6, select *one* entry for each blank from the corresponding column of choices. Fill all blanks in the way that best completes the text.

1. Despite his occasional _____, the professor was, all in all, a tolerant man who avoided judgment of others' views.

Ⓐ epigram
Ⓑ intrepidness
Ⓒ perspicacity
Ⓓ fulmination
Ⓔ equanimity

2. After research began to overwhelmingly support the connection between the consumption of transfats and heart disease and the city's electorate began an outcry against their use, it seemed _____ that lawmakers would refrain from banning them from restaurants.

Ⓐ improbable
Ⓑ plausible
Ⓒ precarious
Ⓓ tacit
Ⓔ furtive

3. The author's current prose is so (i) _____ that it is almost unrecognizable in light of his former writing, which was usually noted for its flourishes and flair but often criticized for those same instances of what many considered to be (ii) _____.

Blank (i)	Blank (ii)
Ⓐ eloquent	Ⓓ grandiloquence
Ⓑ rhetorical	Ⓔ severity
Ⓒ sparing	Ⓕ asceticism

4. The premise that corporations are (i) _____ to the opinions of their stockholders is a concept underlying much of modern investment advice. But in a world where the exhortations of even the largest shareholders are (ii) _____ by many of the world's biggest companies, it can be difficult to imagine how these monoliths might be influenced. Though most large companies are publicly owned, businesses with omnipotent boards of directors are so (iii) _____ that changing the current system seems almost futile.

Blank (i)	Blank (ii)	Blank (iii)
Ⓐ inured	Ⓓ trivialized and disregarded	Ⓖ pervasive
Ⓑ subject	Ⓔ assimilated and utilized	Ⓗ puissant
Ⓒ privy	Ⓕ classified and considered	Ⓘ deviant

5. The renewable energy companies in competition for funding all had compelling ideas, but despite the (i) _____ nature of the solar panel firm and its research, it bested the more inveterate competitors in attendance, (ii) _____ the lion's share of the acclaim at the festival.

Blank (i)	Blank (ii)
Ⓐ veteran	Ⓓ demurring
Ⓑ inchoate	Ⓔ relinquishing
Ⓒ indefatigable	Ⓕ garnering

6. Both the kingdom's poets and princes tended to speak of the storm-plagued mountain range in its northern territory as (i) _____ that (ii) _____ its inhabitants, while the eastern tribes, who were known for their reckless belligerence toward the kingdom, considered it to be a (iii) _____ that even their most savage warriors would not dare to cross.

Blank (i)	Blank (ii)	Blank (iii)
Ⓐ an encumbrance	Ⓓ jeopardized	Ⓖ vulnerability
Ⓑ a boon	Ⓔ stymied	Ⓗ nadir
Ⓒ an augur	Ⓕ safeguarded	Ⓘ juggernaut

Questions 7 to 9 are based on the following reading passage:

As is well-known, Burroughs regards language as a virus that has invaded humanity, making humans dual creatures, alienated from a more interesting (not necessarily truer) universe. Language is a parasite, benefiting from human activity and direct-
Line ing it. Recording could be seen as a way in which language holds, imposing a simple
(5) linearity on experience. Hence, the cut-up is a way of disrupting this. The cutting-up of recording is not just the written cut-up by other means—it is a deeper operation, not because it operates with voice instead of writing, but precisely because it operates through a prosthetic living, a prosthetic speaking, both of which emphasize that there is only ever prosthesis when it comes to the ideas or conditions of living. The mixing
(10) of different recordings intervenes directly in the symbiotic evolution of recording and the human. It refuses the immunity of inoculation (i.e., living with recording, accepting linear, spool-based life) and replaces it with a constant test situation. Disrupting the "natural" progress of recording methods in order to illustrate the chance elements and the "flaws" in systems that allow operation, cutting up recordings, literally or otherwise,
(15) takes the recording into the realm of recombinant DNA. This might seem an obvious and only metaphorical connection, but the working of DNA occurs very much within the thinking induced by recording as medium.

7. The author of the passage would consider which of the following to be most similar to Burroughs' reasoning?

Ⓐ Those who do not contribute to society are less intelligent than those who do.
Ⓑ If a joke is not funny, the words are to blame, not the joke teller.
Ⓒ The act of regarding a star makes it real; until then, it does not exist.
Ⓓ The image of a photograph held in one's mind is illusory; the actual photograph is less real than its subject.
Ⓔ An adult is more encumbered than a newborn baby is in terms of experiencing things that foster excitement and delight.

8. Select the sentence of the passage in which the author expresses skepticism about established wisdom about a topic.

9. In the context in which it appears, "holds" (line 4) most nearly means

Ⓐ grasps
Ⓑ supports
Ⓒ retains
Ⓓ controls
Ⓔ withstands

Questions 10 and 11 are based on the following reading passage:

Line

(5)

(10)

Paglen's work deftly limns the boundaries between art and scholarship, while also suggesting a provocative conjunction of politics and tourism. His unassuming prose requires visitors to read between the lines in order to generate their own interpretations and conclusions. Even if the truth is out there, as Paglen's work argues implicitly, finding answers is not an easy task. As access to unalloyed truth seems increasingly to occupy an elusive position on an infinitely receding horizon, Paglen's rare type of work becomes ever more important. A responsible citizenry may no longer rely (if indeed it ever could) on official pronouncements from corporate and governmental press offices. Instead, those who wish to educate themselves about the world must function as detectives or journalists, following threads and triangulating sources. Paglen's work is exemplary for its insistent look at some of the things we may least want to admit about our government. And his method is ultimately pedagogical, proffering more questions than answers, along with hints about how to uncover the truth for ourselves, if only we have the nerve to do so.

For Question 10, consider each of the choices separately and select *all* that apply.

10. It can be inferred from the passage that the author would agree with which of the following statements?

Indicate *all* that apply.

A The boundary between art and scholarship should be abolished.
B The government should do more to communicate correct information to its people.
C Paglen's work advocates self-responsibility in terms of interpreting its message.

11. The author mentions the "infinitely receding horizon" primarily in order to

Ⓐ draw a parallel to Paglen's lack of forthrightness
Ⓑ support the notion that long-range vision is crucial to setting goals
Ⓒ identify a commonality between politics and tourism
Ⓓ emphasize the difficulty involved in determining facts
Ⓔ indicate the universality of Paglen's message

Question 12 is based on the following reading passage:

Insecticide Q is noteworthy both for its control of pests that attack crops and its benignity toward humans. However, its effects only last 30 days, a period insufficient to protect any major crop until harvest, and a reapplication of Insecticide Q usually kills the crop. Insecticide P, on the other hand, can be reapplied indefinitely without damaging the crop. Therefore, Insecticide Q has no discernible use in protection of major crops.

12.   Which of the following, if true, most seriously undermines the argument?

Ⓐ   There are several minor crops that can be harvested in as few as 20 days.
Ⓑ   A third insecticide not mentioned in the passage protects crops better than either Insecticide Q or P.
Ⓒ   Foods treated with Insecticide P are often banned from organic markets.
Ⓓ   Both Insecticides Q and P can be used on the same crop.
Ⓔ   The production of Insecticide P, once economical, has recently tripled in cost.

DIRECTIONS: For Questions 13 to 16, select the *two* answer choices that, when used to complete the sentence, fit the meaning of the sentence as a whole *and* produce completed sentences that are alike in meaning.

---

13.   Notwithstanding his _____ talents, after walking out onto the expansive stage and feeling the expectant hush of the arena, the young virtuoso felt quite incapable of performing the piece he had so mellifluously played in practice.

A   prodigious
B   exiguous
C   meager
D   multifarious
E   melodious
F   extraordinary

14.   The difficulty inherent in witnessing one's thoughts lies in their _____ nature; but although most thoughts are fleeting, the care necessary to observe them can be worthwhile.

A   ponderous
B   ephemeral
C   evanescent
D   weighty
E   arbitrary
F   efficient

15. Chastised for the _____ manner by which he conducted his research, Kopitsky was repeatedly warned by his professor that, if the delays continued, the funding for the study might be withdrawn.

     A industrious
     B breathless
     C dilatory
     D biased
     E tardy
     F tendentious

16. Modesty, while usually befitting, is not immune to excess; a surfeit of self-effacement can well be considered _____.

     A conceit
     B humility
     C avarice
     D haughtiness
     E meekness
     F timorousness

DIRECTIONS: For Questions 17 to 20, select *one* answer choice unless otherwise instructed.

Questions 17 and 18 are based on this passage.

As a siren approaches an observer, the pitch of its sound seems to get progressively higher. As it passes the observer and moves farther away from him, its pitch seemingly descends. Why does this occur, when it is apparent that the true pitch of the siren remains constant? This effect, commonly known as the Doppler effect, is attributable to the change in frequency of the siren's sound waves relative to the observer, and relies on the theory that sound is emitted in waves. As the siren approaches, each sound wave takes less and less time to reach the observer's ears and as it recedes, each wave takes a longer amount of time to travel back to the observer.

For Question 17, consider each of the answer choices and select *all* that apply.

17. Which of the following statements is supported by the passage?

     Indicate *all* that apply.

     A The Doppler effect is universally accepted by physicists.
     B The pitch from a siren moving away from an observer seems lower than it actually is.
     C The Doppler effect was proposed before the advent of electric sirens.

18. The passage provides information on each of the following except

(A) what happens to the relative pitch of a sound wave as its source approaches an observer
(B) what happens to the relative pitch of a sound wave as its source recedes from an observer
(C) the physical property of sound necessary to produce the Doppler effect
(D) whether the pitch of a sound at the observer's location is the same as its pitch while it is approaching the observer
(E) the distance from the observer at which the sound is most intense

Questions 19 and 20 are based on the following reading passage:

Well before the discovery of the New World, traditional Chinese copper "cash" had served as a model for Japan and Korea's first indigenous currencies. Copper "cash" was also sought after in many parts of Southeast Asia, where previously South-Indian-mod-
Line eled gold and silver currency had been in use, and its possession also was often seen
(5) as a patent to nobility. Notably, in the mid-12th century, Japan imported large amounts of Chinese copper coins, even though it was more copper abundant than China, and not bereft of metallurgic know-how. Invented in China as early as the 11th century yet largely phased out by the 14th century, banknotes came into use in Europe only in the 17th century and spread continuously thereafter. It is arguably this temporal divide that
(10) might help explain the varying degree to which Chinese emperors and European monarchs aimed at enhancing seignorage revenue, i.e., the difference between the face-value and metal value of their coins.

19. In the context in which it appears, "patent to" (line 5) most nearly means

(A) protection of
(B) assurance of
(C) approval for
(D) yearning for
(E) copyright of

20. Which of the following best characterizes the function of the indicated portion of the passage (Notably . . . know-how)?

(A) It contradicts a point made earlier in the passage.
(B) It provides evidence supporting a claim.
(C) It summarizes a point with which the author disagrees.
(D) It puts forward a theory on which a subsequent example is based.
(E) It explains an apparent contradiction in the passage.

SECTION 5—QUANTITATIVE REASONING

TIME: 35 MINUTES—20 QUESTIONS

DIRECTIONS: For Questions 1 to 5, compare Quantity A and Quantity B, using the additional information given, if any, and select *one* of the following four answer choices:

Ⓐ Quantity A is greater.
Ⓑ Quantity B is greater.
Ⓒ The two quantities are equal.
Ⓓ The relationship cannot be determined from the information given.

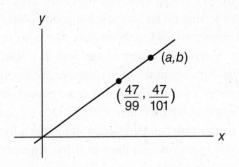

Quantity A	Quantity B
1. a	b

$$2^m = 32$$

Quantity A	Quantity B
2. 3^m	m^3

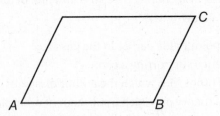

In the parallelogram above,
which is not a rectangle, $AB = 40$ and $BC = 50$.

Quantity A	Quantity B
3. The area of the parallelogram	2,000

$$x^2 + 5x = 6$$

Quantity A	Quantity B
4. $(x+6)(x-1)$	1

Country X is in the shape of a rectangle 80 km wide by 100 km long.
Ann lives on the border of Country X,
and her three children each live inside the country.

Quantity A	Quantity B
5. The sum of the distances from Ann's house to each of her three children's houses	300 km

---

DIRECTIONS: For Questions 6 to 18, select *one* answer choice unless otherwise instructed.

6. Evaluate $1 + \dfrac{1}{1 + \dfrac{1}{1 + \dfrac{1}{1+1}}}$

  Ⓐ 1.4
  Ⓑ 1.5
  Ⓒ 1.6
  Ⓓ 1.7
  Ⓔ 1.8

7. Five people in a room weigh an average of 120 pounds each. When a sixth person enters, the average weight in the room increases to 125 pounds per person. What does the sixth person weigh?

  Ⓐ 130 pounds
  Ⓑ 135 pounds
  Ⓒ 140 pounds
  Ⓓ 145 pounds
  Ⓔ 150 pounds

Questions 8 and 9 are based on the following graph, which shows the number of hours that 10 students studied for a quiz plotted against each student's subsequent quiz score. The line of best fit (trend line) has been plotted for the data. Each dot represents an individual student.

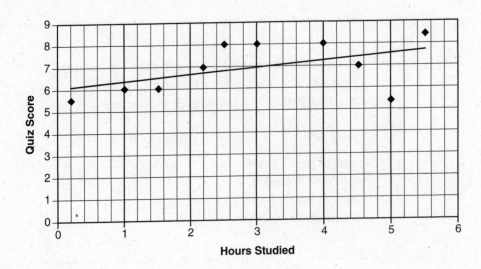

8. What was the quiz score of the student whose score *least* fit the general pattern of data?

    (A) 5
    (B) 5.5
    (C) 6
    (D) 7
    (E) 8

For Question 9, consider each of the answer choices and select *all* that apply.

9. Which of the following statements appear to be true from the data?

    Indicate *all* that apply.

    A The data supports the statement, "Students who studied for more hours tended to receive higher quiz scores."
    B No student who studied for fewer than two hours received a score above six.
    C The mode quiz score was greater than the median quiz score.
    D Some students received the same quiz scores as each other, even though the number of hours they studied differed by more than 1 full hour.

10. $3^{20} + 3^{22}$ is how many *times* greater than 3^{20}?

Ⓐ 9
Ⓑ 10
Ⓒ 20
Ⓓ 27
Ⓔ 3^{20}

11. If $3\left(1+\dfrac{2}{x}\right) = 4\left(2-\dfrac{1}{x}\right)$, then what is the value of x?

Ⓐ $\dfrac{1}{2}$

Ⓑ 1

Ⓒ $\dfrac{3}{2}$

Ⓓ 2

Ⓔ $\dfrac{5}{2}$

12. Eight less than the square of x is less than eight. Which of the following expresses all possible values of x?

Ⓐ $x < 8$
Ⓑ $x < 4$
Ⓒ $x < 0$
Ⓓ $-4 < x < 4$
Ⓔ $x > 4$ or $x < -4$

For Questions 13 and 14, enter your answer in the grid below the question. Equivalent forms of the correct answer, such as 2.5 and 2.50, are all correct. Fractions do not need to be reduced to lowest terms.

13. Five different video games are to be tested on five consecutive weekdays, one game per day. How many different orderings of these games are possible?

14. The sum of two numbers is 40 and their difference is 26. What is their product?

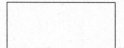

Questions 15 and 16 are based on the following table, which shows student enrollment at College Y over a 7-year period.

Year	Number of males enrolled	Number of females enrolled	Total enrollment
2000	362	571	933
2001	354	537	891
2002	400	450	850
2003	412	416	828
2004	423	390	813
2005	440	360	800
2006	458	302	760

15. What was the greatest percentage decrease in total enrollment from one year to the next?

    Ⓐ 4.6%
    Ⓑ 4.7%
    Ⓒ 4.8%
    Ⓓ 4.9%
    Ⓔ 5.0%

16. In the year 2007 (not shown), n male students and 300 female students enrolled in College Y, and the median total enrollment for the 8 years from 2000 through 2007 became 834.5. What is the value of n?

    Ⓐ 519
    Ⓑ 535
    Ⓒ 540
    Ⓓ 541
    Ⓔ 551

17. Children who ride the roller coaster must be between 24 and 52 inches tall. If x represents the height in inches of a child who may ride the roller coaster, which of the following absolute value inequalities represents all possible values of x?

    Ⓐ $|x - 24| < 52$
    Ⓑ $|x - 28| < 14$
    Ⓒ $|x - 38| < 14$
    Ⓓ $|x - 14| < 38$
    Ⓔ $|x - 28| < 52$

For Question 18, enter your answer in the grid below the question. Equivalent forms of the correct answer, such as 2.5 and 2.50, are all correct. Fractions do not need to be reduced to lowest terms.

18. The ratio of programmers to scientists at a company was 8:5 in the year 2000 and 3:4 in the year 2010. If the total number of programmers *and* scientists at the company was 52 in the year 2000 and 196 in the year 2010, how many more scientists were at the company in 2010 than in 2000?

DIRECTIONS: For Questions 19 and 20, compare Quantity A and Quantity B, using the additional information given, if any, and select *one* of the following four answer choices:

Ⓐ Quantity A is greater.

Ⓑ Quantity B is greater.

Ⓒ The two quantities are equal.

Ⓓ The relationship cannot be determined from the information given.

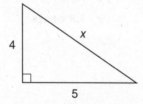   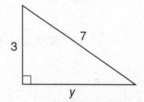

Quantity A	Quantity B
x	y

19.

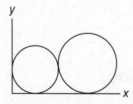

The circle at left above is tangent to the
x- and y-axes, and has radius equal to 3.
The circle at right above is tangent to the x-axis and
to the other circle and has radius equal to 4.

Quantity A	Quantity B
The slope of the line containing the centers of the two circles.	$\dfrac{1}{7}$

20.

ANSWER KEY
Practice Test 3

ANSWER KEY

Section 2: Verbal Reasoning

1. **C**
2. **A**
3. **B, D**
4. **C, D**
5. **A, F**
6. **A, E, G**
7. **D**
8. **C**
9. **A**
10. **B**
11. **E**
12. **A, D**
13. **C, F**
14. **B, C**
15. **A, E**
16. **The last sentence**
17. **D**
18. **D**
19. **E**
20. **C**

Section 3: Quantitative Reasoning

1. **17**
2. **54**
3. **$-\dfrac{3}{2}$ or –1.5**
4. **B**
5. **A**
6. **A**
7. **C, D, E**
8. **C, D**
9. **B, C, D**
10. **$1,360**
11. **C**
12. **B**
13. **$77.6 or $77.60**
14. **12**
15. **2,640**
16. **$78,104**
17. **E**
18. **A, B**
19. **1.8 cents**
20. **5**

Section 4: Verbal Reasoning

1. **D**
2. **A**
3. **C, D**
4. **B, D, G**
5. **B, F**
6. **B, F, I**
7. **E**
8. **Sentence 8**
9. **D**
10. **C**
11. **D**
12. **D**
13. **A, F**
14. **B, C**
15. **C, E**
16. **A, D**
17. **B**
18. **E**
19. **B**
20. **B**

Section 5: Quantitative Reasoning

1. **A**
2. **A**
3. **B**
4. **B**
5. **D**
6. **C**
7. **E**
8. **B**
9. **A, B, C, D**
10. **B**
11. **D**
12. **D**
13. **120**
14. **231**
15. **E**
16. **D**
17. **C**
18. **92**
19. **A**
20. **A**

ANSWER EXPLANATIONS

Section 2—Verbal Reasoning

1. **(C)** The phrase "when in fact" signifies a change in the sentence's direction, so a word such as *accretion* (growth by gradual addition) is a logical shift from "come out of nowhere."

2. **(A)** If the scientist's results matched those from labs with *stringent* (strict) quality standards, it would make sense that finding out that his supplier was *adulterating* (making impure by adding cheaper ingredients) its chemicals would make him *flabbergasted* (shocked).

3. **(B, D)** That lenders were *cognizant* (aware) of the *tenuousness* (uncertainty) of the market would make it all the more *reprehensible* (blameworthy) that they still loaned money. Since they are still loaning money in a worse market, it follows that the author thinks they deserve *censure* (condemnation) from regulators.

4. **(C, D)** Since Phillips seems to think the studies are "misguided," it makes sense that his book is a *disparagement* (belittling) of them. If the "traditionalists" did something unsurprising to this *contrarian's* (one who goes against the norm) views, logically they must have *reprehended* (condemned) those views.

5. **(A, F)** Since the countries didn't want a panic, they must have wanted their people to believe the survival tips would work. They downplayed a potential war's severity to add *credence* (believability) to the tips' *efficacy* (effectiveness). Given their goal, hiring physicists who were *complicit* (acting as an accomplice in a crime) in this deception made sense.

6. **(A, E, G)** The *proliferation* (growth) of online marketplaces would *facilitate* (help) reselling. Since the author poses the question "is it surprising. . .bidder?," one can infer that the artists and critics do not like this fact because the word "though" prefaces a shift from their opinion; therefore, it makes sense they have *reviled* (sharply criticized) this reselling. *Mercenary* (motivated by profit) fits because of the passage's topic: those who buy and sell art for monetary gain.

7. **(D)** This weakens the argument because if cars that are built better last longer, then the cars in City X built before 1980 probably still exist because of the quality with which they were built. Therefore, these existing cars might not represent all cars built before 1980, since many of those cars may have been discarded. Perhaps even most of the pre-1980 cars had poor quality and were quickly discarded.

8. **(C)** The author says that someone who studies the cats and their prey "may benefit from understanding" the cats' tendencies, but then goes on to say that "the capacity to actually estimate" the cats' behavior is "out of reach." Therefore, understanding the leopards' behavior would be more helpful than a scientific or quantitative model.

9. **(A)** The author stops short of saying that ecological methods of prediction do not work ("the gist is not that ecological paradigms are failing") and instead argues that people are expecting too much of these models, saying that they don't always work in practice, especially concerning small populations. Therefore, he is describing the limitations of ecological methods.

10. **(B)** The author cites the "exploitation of (an organism) by indigenous people" as a reason that ecological models should not pretend to be able to predict that organism's population in such cases. In other words, he argues that the typical ecological model could not account for an organism being hunted by humans in its habitat.

11. **(E)** The passage says that accounting for the effect of animals consuming fish "may be warranted," but then calls the prediction of the effect of humans consuming fish a "pretense," saying it is not realistic. Therefore, the effect of animals consuming the species is less likely to invalidate the model described in the passage.

12. **(A, D)** Since those who knew Alvarez are immune, or not fooled by, his portrayal in the press as a *boor* (rude person) and since he is described as having a *veneer* (thin covering) of *churlishness* (rudeness), it can be inferred that instead, he is *genial* (good-natured) or *affable* (friendly).

13. **(C, F)** If red diamonds are only produced in one mine and second only to another mineral in their rarity, they must be extremely uncommon. Both *singular* (unusual) and *anomalous* (abnormal) would describe them well.

14. **(B, C)** The "for instance" is an example of the conventional advice: to choose someone unlike yourself. If someone is *histrionic* (overly emotional), someone who is either *stolid* (unemotional) or *phlegmatic* (calm) would have a contrasting personality.

15. **(A, E)** The described situation is clearly difficult if even a *worldlywise* (experienced) traveler would think so. Therefore, the situation could well be described as an *embroilment* (entanglement) or an *imbroglio* (difficult situation).

16. **(The last sentence: Studies of tribes . . . domains.)** The theory the passage postulates is that "perhaps with a limited amount of land, (they) . . . built structures with a dual purpose." The last sentence supports this theory by providing evidence that other tribes with more territory kept observation and burial separate.

17. **(D)** The passage explains that the ions, which are positive, are attracted to the negative dee, then again attracted to a negative dee after the dee's electric potential has been reversed.

18. **(D)** It can be inferred from the context that the author believes that the ions in the cyclotron act in a predictable way because their behavior is described chronologically and authoritatively; the author therefore uses "regular" to mean "predictable."

19. **(E)** The author explains the magnetic field as a tool with which to direct the ions back toward the dee gap; he is therefore indicating the necessity of that direction for the operation of the cyclotron.

20. **(C)** The first portion in **boldface** is a hypothesis: this year is not over. If that hypothesis is correct, that this year's trees will not produce more oranges than last year's new trees, then the hypothesis supports the argument's conclusion. That conclusion is the second sentence in **boldface**, which postulates that this year's orange crop will not break last year's record.

Section 3—Quantitative Reasoning

*Indicates an alternative way to solve the problem.

1. **(17)** Begin by writing out a few of the numbers to get a feeling for the problem: –8, –7, –6 . . . 0, 1, 2, 3 . . . . They are *consecutive integers* beginning at –8. The question asks how many of these must be added, so that the sum is 0. Look for cancellation! If we extend the list to positive 8, then every positive integer may be paired with its opposite, to make the sum 0.

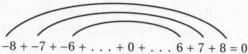

$$-8 + -7 + -6 + . . . + 0 + . . . 6 + 7 + 8 = 0$$

The list now contains $n = 17$ numbers, namely eight positives, eight negatives, and the one number that is neither positive nor negative: zero.

2. **(54)**

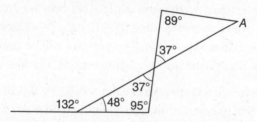

First, find the angle adjacent to the 132° angle along the line segment at bottom, which equals $180 - 132 = 48°$, because the angles comprising a straight line sum to 180°. Then two angles in the lower triangle are known, so we can subtract their sum from 180 to find the third angle. $180 - (48 + 95) = 37°$.

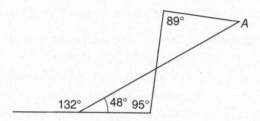

Both the top angle of the lower triangle and the bottom angle of the upper triangle become 37°, because when two lines intersect, the angles directly across from each other, "vertical angles," are equal. Now angle A, the third angle in the upper triangle equals $180 - (89 + 37) = 54°$.

3. **($-\frac{3}{2}$ or –1.5)** The Fundamental Theorem of Algebra states that if 6 is a root of the equation $2x^2 - 9x - 18 = 0$, then $x - 6$ is a factor of the polynomial. So $2x^2 - 9x - 18 = (x - 6)(\underline{\hspace{1cm}} + \underline{\hspace{1cm}})$. Fill in the blanks and thus factor the polynomial by noting that $2x^2$ and -18 must be formed as products, when multiplying by x and -6, respectively: $2x^2 - 9x - 18 = (x - 6)(2x + 3)$. The two solutions are $x - 6 = 0$, so $x = 6$ (already known), or $2x + 3 = 0$, so $x = -\frac{3}{2}$ or –1.5.

4. **(B)** Pick numbers, say 40 for x and –50 for y. Then (A) is $-50 - 40 = -90$, and (B) is $40 - (-50) = 40 + 50 = 90$. So (B) is greater. Quantity (B) will *always* be greater because it will be positive in value (since the double negatives cancel to make a positive), while Quantity (A) will always be negative.

5. **(A)** The probability of any event is between 0 and 1, inclusive; that is, $0 \le p \le 1$, for any probability, p. The probability of two independent events both occurring is the product of their individual probabilities. If the probability of Event C occurring were as low as .09, the value in column (B), then the probability of both events occurring would be less than or equal to .09, since .09 times a number from 0 through 1 would be at most .09. But the given probability of both events occurring is .11, which is greater than .09, so the probability of Event C occurring cannot be as low as .09, and therefore it must be greater than .09, and (A) is correct.

6. **(A)** Let p = the full price, before any discounts. Then Mary, who received 25% marked off the price, paid $p - .25p = .75p$. Since she also paid $201, we know $.75p = 201$. Divide by .75 to obtain $1p = \$268$. Nan received a 15% discount, so she paid $1p - .15p = .85p$, which is $.85 \times 268 = \$227.80$, a little more than $227, so (A) is correct.

7. **(C, D, E)** The easiest way is to pick numbers for the two odds, say $p = 3$, and $m = 5$. Then (A) is $pm = 15$, not an even number, and (B) is $3(3) - 2(5) = -1$, also not even, so (A) and (B) are both incorrect. (C) is always even by definition, because it is written as 2 times another integer. Because $3 + 5 = 8$, (D) is correct. 8 is even, and, in general, the sum of two odds is even. (E) is correct, because the value of the inner parentheses is even (since it is the sum of two odd numbers), and an even times any integer is even. Here, for example, $(3 \times 3 + 5 \times 5) = 9 + 25 = 34$. The answer is (C), (D), and (E).

8. **(C, D)** The triangle inequality states that in a triangle, the sum of any two of the side lengths is always greater than the length of any one. Equivalently, any one side length in a triangle must be less than the sum of the other two, but greater than the difference of the other two side lengths. Here, $17 - 12 < x < 17 + 12$, or $5 < x < 29$. Then the sum of the triangle's three side length, its perimeter, will be greater than $5 + 12 + 17$ but less than $29 + 12 + 17$. This means $34 < \text{perimeter} < 58$. Choices (C) and (D) satisfy this.

9. **(B, C, D)** The restaurant will spend more than $55 + 23 = 78\%$ of its revenue but less than $70 + 28 = 98\%$ of its revenue on food, supplies, and staff salaries combined. Then its remaining net profit, after these expenses are subtracted from revenue, will be between 2% and 22% of revenue, because $100 - 78 = 22$, and $100 - 98 = 2$. Then for a revenue of $80,000, the profit, p, will satisfy $.02 \times 80,000 < p < .22 \times 80,000$, which implies $1600 < p < 17,600$. (B), (C), and (D) satisfy this.

10. **($1,360)** Since Ann spent twice as much on expenses as on savings, we can think of expenses as $2x$ and savings as x, for some unknown x. If she spent an equal amount on food plus rent as on expenses plus savings, then expenses plus savings must account for exactly $\frac{1}{2}$ of all spending. This means that $2x + 1x = \frac{1}{2}$, as long as x represents the *proportion* of spending on savings. Then $3x = \frac{1}{2}$, and multiplying by $\frac{1}{3}$ on each side yields $x = \frac{1}{6}$. In other words, $x = \frac{1}{6}$ of Ann's spending was on savings, and therefore $2x = 2\left(\frac{1}{6}\right) = \frac{2}{6} = \frac{1}{3}$ was for expenses. One-third of the total $4,080 is $4,080 \div 3 = \$1,360$.

11. **(C)** Ann's rent is $.25(4,080) = \frac{1}{4} \times 4,080 = \$1,020$. When this is reduced by $244.80, her rent becomes $1,020 - 244.80 = \$775.20$. This represents $\frac{775.2}{4,080} = .19 = 19\%$ of savings, (C).

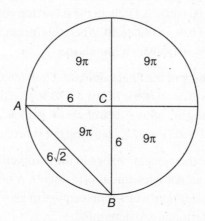

12. **(B)** The area of the full circle is $4 \times 9\pi = 36\pi$. The circle's area is also given by the formula πr^2. So $36\pi = \pi r^2$, and the radius, r, equals 6. Then $AC = BC = 6$. The four sectors are congruent, so the four central angles at point C are all equal, and thus each measures one-fourth of $360°$. (Since are $360°$ in a circle.) That is, angle ACB measures $\frac{1}{4} \times 360° = 90°$. Then triangle ACB is an isosceles right triangle (45-45-90 triangle), the side lengths of which are always in the ratio $x : x : x\sqrt{2}$. This means that the length of hypotenuse AB equals the leg length times $\sqrt{2}$, which equals $6\sqrt{2}$, (B). If you don't have the formula for the 45-45-90 triangle memorized, you can also obtain the last result from the Pythagorean theorem: $6^2 + 6^2 = 36 + 36 = 72 = c^2$, and $c = \sqrt{72} = \sqrt{36 \times 2} = 6\sqrt{2}$.

13. **($77.6 or $77.60)** Set up a ratio to compare the number of books to their cost, aligning the unknown, x, with the desired cost:

$$\frac{\text{books}}{\text{cost}} : \frac{6}{29.10} = \frac{16}{x}$$

Cross multiply to obtain $6x = 465.50$, and divide by 6 to get $x = \$77.6$ or $\$77.60$.

14. **(12)** Copy out the given equation and then add $11x$ and 99 to both sides, in order to combine like terms:

$$
\begin{array}{rcl}
69 - 11x &=& 3x - 99 \\
+99 + 11x & & +11x + 99 \\
\hline
168 &=& 14x
\end{array}
$$

Dividing both sides by 14 yields $x = 12$.

15. **(2,640)** Draw out four blanks to represent the four places in the word to be filled: _____ _____ _____ _____. In each blank, write the number of different ways that particular place can be filled. The total number of combinations will then equal the product of the numbers in the blanks. There are 12 consonants and five vowels in the language. Words fit the CVVC pattern, so we might expect the total number of possible words to equal $12 \times 5 \times 5 \times 12$. But since we are looking for words with

no repeated letters, the number of possibilities for the second vowel and for the second consonant are each reduced by 1, so the answer becomes $12 \times 5 \times 4 \times 11 = 2{,}640$ possible words with four different letters.

16. **($78,104)** When Company D's value decreased by 3%, it retained 97% of its value of $66,000, which is $.97 \times 66{,}000 = \$64{,}020$. In the following year, it increased in value by 22% of this, or $.22 \times \$64{,}020 = \$14{,}084.40$. When this increase is added to 64,020, the final value becomes $78,104.4, which rounds to $78,104.

   *A nice shortcut is to think of the final value as $1.22(.97(66{,}000))$, which is entered on the calculator as $1.22 \times .97 \times 66{,}000 = 78{,}104.4 \approx 78{,}104$. In this approach, we obtain 1.22 mentally by thinking of (value + 22% of value) as $1V + .22V = 1.22V$. Similarly, value minus 3% of value is $1V - .03V = .97V$, justifying the shortcut.

17. **(E)** We are informed of the percent change in the companies' total sales, but we have no information on the actual sales amounts in dollars. A small percentage of a high sales total could be greater than a larger percentage of a low sales total. Therefore, (E), there is not enough information to determine.

18. **(A, B)** For (A), it is easiest to imagine that the company started with sales of $100. After a 10% increase, it had sales of $100 + 10 = \$110$. When the company next experienced a 10% decrease in sales, it lost $.10 \times 110 = \$11$ in sales, so it had only $\$110 - 11 = \$99$ in sales. (Or $.9 \times 110 = \$99$, as in 16* above.) This makes (A) correct, because $99 < 100$, corresponding to a decrease in sales from the starting value. To compute Company B's change in sales for the 2-year period, multiply 1.12 by 1.13 to represent the 12% increase "on top of" a 13% increase (again, see 16* above). This yields $1.12 \times 1.13 \approx 1.266$, or about a 26.6% increase for the 2-year period. Inspection of the other numbers shows that none of the other companies increased by as much, so (B) is correct. You can use the percent change figures to compute Company C's total sales ratio for 2011 to 2009. Assume the figure is $100 in 2009. After a 17% increase, the sales will equal $117. However, to decrease this number, $117, by 5% is not to simply subtract 5 from 117, to obtain 112, and so the ratio will not equal 112:100, and (C) is not correct. Company C's sales in 2011 in this example would equal $.95 \times 117 = 111.15$, and so the proper ratio of sales between the two years would be 111.15:100. The answer is (A) and (B).

19. **(1.8 cents)** Plug the value $x = 9.91$ into the function $D(x) = 6\sqrt{|x - 10|}$, which becomes $6\sqrt{|9.91 - 10|} = 6\sqrt{|-0.9|} = 6\sqrt{.09} = 6(.3) = 1.8$ cents.

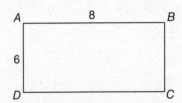 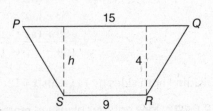

20. **(5)** The area of rectangular region *ABCD* is equal to $6 \times 8 = 48$. The area of a trapezoid is given by $\dfrac{b_1 + b_2}{2} \times h$, where b_1 and b_2 are the bases (the parallel sides)

and h is the height, or perpendicular altitude drawn between the bases. Here, $\frac{b_1+b_2}{2}=\frac{15+9}{2}=\frac{24}{2}=12$. This means that $12 \times h = 48$, since the trapezoid's area equals that of the rectangle, and $h=4$.

Finally, the symmetry of the isosceles trapezoid and the central rectangle allow us to infer that XY, in the figure below, is equal to 9, and that PX and YQ are both equal to $\frac{15-9}{2}=3$. Then QR is the hypotenuse of a right triangle with legs equal to 3 and 4, so $QR=5$, by the Pythagorean theorem, because $3^2+4^2=5^2$.

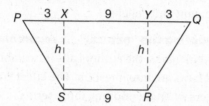

If you forget the formula for area of a trapezoid, you can also find h by setting the sum of the areas of the rectangle and two right triangles in the figure above equal to the known area of 48. That is $9h+2\left(\frac{3 \times h}{2}\right)=48$, so $9h+3h=48$, and $12h=48$, and again $h=4$.

Section 4—Verbal Reasoning

1. **(D)** The word *despite* indicates that the professor's occasional behavior contrasts with his usual tolerance, so *fulmination* (strong condemnation) would work.

2. **(A)** Since the research shows transfats are harmful and the *electorate* (group of voters) has an outcry against them, lawmakers will probably ban them, i.e., it is *improbable* (unlikely) that they'll refrain from banning them.

3. **(C, D)** Since the author's earlier writing was noted for its "flourishes and flair," it must have a decorative, showy style. If blank (i) was *sparing* (restrained), it would make sense that the current work is unrecognizable. Blank (ii) should fit "flourishes and flair" but have a more negative connotation; *grandiloquence* (marked by excess) fits.

4. **(B, D, G)** A clue for blank (i) is provided in the second sentence, with the phrase "it can be difficult to imagine how these *monoliths* (large organizations) might be influenced." Since the second sentence begins with "but," the first sentence must express an idea in contrast to this difficulty, and *subject* (under the power of) creates that contrast. For blank (ii), the same clue can be used, and the phrase "even the largest shareholders" implies that the companies cannot be swayed. Therefore, *trivialized and disregarded* logically fits. Blank (iii) must support the last sentence, and if *omnipotent* (all-powerful) boards of directors are *pervasive* (spread throughout), it would be difficult to effect change.

5. **(B, F)** For blank (ii), *garnering* makes sense because the solar panel company "bested" its competitors. A clue for blank (i) is provided with the word "despite," which signifies that the blank is the opposite of *inveterate* (established), so *inchoate* (in an early stage) would fit.

6. **(B, F, I)** It's easiest to start with blank (iii): if the savage warriors dare not cross the range, they would consider it to be a *juggernaut* (overwhelming force). Then, blank (i) could be *a boon* (something beneficial), since the eastern tribes are known for their *belligerence* (warlike nature) toward the kingdom. Blank (ii) would then have to be *safeguarded* (protected), since the mountains are protecting the inhabitants by keeping out the tribes.

7. **(E)** Only this choice is analogous to Burroughs' portrayal of language as a parasitic virus that makes life less interesting. Therefore, an adult who possesses language would be less likely than a newborn baby to be able to experience interesting things that produce excitement and delight.

8. **(Sentence 8: Disrupting the "natural" . . . recombinant DNA.)** In this sentence, by his use of quotation marks, the author calls the established wisdom about what is natural and what flaws are into question. The effect is as if he is making quotation marks with his fingers when mentioning those terms.

9. **(D)** In this context, "holds" means "controls," since the sentence continues to say that it "impose(s) a simple linearity on experience." This "imposing" implies that language is controlling experience.

10. **(C)** By saying that Palgen's work has "hints about how to uncover the truth for ourselves" and that the reader is required to "read between the lines," the author implies that the work does not merely provide answer, but instead encourages the reader to think and draw her own conclusions.

11. **(D)** The context of the rest of the sentence provides clues. Since the author claims that access to truth is "elusive," the image of a receding horizon logically continues that idea; since the horizon recedes from the viewer, the truth draws farther away, making it more difficult to obtain.

12. **(D)** If both of the insecticides can be used, then the argument, that Insecticide Q has *no* role, is weakened. Perhaps its harmless nature toward humans would make using it for the first 30 days and then using Insecticide P afterward an effective plan.

13. **(A, F)** The word *notwithstanding* (in spite of) creates a shift, so since the *virtuoso* (master musician) feels as though he cannot play, if his talents are *prodigious* (impressive) or *extraordinary*, then there is a surprising outcome as indicated by the shift.

14. **(B, C)** A clue for the blank is given by the description of thoughts' *fleeting* (short-lived) nature; therefore, both *ephemeral* (short-lived) and *evanescent* (short-lived) would also aptly describe the thoughts.

15. **(C, E)** Kopitsky's manner is being criticized, since his professor is *chastising* (criticizing) him and warning him about the consequences of continued delays. Both *dilatory* (tending to delay) and *tardy* (tending toward lateness) would thus describe Kopitsky's research.

16. **(A, D)** If modesty is not immune to excess, then it is vulnerable to being overdone. The semicolon indicates a continuation of the sentence's theme since there are no shifting words, so a *surfeit* (overabundance) of *self-effacement* (modesty) could be called words like *conceit* (an excessively favorable opinion of oneself) or *haughtiness* (pridefulness), both of which are near-opposites of modesty.

17. **(B)** The passage states that the pitch of a siren "seemingly descends" as it moves away from an observer, which supports the assertion that the pitch seems lower but is not actually lower.

18. **(E)** The passage makes no mention of the *intensity* of a sound relative to an observer; it only discusses the changes in relative pitch and frequency of the sound.

19. **(B)** If the coins were sought after, "patent to" in this context means a guarantee or assurance of nobility if the coins were possessed by someone.

20. **(B)** The sentence provides evidence (Japan collected the Chinese coins) that supports a claim (having the coins was desirable and was seen as an indication that the owner of the coins was of a noble class).

Section 5—Quantitative Reasoning

1. **(A)** When a line passes through the origin, $(0, 0)$, the x- and y-coordinates of any point on the line will vary directly with each other. In other words, there is some constant, k, for which $y = kx$, or $\frac{y}{x} = k =$ the slope of the line. $\frac{47}{99} > \frac{47}{101}$, so the x-coordinate of *any* point on the line (in Quadrant I) will be greater than the y-coordinate, and $a > b$, making (A) greater. This is because the constant $k = \dfrac{\frac{47}{101}}{\frac{47}{99}} < 1$, so the slope is less than 1. Think of this as meaning that the "rise" is less than the "run," so that the "up amount" of any point on the line, or its y-coordinate, is less than the "across amount," or its x-coordinate. This makes $b < a$, and $a > b$.

2. **(A)** Solve for m by trial and error. Observe that $2^5 = 2 \times 2 \times 2 \times 2 \times 2 = 8 \times 4 = 32$, so $m = 5$. Then (A) is $3^5 = 3 \times 3 \times 3 \times 3 \times 3 = 243$, while (B) is $5^3 = 5 \times 5 \times 5 = 125$, and (A) is greater.

3. **(B)**

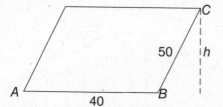

The area of the parallelogram will not equal 40×50, but $40h$, because area is given by base $\times$ height. $h < 50$, because h is the leg of a right triangle with hypotenuse equal to 50. Then area, $40h$, is less than 40×50, so (B), equal to $40 \times 50 = 2{,}000$, is greater.

4. **(B)** Many equations with an x^2 are solved by first getting one side equal to 0. If $x^2 + 5x = 6$ then $x^2 + 5x - 6 = 0$. The left side is factored as $(x + 6)(x - 1)$, since $6x - 1x = 5x$. Quantity (A) exactly matches the factored form $(x + 6)(x - 1)$, which equals 0. Since $1 > 0$, Quantity (B) is greater.

5. **(D)** There are a couple of different ways to draw the picture:

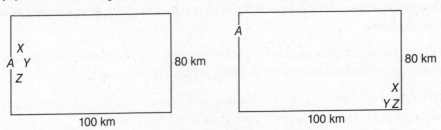

The three children, say *X*, *Y*, and *Z*, might all live quite near Ann, *A*, which would make (B) greater. But the children may also live near the opposite corner of the rectangular region from Ann, which would make each distance greater than 100 and the sum greater than 300. (D) is correct.

6. **(C)** Work your way up from the bottom. $\frac{1}{1+1} = \frac{1}{2}$, and this added to 1 is $1\frac{1}{2}$,

or $\frac{3}{2}$. To divide $\frac{1}{\frac{3}{2}}$, change to multiplication by the reciprocal of the denominator:

$1 \times \frac{2}{3} = \frac{2}{3}$. This added to 1 becomes $\frac{2}{3} + \frac{3}{3} = \frac{5}{3}$. As before, $\frac{1}{\frac{5}{3}} = \frac{3}{5}$. Finally,

$1 + \frac{3}{5} = 1 + .6 = 1.6$, (C).

7. **(E)** If the average weight of five people is 120 pounds per person, then the total weight in the room is $5 \times 120 = 600$ pounds. A moment later there are

$6 \text{ people} \times 125 \frac{\text{pounds}}{\text{person}} = 750$ pounds in the room. This means that the 6th person

brought $750 - 600 = 150$ new pounds to the room, (E).

8. **(B)** By visual inspection, the point in the lower right, (5, 5.5) is farthest from the line, so it represents the student who least fit the general pattern of data. Reading straight across to the left, we see that the score for this student is 5.5, (B).

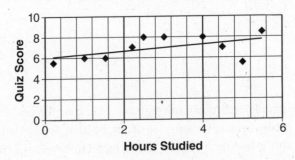

9. **(A, B, C, D)** (A) The trend line, or line of best fit, has a positive slope. It inclines upward as we move from left to right, implying that scores rise with more hours studied. (B) There are three students who studied for less than 2 hours, the 3 points in the lower left. Two of these students scored a 6, but none scored above 6. (C) The most frequently recurring quiz score, or *mode* quiz score, is 8. The median, or middle value on the list, must be below 8, because only four of the scores are as high as 8, while

six of the scores are below 8. Specifically, the median of 10 scores will always be the average of the 5th and 6th highest scores, both of which, here, are less than 8. (D) The two students who scored a 7 differed in their number of hours studied by more than 2 full hours.

10. **(B)** The question is really asking, for what number n will $3^{20} + 3^{22} = 3^{20} \times n$. Factor the left side by factoring out 3^{20}, the greatest common factor of 3^{20} and 3^{22}. Then $3^{20}(1 + 3^2) = 3^{20} \times n$, since exponents are added when multiplying expressions with a common base. So $3^{20}(1 + 9) = 3^{20}(10) = 3^{20}n$, and $10 = n$, to make the two sides match, (B).

11. **(D)** Begin by distributing on both sides to obtain $3 + \dfrac{6}{x} = 8 - \dfrac{4}{x}$. Now combine like terms by subtracting 3 and adding $\dfrac{4}{x}$ to each side. This yields $\dfrac{10}{x} = 5$, so $10 = 5x$, and $x = 2$, (D). Check by putting 2 back in as x to see that $3(1 + 1) = 3 \times 2 = 6$, which also equals $4\left(2 - \dfrac{1}{2}\right) = 4 \times 1\dfrac{1}{2} = 6$.

12. **(D)** Translate the words into math symbols, noting that *eight less than the square of x* translates into x-squared minus 8, so $x^2 - 8 < 8$. Add 8 to both sides, and $x^2 < 16$. Avoid carelessly taking the square-root of each side to obtain $x < 4$, (B), because this approach neglects consideration of negative values. Negative numbers that are more than 4 units from 0 will become positive and greater than 16 when squared, failing to satisfy the inequality. All numbers less than 4 units from 0 in either direction will be less than 16 when squared:

The values of x within the shaded region, $-4 < x < 4$, (D), satisfy the inequality.

13. **(120)** Many students will not get past the initial thought that the answer *must be* 5×5 and will quickly enter 25, which is incorrect. To solve, take a "fill in the blank" approach. Write out five blanks to represent the five weekdays, say Monday through Friday: _____ _____ _____ _____ _____. In each blank, write the number of ways that particular blank can be filled.

On Monday, there are five possible games we could test, so write 5 in the first blank. On Tuesday, there are only four choices left, because the same game will not be tested again. Since five different games need to be tested in the 5-day period, repeats are precluded. Write 4 in the second blank. On Wednesday, there are only three choices remaining, and so forth. By the *Basic Counting Principle*, the total number of combinations equals the product of these numbers. Therefore, there are $5 \times 4 \times 3 \times 2 \times 1$ or 120 total orderings.

14. **(231)** Think of the unknowns as x and y, and set up a linear system:

$$x + y = 40$$
$$x - y = 26$$

If we add the two whole rows together, the y and $-y$ term cancel, and $2x = 66$, so $x = 33$. Substituting this value back into the first row shows that $y = 7$, since $33 + 7 = 40$. Finally, the product means xy, which is $33 \times 7 = 231$.

15. **(E)** Look only at the total enrollment column at the right. This shows a few small yearly decreases and three larger decreases of 42, 41, and 40, in the periods from 2000 to 2001, 2001 to 2002, and 2005 to 2006, respectively. Put each decrease over the starting value of that period, to determine the percent change. The calculator shows that the greatest is $\frac{40}{800} = .05 = 5\%$ (E).

16. **(D)** Conveniently, the numbers are already in (decreasing) numerical order, making it easy to compute the median. The median annual total enrollment through 2006 is simply 828, the number in the middle. If the new value, the 2007 total enrollment, were less than 828, the median would go down and would not equal 834.5, as required. If the 2007 total were more than 850, then the median for the 8 years would be $\frac{828 + 850}{2}$, the average of the two middle values, and again would not equal 834.5. Therefore, the 2007 total enrollment, say x, must have been between 828 and 850, and more importantly, when x is averaged with 828, the result is the median for all 8 years, 834.5. This means $\frac{828 + x}{2} = 834.5$. So $828 + x = 1,669$. Then $x = 1,669 - 828 = 841$. Finally, 300 of these 841 students were female, leaving $841 - 300 = 541$ males, (D).

17. **(C)** Find the average of 24 and 52, which is $\frac{24 + 52}{2} = 38$, in order to find the midpoint of 24 and 52 on a number line. The number 38 is located 14 units from both 24 and 52, so we can think of all permissible heights as those within 14 units of 38. By definition, $|x - 38|$ means the distance from x to 38 on a number line. If we want this to be less than 14, choice (C), $|x - 38| < 14$, properly expresses the relationship.

18. **(92)** In the year 2000, there were eight programmers for every five scientists for every $8 + 5 = 13$ total people. This means that programmers were $\frac{8}{13}$ of all people and that scientists were $\frac{5}{13}$ of all people. (We need only consider these two types of employees as "people.") Then there were $\frac{5}{13} \times 52 = 20$ scientists at the company in 2000. In 2010, there were three programmers for every four scientists for every $3 + 4 = 7$ total people. So scientists were $\frac{4}{7}$ of the 196 employees, which equals $\frac{4}{7} \times 196 = 112$ scientists. Then there were $112 - 20 = 92$ more scientists in 2010.

19. **(A)** This is a direct application of the Pythagorean theorem, $a^2 + b^2 = c^2$, which relates the side lengths in a right triangle. Notice that to solve for x, you are finding the hypotenuse—c in the formula—but that to solve for y, you are finding one of the

legs $-a$ or b in the formula. $4^2 + 5^2 = x^2$, so $16 + 25 = x^2$, and $x = \sqrt{41}$. Furthermore, $3^2 + y^2 = 7^2$, so $9 + y^2 = 49$, making $y = \sqrt{49-9} = \sqrt{40}$. Because $\sqrt{41} > \sqrt{40}$, **(A)** is greater.

20. **(A)**

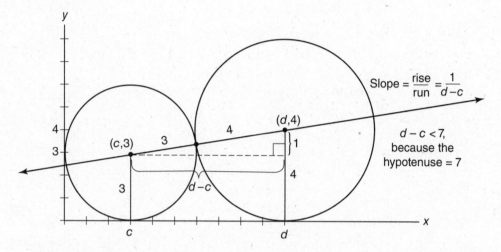

The segment whose endpoints are the centers of the two circles will have a length of $3 + 4 = 7$, because the segment consists of the radii of the two circles meeting endpoint to endpoint on a straight line. Since the circles are *tangent* to the x-axis (intersecting at exactly one point), the radius of each circle, when drawn to the x-axis, will be perpendicular to the x-axis and will determine the center's y-coordinate. That is, one circle's center is 3 units above the x-axis, and one center is 4 units above the x-axis. Then for some constants, c and d, we can think of the coordinates of the two centers as $(c,3)$ and $(d,4)$. To find the slope of the segment, find change in y over change in x, or $\frac{y_2 - y_1}{x_2 - x_1} = \frac{4-3}{d-c} = \frac{1}{d-c}$. We can infer that $d-c$ is less than 7, because it represents the length of the horizontal leg of the right triangle depicted, which must be less than the length of the triangle's hypotenuse, 7. (Specifically, $d - c = \sqrt{7^2 - 1^2} = \sqrt{48} < 7$.) Then $\frac{1}{d-c} > \frac{1}{7}$, so **(A)** is greater. For positive values, a larger number in the denominator makes the fraction smaller.

Practice Test 4

Section 2: Verbal Reasoning

1. Ⓐ Ⓑ Ⓒ Ⓓ Ⓔ
2. Ⓐ Ⓑ Ⓒ Ⓓ Ⓔ
3. Ⓐ Ⓑ Ⓒ Ⓓ Ⓔ Ⓕ
4. Ⓐ Ⓑ Ⓒ Ⓓ Ⓔ Ⓕ
5. Ⓐ Ⓑ Ⓒ Ⓓ Ⓔ Ⓕ
6. Ⓐ Ⓑ Ⓒ Ⓓ Ⓔ Ⓕ
   Ⓖ Ⓗ Ⓘ
7. Ⓐ Ⓑ Ⓒ Ⓓ Ⓔ

8. Ⓐ Ⓑ Ⓒ Ⓓ Ⓔ
9. Ⓐ Ⓑ Ⓒ Ⓓ Ⓔ
10. Ⓐ Ⓑ Ⓒ Ⓓ Ⓔ
11. Ⓐ Ⓑ Ⓒ Ⓓ Ⓔ
12. Ⓐ Ⓑ Ⓒ Ⓓ Ⓔ Ⓕ
13. Ⓐ Ⓑ Ⓒ Ⓓ Ⓔ Ⓕ
14. Ⓐ Ⓑ Ⓒ Ⓓ Ⓔ Ⓕ
15. Ⓐ Ⓑ Ⓒ Ⓓ Ⓔ Ⓕ

16. Highlight sentence in passage.
17. Ⓐ Ⓑ Ⓒ Ⓓ Ⓔ
18. Ⓐ Ⓑ Ⓒ Ⓓ Ⓔ
19. Ⓐ Ⓑ Ⓒ Ⓓ Ⓔ
20. Ⓐ Ⓑ Ⓒ Ⓓ Ⓔ

Section 3: Quantitative Reasoning

1. Ⓐ Ⓑ Ⓒ Ⓓ
2. Ⓐ Ⓑ Ⓒ Ⓓ
3. Ⓐ Ⓑ Ⓒ Ⓓ
4. Ⓐ Ⓑ Ⓒ Ⓓ
5. Ⓐ Ⓑ Ⓒ Ⓓ
6. Ⓐ Ⓑ Ⓒ Ⓓ
7. Ⓐ Ⓑ Ⓒ Ⓓ

8. Ⓐ Ⓑ Ⓒ Ⓓ
9. Ⓐ Ⓑ Ⓒ Ⓓ Ⓔ
10. Ⓐ Ⓑ Ⓒ Ⓓ Ⓔ
11. [   ]
12. [   ]
13. [   ]
14. [   ]

15. [   ]
16. [   ]
17. [   ]
18. [   ]
19. Ⓐ Ⓑ Ⓒ Ⓓ Ⓔ
20. Ⓐ Ⓑ Ⓒ Ⓓ Ⓔ

Section 4: Verbal Reasoning

1. Ⓐ Ⓑ Ⓒ Ⓓ Ⓔ
2. Ⓐ Ⓑ Ⓒ Ⓓ Ⓔ
3. Ⓐ Ⓑ Ⓒ Ⓓ Ⓔ Ⓕ
4. Ⓐ Ⓑ Ⓒ Ⓓ Ⓔ Ⓕ
   Ⓖ Ⓗ Ⓘ
5. Ⓐ Ⓑ Ⓒ Ⓓ Ⓔ Ⓕ
   Ⓖ Ⓗ Ⓘ
6. Ⓐ Ⓑ Ⓒ Ⓓ Ⓔ Ⓕ
   Ⓖ Ⓗ Ⓘ

7. Ⓐ Ⓑ Ⓒ Ⓓ Ⓔ
8. Ⓐ Ⓑ Ⓒ
9. Ⓐ Ⓑ Ⓒ Ⓓ Ⓔ
10. Ⓐ Ⓑ Ⓒ
11. Ⓐ Ⓑ Ⓒ
12. Ⓐ Ⓑ Ⓒ Ⓓ Ⓔ Ⓕ
13. Ⓐ Ⓑ Ⓒ Ⓓ Ⓔ Ⓕ
14. Ⓐ Ⓑ Ⓒ Ⓓ Ⓔ Ⓕ
15. Ⓐ Ⓑ Ⓒ Ⓓ Ⓔ Ⓕ

16. Ⓐ Ⓑ Ⓒ
17. Highlight sentence in passage.
18. Ⓐ Ⓑ Ⓒ Ⓓ Ⓔ
19. Ⓐ Ⓑ Ⓒ Ⓓ Ⓔ
20. Ⓐ Ⓑ Ⓒ Ⓓ Ⓔ

Section 5: Quantitative Reasoning

1. Ⓐ Ⓑ Ⓒ Ⓓ
2. Ⓐ Ⓑ Ⓒ Ⓓ
3. Ⓐ Ⓑ Ⓒ Ⓓ
4. Ⓐ Ⓑ Ⓒ Ⓓ
5. Ⓐ Ⓑ Ⓒ Ⓓ
6. [   ]
7. [   ]

8. [   ]
   ──────────
   [   ]
9. [   ]
10. Ⓐ Ⓑ Ⓒ Ⓓ Ⓔ
11. Ⓐ Ⓑ Ⓒ Ⓓ Ⓔ
12. Ⓐ Ⓑ Ⓒ Ⓓ Ⓔ
13. Ⓐ Ⓑ Ⓒ Ⓓ Ⓔ

14. Ⓐ Ⓑ Ⓒ Ⓓ Ⓔ
15. Ⓐ Ⓑ Ⓒ
16. Ⓐ Ⓑ Ⓒ Ⓓ Ⓔ Ⓕ
17. Ⓐ Ⓑ Ⓒ Ⓓ
18. Ⓐ Ⓑ Ⓒ Ⓓ Ⓔ
19. [   ]
20. [   ]

SECTION 1—ANALYTICAL WRITING

TIME: 60 MINUTES—2 WRITING TASKS

TASK 1: ISSUE EXPLORATION

TIME: 30 MINUTES

The topic is presented in a one- to two-sentence quotation commenting on an issue of general concern.

Your essay will be judged on the basis of your skill in the following areas:

- response to the specific task instructions
- consideration of the complexities of the issue
- organization, development, and expression of your ideas
- support of your position with relevant reasoning and examples
- control of the elements of standard written English

> **TOPIC**
>
> Colleges should require all students to demonstrate proficiency in at least one foreign language.

DIRECTIONS: Write a response in which you discuss the extent to which you agree or disagree with the recommendation and explain your reasoning for the position you take. In developing and supporting your position, describe specific circumstances in which adopting the recommendation would or would not be advantageous and explain how these examples shape your position.

TASK 2: ARGUMENT ANALYSIS

TIME: 30 MINUTES

Your essay will be judged on the basis of your skill in the following areas:

- identification and assessment of the argument's main elements
- organization and articulation of your thoughts
- use of relevant examples and arguments to support your case
- handling of the mechanics of standard written English

TOPIC

Our school is the best choice for students considering a career in theatre. First, our school does not require an audition and encourages applicants of all acting experience levels to apply. Second, our students are trained in all major schools of acting methods. Finally, many of our graduates have gone on to achieve acting roles in Broadway productions and Hollywood films.

DIRECTIONS: Write a response in which you discuss what questions would need to be addressed in order to decide whether the conclusion and the argument on which it is based are reasonable. Be sure to explain how the answers to the questions would help to evaluate the conclusion.

SECTION 2—VERBAL REASONING

TIME: 30 MINUTES—20 QUESTIONS

> **DIRECTIONS:** For Questions 1 to 6, select *one* entry for each blank from the corresponding column of choices. Fill all blanks in the way that best completes the text.

1. Far from the plodding predictability of most of the genre, the plots of the author's mysteries are _____ in that they seem driven mostly by whim and fancy.

Ⓐ reliable
Ⓑ constant
Ⓒ malleable
Ⓓ capricious
Ⓔ jejune

2. The victim of an accidental mushroom poisoning, the botanist considered that the culprit must have been a rogue foreign species, since he was familiar with all of the flora _____ to his region.

Ⓐ endemic
Ⓑ alien
Ⓒ amorphous
Ⓓ profligate
Ⓔ superfluous

3. Condominium owners have become so accustomed to the tax advantages derived from their rental properties that a fiscal policy designed to withdraw these benefits would invite (i) _____. Indeed, implementation of such a policy would be akin to trying to (ii) _____ a bone from the jaws of a starving dog.

   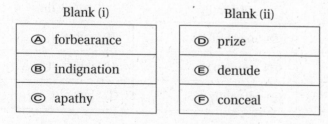

Blank (i)	Blank (ii)
Ⓐ forbearance	Ⓓ prize
Ⓑ indignation	Ⓔ denude
Ⓒ apathy	Ⓕ conceal

4. The need for a fresh perspective on the criteria by which university administrators design curricula is readily apparent, according to Boon. In his new book, he (i) _____ a plan whereby (ii) _____ transformation of the status quo can be effected. Boon's detractors, however, seem unified in their disparagement of his ideas, calling for an expeditious program of action.

Blank (i)	Blank (ii)
Ⓐ retracts	Ⓓ an abrupt
Ⓑ respects	Ⓔ an equivocal
Ⓒ delineates	Ⓕ an incremental

5. Contrary to what might seem logical, alpha males of many species engage in what might be dubbed "forced charity." The (i) _____ male bird in a group, for instance, certainly could command the lion's share of the food due to his status, but instead has been known to force feed other males, which usually accept their gifts passively. This display—both the dominance of the alpha and the resulting (ii) _____ of the lower status male—is undoubtedly an instinctive attempt to impress the females in the vicinity.

Blank (i)	Blank (ii)
Ⓐ preeminent	Ⓓ contention
Ⓑ representative	Ⓔ acquiescence
Ⓒ subordinate	Ⓕ demurral

6. It was only after witnessing the ingenue's (i) _____ performance that the film critic realized he had been presumptuous in his judgment of her ability, and he berated himself for not realizing it sooner. On screen, her impassive delivery combined with her (ii) _____ mannerisms reminded him of a mannequin (iii) _____ with just enough life to pass as a human, and he found himself dreading the next time her character would speak.

Blank (i)	Blank (ii)	Blank (iii)
Ⓐ breathtaking	Ⓓ mawkish	Ⓖ imbued
Ⓑ grating	Ⓔ wooden	Ⓗ divested
Ⓒ passable	Ⓕ sprightly	Ⓘ inflated

7. Reports that a popular brand of athletic shoe had been manufactured by workers deprived of basic labor rights seemed to have a negligible effect on consumers. When surveyed, few consumers said that they planned to change their brand preferences in spite of the damning reports. However, a month after the reports had been broadcast, retail sales of the brand of athletic shoe had dropped sharply.

    Which of the following, if true, best explains the apparent contradiction described in the passage?

    Ⓐ Consumer advocates did not believe that the majority of the company's workers were deprived of their rights.

    Ⓑ The reports did not mention any other footwear manufacturers, many of which have been accused of exploiting workers.

    Ⓒ The report aired on both television and public radio.

    Ⓓ So many reports about worker exploitation had been recently aired that consumers had become desensitized to such reports.

    Ⓔ Many retailers removed the brand from their shelves in response to the report.

Questions 8 to 11 are based on the following passage:

Poverty indexes are determined by pretax money income only and are adjusted annually for changes in the national cost of living, as reflected by the Consumer Price Index for urban dwellers. The official poverty threshold for a family of four, for example, has
Line grown from $2,973 in 1959 to $22,314 in 2010. However, the indexes and thresholds
(5) are not adjusted for regional differences in living costs. Consequently, since the cost of living in the Chicago metropolitan area is 18% greater than the national average for all urban areas, 23% greater in Los Angeles/Long Beach, and 140% greater in New York City, poverty is substantially underestimated in each of the three most populous urban centers.

(10) Counts and incidences of U.S. poverty are constructed from definitions and procedures adopted by the Bureau of the Census. These official estimates are universally employed by governmental agencies at all jurisdictional levels and have been used consistently since their original development by the Social Security Administration. In 1969, the Bureau of the Budget (now the Office of Management and Budget) formally prescribed
(15) the poverty thresholds as the official standard to be used by all federal agencies.

Yet, the estimates have been criticized and been modified over the years by several federal inter-agency committees. Some major points of criticism that still remain include that non-cash benefits (such as food stamps, school lunches, health benefits, subsidized housing, income-in-kind, and deferred benefits) as well as assets are excluded
(20) from the determination of poverty status; either median income or disposable income would be a more appropriate benchmark for poverty; money income is under-reported by recipients; inter-household transfers are unreliably estimated; intra-household

transfers are ignored; poor Blacks, Hispanics, and the homeless are particularly under-counted; the mix and cost of a nutritionally adequate diet needs to be updated.

(25) Nevertheless, as stated by Wendell Primus, "The real importance of a . . . poverty measure is not the number who is poor in any one year but the indicator's ability to show whether the number is decreasing or increasing over time." Despite modifications and numerous criticisms, it appears that the Census Bureau will continue to use the present definition of U.S. poverty and its methods of tabulation for the foreseeable future.

(30) There can be a wide variety of economic, social, psychological, and chance influences on the levels, trends, and divergences of the rates of poverty. Further, exogenous common factors may likely have affected the individual demographic groups in distinct ways. For example, a period of economic contraction does not provide a blanket of uniform hardship upon all subgroups. Ultimately, the end goal is to prevent and coun-
(35) teract those factors that cause poverty. The factors are likely to have time-, location-, and group-specific influences.

8. According to the passage, which of the following is true regarding U.S. poverty definitions?

    Ⓐ Federal poverty estimates and definitions have gone unchanged since 1969.
    Ⓑ Despite heavy criticism, poverty indexes have not been adjusted for the national cost of living for many years.
    Ⓒ Subsidized housing has recently been included in the determination of poverty status.
    Ⓓ The current definition of poverty has shown that the number of poor has increased recently.
    Ⓔ A city with a cost of living below the national average would have its poverty level overestimated.

9. In the fourth paragraph of the passage, the author is concerned primarily with

    Ⓐ responding to critics who claim the poverty level in the U.S. has risen
    Ⓑ pointing out an argument against the assertion that the current definition of poverty in the U.S. can be measured
    Ⓒ suggesting a reason behind the persistence of the current definition of poverty in the U.S.
    Ⓓ tracing the recent history of the Census Bureau's stance on the definition of poverty in the U.S.
    Ⓔ discussing the implications of a radical modification of the current definition of poverty in the U.S.

10. According to the passage, which of the following would NOT be considered an improvement to the current definition of poverty by one of the critics mentioned in the passage?

Ⓐ Include health care benefits in the determination of poverty status.

Ⓑ Include owned vehicles and real estate in the determination of poverty status.

Ⓒ Determine poverty status by using a family's income before taxes have been taken out of it.

Ⓓ Instill a method to increase the accuracy of reported money income by recipients.

Ⓔ Conduct a review of whether the current allotment of money for food is sufficient to buy healthy food.

11. Which of the following statements can be inferred from the passage?

Ⓐ The Consumer Price Index is the most accurate measure of the national cost of living.

Ⓑ The Bureau of the Budget had its name changed to reflect its expanded role in managing welfare programs.

Ⓒ Of the poverty in all U.S. cities, the poverty in New York City is the most underestimated.

Ⓓ The number of poor Blacks and Hispanics is larger than the number of poor whites in most U.S. cities.

Ⓔ During a recession, certain groups that fit the federal definition of poverty suffer less economic hardship than other groups do.

DIRECTIONS: For Questions 12 to 15, select the *two* answer choices that, when used to complete the sentence, fit the meaning of the sentence as a whole *and* produce completed sentences that are alike in meaning.

12. Although the sheriff had become accustomed to a certain level of _____ from the town's elected officials, he was still surprised by the way the new mayor quickly acceded to his requests.

A deference

B dissent

C yielding

D disapproval

E bureaucracy

F regulation

13. The positions of electrons were once thought to be definable; however, recent research has shown that, since measuring an electron affects its position, their locations are, in fact, _____.

   A ubiquitous
   B nebulous
   C straightforward
   D unequivocal
   E enigmatic
   F abundant

14. Dubbed a "walking contradiction" by his friends, the man offered sweet compliments from a gruff visage and offered _____ debate that belied his usually languid manner.

   A glacial
   B placid
   C languorous
   D spirited
   E mettlesome
   F insightful

15. The saleswoman thought that she had been both friendly and polite to the new customer; her boss agreed, but pointed out that she had also been overly _____ when she inquired about the health of their client's goldfish.

   A solicitous
   B felicitous
   C inappropriate
   D generous
   E altruistic
   F attentive

Question 16 is based on the following passage:

In autism, perception of the eyes in the context of a face is atypical. Children with autism demonstrate an advantage in face recognition when only the mouth or lower-face features are presented whereas typical children benefit more from the eyes. Chil-

Line dren with autism benefit more from the lower half of the face than from the upper face

(5) when making judgments about emotional expressions, in contrast to typical children. Similar findings have been made for adults with autism. When watching actors on screen, adults with autism look more at the mouth and less at the eyes than do typical adults. This bias toward looking at the mouth is unlikely to be a developmental delay: from the age of seven weeks, infants will fixate more on the eye region of the face when

(10) an adult begins to talk.

16.   Select the sentence in which the author provides support for a parallel drawn to a finding stated earlier in the passage.

Questions 17 to 19 are based on the following passage:

Cognitive brain functions including sensory perception and control of behav-ior are ascribed to computation in networks of neurons. In each biological neu-ron, dendrites receive and integrate synaptic inputs to a threshold for axonal firing

Line as output. Even though the behavior of an actual biological neuron is quite com-

(5) plex, in replicating complex behaviors, neurons are frequently modeled as simple integrate-and-fire neurons. Neuronal firings and their chemical synaptic transmis-sions are presumed to act like "bit states" in silicon computers. Information flows directionally through landscapes of integrate-and-fire neurons in feed-forward and feedback networks, accounting for various forms of brain cognition. However, cog-

(10) nition and consciousness may, or may not, coincide. Complex behaviors like walk-ing or driving are at times non-conscious autopilot functions and at other times accompanied by conscious perception and control. For example, we may drive to work on non-conscious autopilot while daydreaming—our conscious minds roaming elsewhere. But if a horn sounds or a light flashes, our conscious mind returns to con-

(15) scious perception and control. Studies of stimulus-independent thought ("mind wan-dering") show activity literally moving around the brain as the content of consciousness changes.

17.   In the context in which it appears, "ascribed" (line 2) most nearly means

Ⓐ inscribed
Ⓑ attributed
Ⓒ compared
Ⓓ allowed
Ⓔ imparted

18. The author of the passage mentions "autopilot functions" primarily in order to

Ⓐ argue that computation models of neuron behavior are oversimplified

Ⓑ suggest an alternate explanation for the behavior of dendrites

Ⓒ provide an example of neuron-produced computation that coincides with consciousness

Ⓓ cast doubt on the theory that cognition and consciousness are necessarily linked

Ⓔ warn against the dangers of non-conscious behavior

19. Which of the following can be inferred based on the information provided in the passage?

Ⓐ The behavior of neurons is too complex to be realistically modeled.

Ⓑ Early neuroscientists primarily compared brain functions to computer processes.

Ⓒ At least some of the time, sensory perception occurs during consciousness.

Ⓓ A dangerous stimulus is required for a rapid shift from autopilot behavior to consciously controlled behavior.

Ⓔ Humans are unable to go without daydreaming for more than a few hours at a time.

Question 20 is based on the following passage:

Musicians typically record most of their albums before the age of 35. Some have argued that this phenomenon is the result of older age diminishing creative processes. **But most musicians who record albums after the age of 35 started to record music only**
Line **after they turned 30**. Additionally, by the time most musicians have turned 30, they
(5) have been recording music for several years. So instead of arguing that old age reduces creativity, it can instead be suggested that **many musicians over the age of 35 produce fewer albums because they have been making music for too long to write compelling new music**.

20. In the argument given, the two portions in **boldface** play which of the following roles?

Ⓐ Each provides support for the primary explanation for the phenomenon described in the passage.

Ⓑ The first is a rebuttal of an assertion made by the argument; the second is that assertion.

Ⓒ The first provides evidence in support of an explanation that the argument challenges; the second is that explanation.

Ⓓ The first offers evidence in support of an explanation with which the argument agrees; the second is that explanation.

Ⓔ The first offers evidence in support of an explanation that the argument challenges; the second is an explanation with which the argument agrees.

SECTION 3—QUANTITATIVE REASONING

TIME: 35 MINUTES—20 QUESTIONS

DIRECTIONS: For Questions 1 to 8, compare Quantity A and Quantity B, using the additional information given, if any, and select *one* of the following four answer choices:

- Ⓐ Quantity A is greater.
- Ⓑ Quantity B is greater.
- Ⓒ The two quantities are equal.
- Ⓓ The relationship cannot be determined from the information given.

Team A has a 50% chance of winning any game that it plays. Team B has a 60% chance of winning any game that it plays.

	Quantity A	Quantity B
1.	The probability that Team A will win its next three games in a row	The probability that Team B will win its next four games in a row

	Quantity A	Quantity B
2.	The greatest common factor of 84 and 700	The least common multiple of 6 and 15

	Quantity A	Quantity B
3.	$(-2)^{16}$	8^5

$$(x^2 + 9)(x + 9)(x - 5) = 0$$

	Quantity A	Quantity B
4.	x	7

The number of pull-ups performed
in 1 minute by 10 kids in a class is given
by set $S = \{0, 0, 0, 2, 9, 11, 11, 14, 16, 17\}$

Quantity A	Quantity B
5.	The median number of pull-ups performed by the 10 kids	The mean (average) number of pull-ups performed by the 10 kids

---

Account M earns 4.3% interest, compounded annually.
Account N earns 2.9% interest, compounded annually.
Joe opens one account of each type on January 1, 2000.

Quantity A	Quantity B
6.	The amount of interest that Joe earns from leaving $X in account M for 6 years.	The amount of interest that Joe earns from leaving $Y in account N for 9 years.

---

x is a real number.

Quantity A	Quantity B
7.	$x^2 + 3$	$3x - 2$

Quantity A	Quantity B
8.	The number of hours in d days	The number of minutes in $\dfrac{d}{2.5}$ hours

9. The measure of one angle in an isosceles triangle is 120°. If the length of the side opposite this angle equals $12\sqrt{3}$, then what is the perimeter of the triangle?

   Ⓐ $18 + 12\sqrt{3}$

   Ⓑ $21 + 12\sqrt{3}$

   Ⓒ $24 + 12\sqrt{3}$

   Ⓓ $30 + 12\sqrt{3}$

   Ⓔ $36 + 12\sqrt{3}$

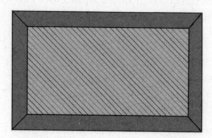

10. The diagram above represents a rectangular picture (inner region) surrounded by a picture frame of uniform width (darker region). The picture measures 8 inches by 12 inches. The area of the picture frame is equal to the area of the picture itself. What is the width of the frame?

   Ⓐ 0.5 inches
   Ⓑ 1 inch
   Ⓒ 1.5 inches
   Ⓓ 2 inches
   Ⓔ 4 inches

11. How many whole numbers between 100 and 200 are *not* equal to the square of another integer?

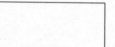

For Questions 12 to 18, enter your answer in the answer box below the question. Equivalent forms of the correct answer, such as 2.5 and 2.50, are all correct. Fractions do not need to be reduced to lowest terms.

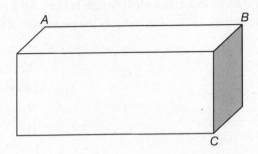

12. In the figure above, the shaded region is a square with area equal to 256. If *AB* = 8, then what is the length of diagonal *AC*?

13. A business is currently selling 30 chairs per day for a price of $25 per chair. A worker predicts that if the business chooses to lower the cost of the chairs, then for every $1 the price is lowered, one more chair will be sold. If the prediction is accurate, what is the maximum revenue the business can earn in a day from selling chairs? (*Revenue* is the amount of money that the business takes in, without consideration of expenses or other costs.)

$

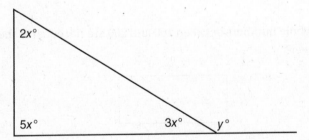

14. In the figure above, what is the value of *y*?

15. The ratio of boys to girls in a room is 7 to 5. The room contains 312 children. How many more boys than girls are in the room?

16. In a certain game, a player flips a coin to determine movement. Every toss of the coin lands with either a head facing up or a tail facing up. If a head is facing up, the player moves forward 10 squares, and if a tail is facing up, he moves backward 13 squares. After flipping the coin 120 times, the player is four squares forward of his starting position. How many of the 120 flips showed a head facing up?

17. A nurse has 80 ml of a solution that has a concentration of 5% Drug X in water. How many milliliters of pure water containing none of the drug must the nurse add to dilute the concentration to 2% Drug X in water?

ml

Appetizer	Entrée	Dessert
Fruit	Fish	Ice Cream
Salad	Steak	Cookie
Soup	Hamburger	Brownie
Nuts	Pizza	Milkshake
Dumpling		Pie
Tofu Skewer		

18. From the menu above, a restaurant offers customers two choices of appetizer and one choice each of entrée and dessert. If the appetizers must be different from each other, how many different meal combinations are available to customers?

Questions 19 and 20 are based on the following graph, which shows how the weight of three animals varied during a study in which the animals were fed an experimental diet. The weights at left are in kilograms.

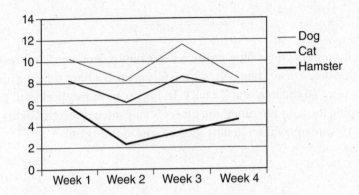

19. For the animal whose final weight differed most from its starting weight, what was the approximate change in weight from the beginning of the study to the end?

Ⓐ 1.0 kg
Ⓑ 1.5 kg
Ⓒ 2.0 kg
Ⓓ 2.5 kg
Ⓔ 3.0 kg

20. The data supports which of the following claims?

Ⓐ No animal gained or lost more than 50% of its body weight in one week.
Ⓑ The dog's weight throughout the study was always at least 2 kg greater than the cat's weight.
Ⓒ At least one animal weighed more at the end of the study than at the beginning.
Ⓓ At least one animal reached its maximum weight during week 3 of the study.
Ⓔ Each animal's weight first decreased, then increased, then decreased again during the study.

DIRECTIONS: For Questions 1 to 6, select *one* entry for each blank from the corresponding column of choices. Fill all blanks in the way that best completes the text.

---

1. Often considered by his peers to be a purveyor of _____, Simmons had to look to his students for admiration, who, in contrast to his more seasoned colleagues, often praised the sincerity and profundity with which he wrote.

Ⓐ rationality
Ⓑ claptrap
Ⓒ esoterica
Ⓓ indecency
Ⓔ prolixity

2. Despite its wealth of ingenuity, science fiction has never been known for the accuracy of its foresight; however, a notable minority of its authors have managed more than a middling degree of _____, correctly predicting such inventions as the Internet.

Ⓐ veracity
Ⓑ prescience
Ⓒ myopia
Ⓓ blandishment
Ⓔ synthesis

3. Most of the theatregoers agreed that the critic's review had been (i) _____ because it (ii) _____ the cordiality of which was her newspaper's hallmark in favor of belittling criticism.

Blank (i)	Blank (ii)
Ⓐ pejorative	Ⓓ dispensed with
Ⓑ magnanimous	Ⓔ alluded to
Ⓒ diffuse	Ⓕ coincided with

4. The group's new album, rather than (i) _____ the clues provided by their previous record, actually (ii) _____ its prior intimations, making one's discernment of their message more (iii) _____ than before.

Blank (i)	Blank (ii)	Blank (iii)
Ⓐ clarifying	Ⓓ enfolds	Ⓖ clear
Ⓑ enshrouding	Ⓔ muddles	Ⓗ negative
Ⓒ elucidating	Ⓕ explicates	Ⓘ grotesque

5. The popularity of electronic books will undoubtedly have (i) _____ effect on young readers. In addition to inducing children to be more (ii) _____ with their reading, they will drive parents to purchase educational books that were not (iii) _____ in the days when only printed books existed.

Blank (i)	Blank (ii)	Blank (iii)
Ⓐ an unforeseen	Ⓓ backward	Ⓖ jarring
Ⓑ a beneficial	Ⓔ indolent	Ⓗ available
Ⓒ a deleterious	Ⓕ venturesome	Ⓘ harmless

6. Those who most (i) _____ proclaim their allegiances and credos and by doing so seek to claim the (ii) _____ of conviction that often seems so tantalizingly accessible to the uninitiated might well take heed of the wisdom that any good truth is worth testing, and that many who speak loudly do so to compensate for (iii) _____ surety in their own beliefs.

Blank (i)	Blank (ii)	Blank (iii)
ⓐ vociferously	ⓓ febrility	ⓖ a comprehensive
ⓑ plaintively	ⓔ susceptibility	ⓗ a vigorous
ⓒ subtly	ⓕ invulnerability	ⓘ an ersatz

DIRECTIONS: For Questions 7 to 11, select *one* answer choice unless otherwise instructed.

Questions 7 to 9 are based on the following passage:

The question of aesthetics and politics takes on surprising new turns in relation to the medium of the computer. In 1985, the Centre Pompidou opened an exhibit, "The Imma-terials," curated by Jean-François Lyotard that featured the use of computers in art. One
Line installation consisted of several Minitels, each containing a document in which intel-
(5) lectuals, writers, and artists responded to the curator's request to define certain words (such as freedom, matter, maternal, and so forth). The goal of the installation was to destabilize accepted meanings and to explore the polysemy or "immateriality" of lan-guage. While computers were not necessary for the exhibit, they did allow a form of browsing that amplified the exhibit's purpose. On the screen, words were electronic and
(10) presumably became less material. In another room, an installation wired each square of the floor, which was activated by the movement of the participant. As one walked through the space of the installation, one's body provided inputs to a computer. Sounds and lights changed based on an algorithm programmed into a computer, transforming the participants' input into data, and then into sound and light configurations. In both
(15) cases, the use of computers facilitated the questioning of the stability or materiality of cultural forms and automatically included the audience in the work of art. Already, the position of the audience had changed from the disinterested contemplation of the tra-ditional gallery of paintings to the distracted participation of computerized art.

7. Which of the following best describes the organization of the passage?

ⓐ A hypothesis is criticized, and an alternative theory is put forward.
ⓑ An observation is made, then the basis for that observation is explained.
ⓒ A modification of a currently accepted theory is proposed, then the modification is supported.
ⓓ A challenge to a longstanding theory is examined and debunked.
ⓔ A specific instance is explained, then deconstructed.

For Question 8, consider each of the choices separately and select *all* that apply.

8. The author suggests which of the following about the art installation described in the passage?

   Indicate *all* that apply.

   A The use of computers was crucial in order to provide a medium with which to expose the multiple meanings of certain words.

   B The content of the exhibit was less important than the experience of the exhibit.

   C Computerized art, by nature, is superior to traditional painting.

9. In the context in which it appears, "amplified" (line 9) most nearly means

   Ⓐ increased
   Ⓑ added to
   Ⓒ exaggerated
   Ⓓ loudened
   Ⓔ varied

Questions 10 and 11 are based on the following passage:

Can theory be used to bring about practical effects? And, if so, are there limits to its field of applicability? Smoking is, after all, an "everyday practice" of the smoker. If one wanted to effect a "life change" of this order one might, more likely, turn to the genre of
Line "self-help" literature directed at everyday life than to high theory. Alternatively, a cul-
(5) tural studies investigation of the political economy of the tobacco trade or of tobacco advertising, conceivably for some smokers might change their understanding of their habit and the source of their compulsion by revealing its imbrications in broader cultural contexts and issues. Anti-smoking propaganda, too, might, with the intention of intervention, address populations of smokers and smoking as a cultural habit. Turning
(10) to deconstruction: is there any sense in which or any "scale" on which its relation to the everyday could produce results? Can such a theory be used to intervene concretely, to make an alteration to a particular instance of the everyday life—of an individual or a population, for example?

For Questions 10 and 11, consider each of the choices separately and select *all* that apply.

10. According to the passage, which of the following are ways in which the author hypothesizes that smokers might be able to change their habit?

    Indicate *all* that apply.

    A Read books designed to aid with self-help that are written in a manner that is more theoretical than realistic.

    B Research the ways by which tobacco companies attempt to influence the public via marketing.

    C Peruse material written with the intention of dissuading people from smoking.

11. The passage suggests which of the following about theory's potential role in helping people quit smoking?

Indicate *all* that apply.

A Self-help literature written in a practical way is more useful than that written at a more theoretical level.

B Learning the everyday workings of tobacco companies' attempt to influence politicians is not theoretical enough to help people effect change.

C Adding a graphic warning label to a pack of cigarettes would reduce cigarette consumption.

DIRECTIONS: For Questions 12 to 15, select the *two* answer choices that, when used to complete the sentence, fit the meaning of the sentence as a whole *and* produce completed sentences that are alike in meaning.

---

12. The politician's debate strategy, to capitalize on his opponent's _____ by drawing her into a discussion of her favorite topic, tax law, and luring her into boring their audience, backfired when she explained her ideas about the law succinctly and powerfully.

A idiosyncrasies

B proclivities

C predilections

D disinclinations

E aversions

F eccentricities

13. Stranded far at sea in a lifeboat, the survivors of the shipwreck faced a quandary: they could hardly _____ seawater, for they knew that it might hasten their demise, but they could also not go more than another day without drinking something.

A consume

B evoke

C dispel

D avoid

E shirk

F drink

14. The intrinsic complications of the appropriately named tax code have spawned an entire industry devoted to its esoterica; it is a small wonder that the layman often finds himself _____ the code's intricacies.

A confused by

B frustrated with

C beholden to

D emboldened by

E irked by

F awash in

15. The breadth and depth of his masterwork stunned most of Salk's contemporaries and perplexed many of them; indeed, in private, some admitted they found the work to be _____.

A discriminating
B confounding
C august
D bombastic
E recondite
F abstruse

DIRECTIONS: For Questions 16 to 20, select *one* answer choice unless otherwise instructed.

Questions 16 and 17 are based on the following passage:

The modes for measuring life are numerous: fingerprinting, hand scans, iris scans, retina scans, voice and face recognition. Less robust technologies are also being developed on gait, keystroke patterns, and odor. But the principle is essentially the same: the
Line identification of unique bodily characteristics via the algorithmic techniques of pattern
(5) matching. How robust any of these technologies are, depend, naturally enough, on the ecology of usage. For instance, retina scanning in which the eye is pressed against a laser light scanner in order to verify against the patterning of the blood vessels at the back of the eye is highly efficient (few false matches and false non-matches). It is also fast: the template for a retina match can be 10 times smaller than that for an iris match.
(10) Yet retina scans require bodily contact with a machine, and this contact aspect often creates end user problems—seen by many as unhygienic. Thus the body must be captured, coded, and scanned but not touched.

Currently, the preferred systems for trialing are those in which the user is aware they are being scanned but have no physical contact with the machine. Also preferred are
(15) systems that avoid the rather obvious associations of biometrics to criminality, such as fingerprints. It seems strange that there isn't more concern being expressed about how quickly we are being compelled to patch our bodies into multiple networks of regulation (and expansion), given the rather transparent connections between the structures and operations of criminality and biometrics. Indeed, in the public sphere, biometrics
(20) systems have been initially trialed on those exceptional cases with the fewest rights, such as "known criminals" in Florida and asylum seekers in Britain.

For Question 16, consider each of the choices separately and select *all* that apply.

16. It can be inferred from the passage that the author would agree with which of the following statements?

    Indicate *all* that apply.

    A For the majority of Americans, lack of cleanliness is more concerning than being scanned.
    B Biometrics systems are often linked with those who break the law.
    C Public perception of biometrics is an important factor in its utilization.

17. Select the sentence in the passage in which the author expresses skepticism about a term.

Question 18 is based on the following passage:

Some would argue that, since the number of pandas photographed in the wild has greatly increased, the species is no longer as endangered as it once was. However, this argument is unfounded for the same reason that it would be incorrect to assume that
Line an increase in frequency with which a rare flower is spotted by naturalists indicates
(5) the flower is no longer as rare. The true cause of the increase in photographs of pandas is advances in their behavior prediction.

18. Which of the following conclusions is best supported by the argument?

    Ⓐ Technology is having a detrimental effect on nature.
    Ⓑ The number of pandas in the wild can be determined by a method other than photography.
    Ⓒ The number of pandas photographed each year is as large as the instances of observation of the rare flower.
    Ⓓ Modern behavior prediction of pandas impinges upon their habitats.
    Ⓔ Pandas are still an endangered species.

Questions 19 and 20 are based on the following passage:

The purposeful use of language makes knowing possible. As the Sophists (and many others subsequently) noted, language necessarily affects the truths that it can say or name. How we write is as important as what we write. From this perspective, rhetoric
Line aims at knowledge, or makes it available. How it is made available will vary according to
(5) the apparatus in which it is generated. It could be argued that the academic essay, as it has come to be institutionalized within the humanities, is a writing that demonstrates all the virtues of mainstream literacy—unity, coherence, perspicuity, closure, and correctness. However, what students learn from the process of writing essays which, rhetorically, have been stripped of the art of invention, is to close discourse down, to let the
(10) conclusion dictate their thinking, and to necessarily censor whatever imagined possibilities seem irrelevant or inappropriate. What they learn is a trained incapacity to speculate or raise questions, to try stylistic and formal alternatives.

19. The author of the passage attributes students' "incapacity to speculate or raise questions" (lines 11–12) in part to

   Ⓐ the limitations of their vocabulary
   Ⓑ the structure of the typical academic essay
   Ⓒ their experimentation with stylistic and formal alternatives
   Ⓓ the lack of breadth in the usual academic curriculum
   Ⓔ an overuse of rhetoric

20. The author of the passage mentions Sophists primarily in order to

   Ⓐ illustrate how a certain group's rhetoric influenced their ability to influence others
   Ⓑ contrast one group's ability to ascertain the truth from language to another group's ability to do the same
   Ⓒ argue that past intellectuals were more innovative than present thinkers
   Ⓓ explain how the Sophists were the first group to understand how language affects truth
   Ⓔ identify an example of a group that was aware of the limitations of language

TIME: 35 MINUTES—20 QUESTIONS

DIRECTIONS: For Questions 1 to 5, compare Quantity A and Quantity B, using the additional information given, if any, and select *one* of the following four answer choices:

Ⓐ Quantity A is greater.

Ⓑ Quantity B is greater.

Ⓒ The two quantities are equal.

Ⓓ The relationship cannot be determined from the information given.

Points *A*, *B*, and *C* are three different
points on a circle, which has area equal to 64π.

	Quantity A	Quantity B
1.	$AB + AC$	32

$$xy = -60, \ yz = -50$$

	Quantity A	Quantity B
2.	xz	0

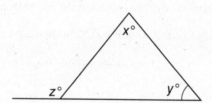

	Quantity A	Quantity B
3.	$x + y$	z

The function *f* is defined as follows:
$$f(x) = 3x^4 + 5x^2 + 7.$$

	Quantity A	Quantity B
4.	$f(32)$	$f(-32)$

The circumference of a circle is $2\pi^2$.

Quantity A	Quantity B
5. The area of the circle	27

DIRECTIONS: For Questions 6 to 9, enter your answer in the grid below the question. Equivalent forms of the correct answer, such as 2.5 and 2.50, are all correct. Fractions do not need to be reduced to lowest terms.

---

6. Sixty stones are placed into four jars in such a way that the ratio of stones in the four jars is 1:2:3:4. What is the least number of stones that can be moved, so that the ratio of stones in the four jars becomes 1:1:1:1?

7. $3^x \times 3^y \times 3^z = 729$. If x, y, and z are three different positive integers and $z = x + y$, then what is the value of 3^z?

8. Cup A is $\frac{2}{9}$ full. Cup B is twice as large as Cup A and is $\frac{5}{8}$ full. If the contents of Cup A are poured into Cup B, Cup B will then be what fraction full?

9. A builder wants to build a building with the following two properties: each floor has at least one room, each floor has at least twice as many rooms as the floor above it. What is the minimum number of rooms the builder will need for a seven-floor building?

10. At a conference, $\frac{1}{3}$ of the 900 participants are female, and the rest are male. Of the female participants, $\frac{1}{4}$ are retired. Of the male participants, $\frac{5}{8}$ are retired. What fraction of all participants at the conference are retired?

(A) $\frac{1}{3}$

(B) $\frac{1}{2}$

(C) $\frac{2}{5}$

(D) $\frac{3}{5}$

(E) $\frac{2}{3}$

11. Which of the following equations has no solutions for x?

(A) $x^2 + 8x = -17$
(B) $x^2 + 8x = -13$
(C) $x^2 + 8x = 0$
(D) $x^2 + 8x = 1$
(E) $x^2 + 8x = 16$

12. If $\frac{21^{60}}{n}$ is a positive integer, which of the following could be n?

(A) 2
(B) 3
(C) 4
(D) 5
(E) 6

13. Zoe needs to drive 879 miles in 24 hours. She will need seven rest breaks of a half hour each, during which she will not be driving. Approximately what speed, in miles per hour, will she need to average during the periods when she is driving to finish the journey in time?

Ⓐ 40
Ⓑ 41
Ⓒ 42
Ⓓ 43
Ⓔ 44

For Questions 14 to 17, consider each of the choices separately and select *all* that apply.

14. Which of the following functions has as its domain the set of all real numbers?

Indicate *all* that apply.

A̅ $f(x) = \dfrac{4}{x+4}$

B̅ $f(x) = \dfrac{4}{x^2+1}$

C̅ $f(x) = \sqrt{4x^3}$

D̅ $f(x) = \sqrt{(-4x)^2}$

E̅ $f(x) = \sqrt[3]{4x}$

15. A set of test scores at a large university is normally distributed with a mean of 74 and a standard deviation of 7. Which of the following is true?

Indicate *all* that apply.

A̅ More students scored above 83 than scored below 63.
B̅ At least 65% of students scored between 67 and 81.
C̅ More than half the students scored above 75.

16. Line *l* passes through the points (3, 4) and (6, 5) in the *xy*-plane. Which of the following could be the equation of a line parallel to line *l*?

Indicate *all* such equations.

A $y = 2x + 7$

B $y = 3x - 4$

C $y = \dfrac{1}{3}x - 5$

D $y = \dfrac{1}{3}x + 2$

E $y = 3x + 2$

F $y = x - 3$

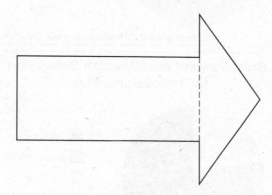

(figure not to scale)

17. A sign in the shape of an arrow (above) is cut along the dotted line to create a rectangle and a triangle. Which of the following must be true?

Indicate *all* that apply.

A The sum of the side lengths of the rectangle is greater than the sum of the side lengths of the triangle.

B The area of the rectangle is greater than the area of the triangle.

C The sum of the measures of the angles of the rectangle, in degrees, is greater than the sum of the measures of the angles of the triangle, in degrees.

D The number of acute angles in the triangle is greater than the number of acute angles in the rectangle.

Questions 18 to 20 are based on the following pie charts, which show the breakdown of 600 participants in a conference by nationality, and the breakdown of the Canadian delegation by occupation (professional field).

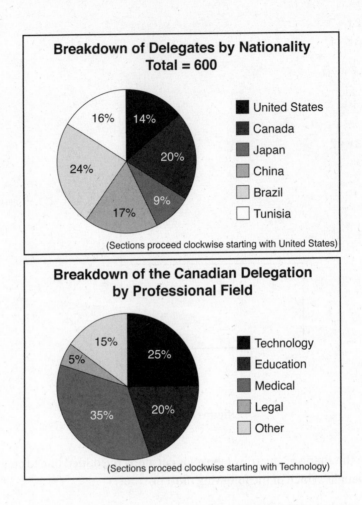

18. How many Canadians from the medical field attended the conference?

   Ⓐ 32
   Ⓑ 35
   Ⓒ 38
   Ⓓ 40
   Ⓔ 42

For Questions 19 and 20, enter your answer in the answer box below the question. Equivalent forms of the correct answer, such as 2.5 and 2.50, are all correct. Fractions do not need to be reduced to lowest terms.

19. How many more delegates attended the conference from Brazil than from Tunisia?


```
┌─────────────────┐
│                 │
│                 │
└─────────────────┘
```

20. For all countries other than Canada, an average of 10% of delegates were from the field of education. What percent of all delegates were occupied in the education field?

```
┌─────────────────┐
│                 │  %
└─────────────────┘
```

Section 2: Verbal Reasoning

1. **D**
2. **A**
3. **B, D**
4. **C, F**
5. **A, E**
6. **B, E, G**
7. **E**
8. **E**
9. **C**
10. **C**
11. **E**
12. **A, C**
13. **B, E**
14. **D, E**
15. **A, F**
16. **Sentence 5**
17. **B**
18. **D**
19. **C**
20. **D**

Section 3: Quantitative Reasoning

1. **B**
2. **B**
3. **A**
4. **B**
5. **A**
6. **D**
7. **A**
8. **C**
9. **C**
10. **D**
11. **95**
12. **24**
13. **$750**
14. **126**
15. **52**
16. **68**
17. **120 ml**
18. **300**
19. **C**
20. **D**

Section 4: Verbal Reasoning

1. **B**
2. **B**
3. **A, D**
4. **B, F, G**
5. **B, F, H**
6. **A, F, I**
7. **E**
8. **B**
9. **B**
10. **B, C**
11. **A**
12. **B, C**
13. **A, F**
14. **B, E**
15. **E, F**
16. **B, C**
17. **The last sentence**
18. **E**
19. **B**
20. **E**

Section 5: Quantitative Reasoning

1. **B**
2. **A**
3. **C**
4. **C**
5. **A**
6. **12**
7. **27**
8. **$\dfrac{53}{72}$**
9. **127**
10. **B**
11. **A**
12. **B**
13. **D**
14. **B, D, E**
15. **A, B**
16. **C, D**
17. **C, D**
18. **E**
19. **48**
20. **12%**

ANSWER EXPLANATIONS

Section 2—Verbal Reasoning

1. **(D)** If the plots of the author's mysteries are "far from" predictable and "driven mostly by whim and fancy," they could be described as *capricious* (unpredictable).

2. **(A)** If the botanist was familiar with the *flora* (plants) *endemic* (native) to his region, it makes sense that he would be only vulnerable to poisoning from a foreign fungus.

3. **(B, D)** Since the owners are accustomed to the advantages, taking them away might logically produce *indignation* (anger) from them. If blank (ii) is *prize* (pry), then the comparison makes sense, since neither the dog nor the owner want to give up what they have.

4. **(C, F)** Given the options, only *delineates* (describes) is an appropriate word to talk about how a book might discuss a plan. A clue for blank (ii) is provided by the third sentence, which says that Boon's *detractors* (critics) *disparage* (put down) his ideas and argue for an *expeditious* (quick) plan, which would mean Boon's plan advocates *an incremental* (step-by-step) change.

5. **(A, E)** A clue for blank (i) is given in the rest of its sentence, since the described bird "could command the lion's share of the food due to his status." *Preeminent* (having the highest rank or position) would thus describe this bird. Since the other male bird accepts the food passively, this acceptance can be termed *acquiescence* (giving in without protest).

6. **(B, E, G)** Clues are provided by the description of the ingenue's delivery as *impassive* (emotionless) and the critic's view of her as a mannequin with just enough life to pass as a human. Of the choices for blank (i), *grating* (irritating) fits, especially because the critic found himself "dreading" her next line. For blank (ii), *wooden* (expressionless) fits the ingenue's impassive manner, and *imbued* (infused) makes sense because the mannequin would have had to gain some life to pass as a human.

7. **(E)** If retailers removed the brand from their shelves, retail sales would drop even if consumers' preferences were unaffected by the reports.

8. **(E)** Since the author indicates that cities with a higher cost-of-living than average have underestimated poverty levels, it can be inferred that cities with a lower cost-of-living than average have overestimated poverty levels since their inhabitants do not have to spend as much money on things like food and housing.

9. **(C)** In the last sentence of the fourth paragraph, the author indicates that the U.S. Census Bureau is likely to continue using its current definition of poverty "for the foreseeable future." He prefaces this statement with the quote from Wendell Primus, which essentially says that a definition of poverty's worth depends on its ability to measure whether the number of poor is increasing or decreasing. It can thus be inferred that the author is suggesting the current definition is persisting because it can make that distinction.

10. **(C)** In the first paragraph, the author states that the current definition of poverty uses pretax income, i.e., using income before taxes have been withdrawn would not change the current system nor appease a critic of that system.

11. **(E)** In the last paragraph, the author says that "a period of economic contraction does not provide a blanket of uniform hardship upon all subgroups." In other words, during a recession, it can be inferred that some of these subgroups suffer more hardship than others do.

12. **(A, C)** Since the sheriff is "still surprised" by the way the new mayor quickly *acceded* (agreed), it is implied that he is surprised even though he has become accustomed to such behavior. Therefore, he would be accustomed to either *deference* (submission) or *yielding* (giving way to).

13. **(B, E)** The phrase "in fact" indicates a shift, so if the positions of electrons were once thought to be definable, they must now be the opposite. Both *nebulous* (vague) and *enigmatic* (mysterious) create the necessary contrast.

14. **(D, E)** If the man is a walking contradiction and his manner is usually *languid* (lacking energy), an appropriate contrast could be created with *spirited* (lively) or *mettlesome* (full of vitality and energy).

15. **(A, F)** Inquiring about the health of someone's goldfish, in most cases, goes beyond politeness to the realm of being overly *solicitous* (concerned about the well-being of) or overly *attentive* (considerate).

16. **(Sentence 5: When watching . . . adults.)** This sentence supports the assertion in the preceding sentence by giving an example of a finding in adults. The preceding sentence draws a parallel to the similar finding stated earlier in the passage regarding children.

17. **(B)** In this context, "ascribed" means "attributed," especially since the author goes on to explain how may neurons accomplish the indicated brain functions.

18. **(D)** The author states that cognition and consciousness "may, or may not, coincide," and his description of "autopilot" behavior supports this assertion, in effect, arguing against the converse, that the two are always linked.

19. **(C)** "At least some of the time" is not hard to prove, and the passage indicates that the shift to conscious control can be the result of a dangerous stimulus, a situation where sensory perception (hearing, seeing, etc.) would certainly occur.

20. **(D)** The argument supports the explanation offered in the last sentence, that "many musicians over the age of 35 produce fewer albums because they have been making music for too long to write compelling new music." The first portion in **boldface** offers evidence that supports an alternative to the first explanation for the phenomenon—that musicians record most of their albums before age 35. The second portion in **boldface** states the explanation—that this is mostly due to the length of musicians' careers.

Section 3—Quantitative Reasoning

*Indicates an alternative way to solve the problem.

1. **(B)** To find the probability of several independent events all occurring, multiply the probabilities of each event. For Team A to win all three of its next three games, the probability is $.5 \times .5 \times .5 = .125$. For Team B to win four games in a row, the probability is $.6 \times .6 \times .6 \times .6 = .1296$, so (B) is greater. (Note: 50% = .5 and 60% = .6.)

2. **(B)** To find the greatest common factor (GCF) of 84 and 700, factor each into primes. A tree might help:

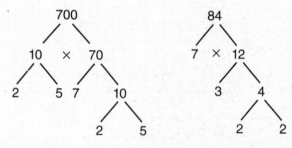

   Looking at the prime numbers, those at the bottom of every branch, we see that 84 and 700 have $2^2 \times 7$ in common. Then the GCF, Quantity (A), is $2^2 \times 7 = 28$. The easiest way to find the least common multiple of 6 and 15 is to list multiples of the larger number until reaching one that is also a multiple of the smaller: 15, 30, 45. . . . Notice that the second multiple of 15 is 30, which is also a multiple of 6, because $6 \times 5 = 30$. Since $30 > 28$, (B) is greater.

3. **(A)** Don't waste time trying to compute the quantities. In Column (B), $8 = 2^3$, so $8^5 = (2^3)^5 = 2^{15}$. In Column (A), recall that a negative number to an even power is positive, so $(-2)^{16} = 2^{16}$. Since $2^{16} > 2^{15}$, (A) is greater.

4. **(B)** The product of the three quantities is zero, so one of the individual factors $(x^2 + 9)$, $(x + 9)$, or $(x - 5)$ must equal zero. $x^2 + 9 = 0$ has no real solution, because x^2 can't equal -9, or any negative. If $x + 9 = 0$ then $x = -9$, and if $x - 5 = 0$, then $x = 5$. So the two possible values of x are -9 and 5, both less than 7. Then Quantity (B), 7, is greater.

5. **(A)** To find the median of the list, begin crossing out the lowest and highest numbers in turn until one or two are left in the middle: ~~0~~, ~~0~~, ~~0~~, ~~2~~, 9, 11, ~~11~~, ~~14~~, ~~16~~, ~~17~~. After four values have been crossed off either end, 9 and 11 remain in the middle, making the median equal to $\frac{9+11}{2} = 10$. To find the average of the ten numbers on the list, add all the numbers and divide by 10, which is $\frac{80}{10} = 8$. Since $10 > 8$, (A) is greater. You can also save time and spot visually that the average will be less than 10 by noticing the three 0s and no numbers greater than 17 on the list.

6. **(D)** The amounts of money, X and Y, that are invested in the two accounts are unknown, so we cannot determine the dollar amount of interest each account earns, (D).

7. **(A)**

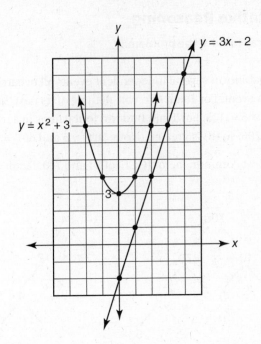

Graph the equations $y = 3x - 2$ and $y = x^2 + 3$ in the xy-plane, noting that the first is a line with slope 3 and y-intercept $(0, -2)$, and that the second is an upward pointed parabola with y-intercept $(0, 3)$. The parabola is always above the line, having a greater y value, so $x^2 + 3 > 3x - 2$ for all values of x. (A).

*Plug in numbers for x. For $x < 0$, (A) is positive, while (B) is negative, so (A) is greater. If $x = 0$, then (A) = 3 > (B) = –2. If $x = 1$, then (A) = 4 > (B) = 1. For large values of x, $x^2 > 3x$, so (A) is greater.

8. **(C)** There are 24 hours in 1 day, so there are $24d$ hours in d days. Quantity (B) is

$$\frac{d}{2.5} \ \text{hours} \times 60 \ \frac{\text{minutes}}{\text{hour}} = d \times \frac{60}{2.5} \ \text{minutes} = 24d \ \text{minutes}.$$ The quantities are both

equal to $24d$, **(C)**.

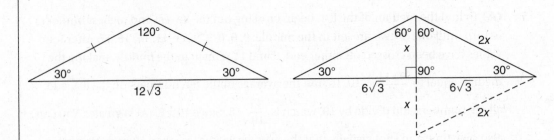

9. **(C)** First, since the triangle is isosceles, two side lengths are equal, and two angles are equal. The value of the two equal angles is $\frac{180 - 120}{2} = \frac{60}{2} = 30°$. Next, draw the perpendicular from the upper vertex to the base, creating two congruent 30–60–90 triangles, each with base $\frac{12\sqrt{3}}{2} = 6\sqrt{3}$. If you remember the $s - s\sqrt{3} - 2s$ pattern

for the side lengths of 30–60–90 triangles, you can quickly obtain 6, $6\sqrt{3}$, and 12 as the three side lengths, meaning that $x = 6$ and $2x = 12$ in the diagram. This makes the perimeter of the original isosceles triangle $12 + 12 + 12\sqrt{3} = 24 + 12\sqrt{3}$, (C). If you forget the formula for 30–60–90 triangles, draw the dashed reference lines, and observe that the symmetry of the larger equilateral triangle thus created implies the $1x$ to $2x$ ratio of side lengths in the upper right triangle. Then, from the Pythagorean theorem, $x^2 + (6\sqrt{3})^2 = (2x)^2$. So $x^2 + 36 \times 3 = 4x^2$, which yields $108 = 3x^2$ and $36 = x^2$. This again makes $x = 6$ and perimeter equal to $4x + 12\sqrt{3} = 24 + 12\sqrt{3}$.

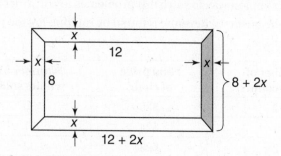

10. **(D)** Call the uniform width x, and the outer dimensions of the picture together with the frame become $8 + 2x$ and $12 + 2x$, because the frame's width adds to both the top and bottom and the left and right of the picture. The full area of the picture together with frame is then $(8 + 2x)(12 + 2x) = 96 + 16x + 24x + 4x^2 = 4x^2 + 40x + 96$. This expression must equal $2 \times 8 \times 12 = 192$, because the frame's area is equal to the picture's, implying that the area enclosed by the frame and picture together must equal twice the area of the picture alone. So $4x^2 + 40x + 96 = 192$. Subtract 192 to obtain $4x^2 + 40x - 96 = 0$, and divide by 4 on both sides: $x^2 + 10x - 24 = 0$. The left side factors as $(x + 12)(x - 2)$, since $12x - 2x = 10x$, and so $x = 2$ or -12. Only $x = 2$, (D), works in context of the problem, because a length cannot be negative. You can also get this result using a trial and error approach with the answer choices. When $x = 2$, the outer dimensions become 12×16, for a total area of 192. This makes the picture's area, $8 \times 12 = 96$, the same as the frame's area, $192 - 96 = 96$.

11. **(95)** The whole numbers between 100 and 200 consist of 101, 102, 103 . . . 199, and thus include 99 numbers. Of these, four numbers *are* equal to the square of another integer: 121, 144, 169, and 196, because $121 = 11^2$, $144 = 12^2$, $169 = 13^2$, and $196 = 14^2$. Notice that $10^2 = 100$ and $15^2 = 225$ fall outside the specified range. This leaves $99 - 4 = 95$ whole numbers that are *not* the square of an integer.

12. **(24)**

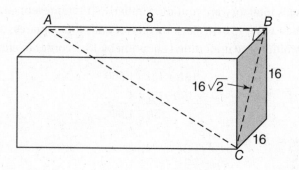

Note: As in many GRE geometry problems, the figure is not drawn to scale. Since the shaded region has area equal to 256, the length of each side of the square is $\sqrt{256} = 16$. Then $\overline{BC}$ is the hypotenuse of an isosceles right triangle with legs of length 16. So $BC = \sqrt{16^2 + 16^2} = \sqrt{16^2 \times 2} = 16\sqrt{2}$ (or $\sqrt{512}$), by the Pythagorean theorem. Then $16\sqrt{2}$ and $AB = 8$, are the lengths of two legs in the separate right triangle ABC. Find hypotenuse AC by again applying the Pythagorean theorem. $8^2 + (16\sqrt{2})^2 = AC^2$. So $64 + 256 \times 2 = AC^2$. Finally, $AC = \sqrt{64 + 512} = \sqrt{576} = 24$.

13. **($750)** The simplest way to solve this problem is to construct a table listing possible options for the business. Revenue is found by multiplying the price per chair times the number of chairs.

Number of $1 discounts	Final price of chair	Number of chairs sold	Revenue
0	$25	30	$750
1	$24	31	$744
2	$23	32	$736
3	$22	33	$726

We see that lowering the price only decreases revenue, so the business generates the most revenue by leaving the price at $25. The maximum is $750.

14. **(126)** The sum of the measures of the three angles in a triangle is 180°, so $2x + 3x + 5x = 180$. Then $10x = 180$, and $x = 18$. Then the $3x$ angle measures $3(18) = 54°$. Since the sum of angles that comprise a straight line is 180°, $54 + y = 180$, and $y = 126$.

15. **(52)** There are seven boys for every five girls for every $7 + 5 = 12$ children. Then boys are $\frac{7}{12}$ of all children and girls are $\frac{5}{12}$. Out of 312 total children, there are $\frac{7}{12} \times 312 = 182$ boys, and $\frac{5}{12} \times 312 = 130$ girls. Then there are $182 - 130 = 52$ more boys.

*For every 12 children, there are 7 boys – 5 girls = 2 more boys. Then $\frac{2}{12}$ of all children are the number of "more boys": $\frac{2}{12} \times 312 = \frac{1}{6} \times 312 = 52$.

16. **(68)** Suppose that of the 120 tosses, h lands heads up and t lands tails up. Then $\underline{h + t = 120}$. If each of the h heads moves the player forward 10 units, then $10h$ represents his total forward motion. Similarly, $-13t$ represents the player's backward motion. Then $10h - 13t = 4$, since the player ends four squares forward of his starting position. Multiply the underlined equation by 13, in order to eliminate the t variable:

$$13h + 13t = 1{,}560$$
$$\underline{+\ 10h - 13t = 4}$$
$$23h = 1{,}564$$

So $h = 1{,}564 \div 23 = 68$.

17. **(120 ml)** Drug X is 5% of the 80 ml solution, so there are .05 × 80 = 4 ml of Drug X. We want to dilute the solution to a 2% concentration, so this 4 ml of the drug will be 2% of some total volume, say T. That is, 4 = .02T. Then T is 4 ÷ .02 = 200. If the total volume after adding water will be 200 ml, then the amount added must be 200 minus the initial volume: 200 – 80 = 120 ml are added.

18. **(300)** Find the number of choices for appetizers with the "choose" function, written as $_nC_k$ or $\binom{n}{k}$ and defined for positive integers by the formula

$$\binom{n}{k} = \frac{n!}{k!(n-k)!} \text{ for } 0 \le k \le n.$$

Recall that $n!$ means the product of all positive integers from 1 through n, inclusive. From six appetizers, we choose two, so there are $_6C_2$ combinations, which equals $\frac{6 \times 5}{2 \times 1} = 15$, after canceling duplicate numbers in the numerator and denominator.

You can also compute this by "brute force." Label the appetizers A, B, C, D, E, and F, and then list all combinations of two appetizers as follows: AB, AC, AD, AE, AF, BC, BD, BE, BF, CD, CE, CF, DE, DF, EF. There are 5 + 4 + 3 + 2 + 1 = 15 combinations in all. Multiply the number of choices for appetizer by the four choices for entrée and the five choices for dessert to obtain 15 × 4 × 5 = 300 total menu combinations.

19. **(C)** Examine only the beginning and ending weights for all three animals. For the cat and hamster, the difference between the original and final weights was less than 2 kg. For the dog, the initial weight was a little more than 10 kg, while the final weight was a little more than 8 kg. The dog's weight changed by 10 – 8 = 2 kg, which is the greatest change for the three animals. (C).

20. **(D)** The hamster's weight changed from nearly 6 kg in week 1 to just above 2 kg in week 2, a change of over 50% in 1 week, so (A) is not correct. The dog's weight parallels the cat's fairly closely throughout the study and is usually about 2 kg greater than the cat's, except in week 4, when their weight graphs move closer together, showing that (B) is not correct. Each animal had a lower final weight than starting weight, so (C) is not correct. An examination of the week 3 weights for the animals shows that the dog did reach its maximum weight in week 3, so (D) is correct. The dog's and cat's weights did follow the "decrease-increase-decrease" pattern throughout the study, but the hamster's weight simply decreased then increased, so (E) is not correct.

Section 4—Verbal Reasoning

1. **(B)** If Simmons's students think he is sincere and profound, and his colleagues are in contrast to those students, it would make sense that they think his work is *claptrap* (trash).

2. **(B)** The "however" in the sentence creates a shift from the fact that science fiction has not been known for its *foresight* (ability to look forward). Therefore, the authors mentioned must have *prescience* (ability to predict the future), especially since they have "correctly predicted" inventions.

3. **(A, D)** The review favors *belittling* (putting down; disparaging) criticism, so it could be described as *pejorative* (disparaging). Such a review would necessarily have *dispensed with* (gotten rid of) *cordiality* (cheerfulness; warmth).

4. **(B, F, G)** Only one combination of blanks produces a logical sentence here. If the new album, rather than *enshrouding* (covering up) the clues *explicates* (explains) its prior *intimations* (implications), then one's *discernment* (perception) would become more clear.

5. **(B, F, H)** Again, only one combination of blanks will produce a logical sentence. If the popularity of the books will have *a beneficial* (good) effect, then children would be more *venturesome* (adventurous) with their reading, and parents would buy books not *available* before electronic books.

6. **(A, F, I)** Beginning with blank (iii), if the people being discussed are compensating, then using *ersatz* (artificial) to describe their *surety* (sureness) would work. For blank (ii), the phrase "tantalizingly accessible" is used to describe the preceding phrase, so using *invulnerability* (immunity to attack) of conviction would logically be tantalizing to those considering their "allegiances and *credos* (beliefs)." A clue for blank (i) is given by the phrase "many who speak loudly": *vociferously* (loudly) is also the only word that fits given the choices.

7. **(E)** In the passage, the author describes a specific art installation, then proceeds to *deconstruct* (examine by breaking a whole into parts) the elements of the art exhibit and their meanings.

8. **(B)** The author spends little time describing the exhibit (he doesn't bother to catalog all the words defined, for instance) and instead emphasizes that its goals were to explore the *polysemy* (multiple meanings) of language, and to foster participation rather than contemplation. The last sentence, in particular, highlights this change. It can therefore be inferred that the viewer's response to the exhibit is more important than the exhibit itself.

9. **(B)** Since the author is using "amplified" to describe the exhibit's purpose, in this context, "amplified" means "added to."

10. **(B, C)** Both Choices (B) and (C) are accurate paraphrases of sentences in the passage. Choice (B) paraphrases the sentence, "Alternatively, a cultural . . . issues," and Choice (C) is a paraphrase of "Anti-smoking propaganda, too . . . habit."

11. **(A)** The author says that to produce a life change, it is "more likely" that self-help directed at "everyday life" is more useful than that in the realm of high theory; he thereby argues that practical self-help is more useful in helping people stop smoking.

12. **(B, C)** The politician is trying to draw his opponent into a topic that he thinks will work against her. "Favorite topic" indicates that she likes the topic, so either *proclivities* (inclinations toward something) or *predilections* (preferences) would make sense.

13. **(A, F)** Start with the shift: "*but* they could also not go . . . without drinking." Since there is a shift to this statement, the first part of the sentence must be something nearly opposite. Using either *consume* or *drink* creates the necessary shift from drinking to not drinking.

14. **(B, E)** The tax code must be difficult for the *layman* (nonprofessional), since it is *intrinsically* (by nature) complicated and because an industry is devoted to its *esoterica* (things known only to a select few). Of the choices, only *frustrated with* and *irked* (annoyed) *by* are synonyms.

15. **(E, F)** Of the choices given, only *recondite* (difficult to understand) and *abstruse* (difficult to understand) create sentences with the same meaning; both are also supported by the fact that Salk's contemporaries are *perplexed* (confused) by his work.

16. **(B, C)** Choice B is supported by the author's statements in the second paragraph that there are obvious associations and connections between biometrics and criminality. Choice C is supported by the author's statements in the beginning of the second paragraph, since both refer to a public preference, which indicates that public perception is an important consideration.

17. **(The last sentence: Indeed, in the . . . Britain.)** By surrounding the term "known criminals" with quotation marks, the author is implying that the conventional use of this term may be either invalid or based on questionable evidence.

18. **(E)** By saying that the argument, that photographs of pandas indicate their numbers, is unsound in determining whether they are less endangered, the author argues that the pandas are, in fact, still threatened. His example about the rare flower is also used to discredit the argument.

19. **(B)** The author points out the merits of the academic essay, but then proceeds to argue that it is this very structure that induces students to avoid experimentation and to discard observations that do not match their conclusions.

20. **(E)** The author says that the Sophists were aware that language "affects the truths that it can say or name," and then goes on to say that language's apparatus affects how the truth will be made available. In other words, the Sophists are an example of a group who understood that the nature of language partially determines what it can communicate; therefore, different kinds of language have different limitations.

Section 5—Quantitative Reasoning

*Indicates an alternative way to solve the problem.

1. **(B)** Use the area formula for a circle: Area $= \pi r^2$. So $64\pi = \pi r^2$, and $r = 8$. More importantly, the diameter $= 2r = 2 \times 8 = 16$.

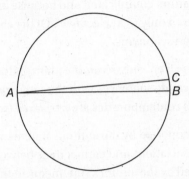

There are many ways to place points A, B, and C, but the diagram may look like the above. If $\overline{AB}$ is a diameter, then $AB = 16$. But C is a point distinct from B, making $\overline{AC}$ not a diameter. Then $AC < 16$, because any chord in a circle that is not the diameter is smaller than the diameter. Therefore, $AB + AC < 16 + 16 = 32$, (B).

2. **(A)** If y is positive, then x and z must both be negative, in order to make the products xy and yz negative. Then xz is the product of two negative numbers and is thus positive and greater than zero. On the other hand, if y is negative, x and z must both be positive in order to make the products xy and yz negative. Then xz is the product of two positives, and again $xz > 0$, so (A) is greater.

3. **(C)**

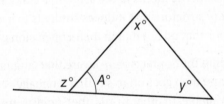

Consider the angle marked A. The angles of a triangle sum to $180°$, so $A + x + y = 180$. But the sum of angles that comprise a straight line is also $180°$, so $A + z = 180$. Then $A + x + y = A + z$. Subtract A from both sides, and the As cancel to yield $x + y = z$, (C).

4. **(C)** We can find $f(32)$ for the function $f(x) = 3x^4 + 5x^2 + 7$ by plugging in 32 for x. But this is time-consuming and unnecessary. A negative number raised to an even power is positive, and since x appears only to even powers in $f(x)$, $f(-32)$ must equal $f(32)$. (C).

5. **(A)** Use the formula for the circumference of a circle: $C = 2\pi r$, where r is the radius and C is the circumference. We're given $C = 2\pi^2$, so $2\pi^2 = 2\pi r$. Dividing by 2π on both sides shows that $\pi = r$. Now use the area formula for a circle: Area $= \pi r^2$. Then area $= \pi \times \pi^2 = \pi^3$. Since $\pi > 3$, $\pi^3 > 3^3 = 27$, (A).

6. **(12)** Since the ratio is 1:2:3:4, we can think of the jars containing $1x$, $2x$, $3x$, and $4x$ marbles for some whole number, x. Then $1x + 2x + 3x + 4x = 60$, so $10x = 60$, and $x = 6$. This makes the current count of marbles in the jars $1(6)$, $2(6)$, $3(6)$, and $4(6)$, or 6, 12, 18, and 24. If each jar were to contain $60 \div 4 = 15$ marbles, the ratio would become $15 : 15 : 15 : 15$, which reduces to 1:1:1:1, as required. The minimum number of stones that must be moved to effect this change is $3 + 9 = 12$, because three stones moved from the 18 jar to the 12 jar would leave those jars with 15 stones each, and nine stones moved from the 24 jar to the 6 jar would give those jars 15 each.

7. **(27)** By the law of exponents, $3^x \times 3^y \times 3^z = 3^{x+y+z}$. Think of this situation as 3 raised to some power must equal 729, and use trial and error on your calculator to obtain the proper exponent. You might worry that this will take too long, but exponential functions grow quickly, and in a few seconds you should obtain $729 = 81 \times 9 = 3^4 \times 3^2 = 3^6$. This means that $x + y + z = 6$. Observe that $1 + 2 + 3 = 6$. For three different positive integers, this is the only solution, since all other such sums will be greater than 6. Given $z = x + y$, then z is 3, and x and y are 1 and 2 in either order. Finally, $3^z = 3^3 = 27$.

8. $\left(\dfrac{53}{72}\right)$ The volume of cup B when full is twice that of cup A, so it is natural to represent these quantities as $2x$ and x. But the question asks about cup B, so it is easier to let $x =$ the volume of cup B, and let $\dfrac{1}{2}x =$ the volume of cup A (when full). Since A is now $\dfrac{2}{9}$ full, it contains $\dfrac{2}{9}\left(\dfrac{1}{2}x\right) = \dfrac{1}{9}x$ units of fluid or other contents. This $\dfrac{1}{9}x$ is to be added to the $\dfrac{5}{8}x$ currently in cup B. Add the fractions by using the common denominator: $9 \times 8 = 72$. Then $\dfrac{1}{9}x + \dfrac{5}{8}x = \dfrac{8}{72}x + \dfrac{45}{72}x = \dfrac{53}{72}x$, meaning the cup is $\dfrac{53}{72}$ full.

9. **(127)** The minimum occurs when the top floor has one room, and each additional floor has exactly 2 times the number of rooms as the floor above. The total is $1 + 2 + 4 + 8 + 16 + 32 + 64 = 127$ rooms.

10. **(B)** There are $\dfrac{1}{3} \times 900 = 300$ females and, therefore, $900 - 300 = 600$ males. For the category of retired individuals, there are $\dfrac{1}{4} \times 300 = 75$ retired females, and $\dfrac{5}{8} \times 600 = 375$ retired males. This means that $75 + 375 = 450$ people are retired in all. This represents $\dfrac{450}{900} = \dfrac{1}{2}$ of all participants, (B).

11. **(A)** For each answer choice, get zero on one side first. For example, (A) becomes $x^2 + 8x + 17 = 0$. You can determine the number of real solutions by considering the *discriminant*, $b^2 - 4ac$, from the Quadratic Formula. Here, $a = 1$, $b = 8$, and $c = 17$. Then $b^2 - 4ac = 8^2 - 4 \times 1 \times 17 = 64 - 68 = -4$. When the discriminant is negative, there are no

solutions, since it is not possible to take the square root of a negative number within the real number system. (The discriminant appears under the radical sign in the

Quadratic Formula: $x = \dfrac{-b \pm \sqrt{b^2 - 4ac}}{2a}$.) Only **(A)** makes $b^2 - 4ac$ negative.

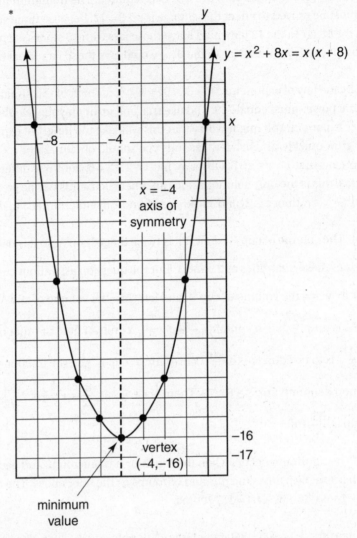

minimum value

Graph the equation $y = x^2 + 8x$ in the xy-plane. First, find the x-intercepts by setting y equal to zero. So $0 = x^2 + 8x = x(x + 8)$, and $x = 0$ or -8. Due to the symmetry of the parabola, the vertex will occur halfway between $x = 0$ and $x = -8$, meaning that

$x = \dfrac{0 + -8}{2} = -4$ is the graph's axis of symmetry. Plug $x = -4$ into $y = x^2 + 8x$, and

$y = (-4)^2 + 8(-4) = 16 - 32 = -16$. This means that the vertex has coordinates $(-4, -16)$. The y-coordinate of the vertex in an upward pointed parabola is the graph's minimum value. Because $-17 < -16$, y can never equal -17, and (A) is correct.

*If you are stuck, you may be able to guess the correct answer by reasoning that x^2 is usually "big," because it is both non-negative and generally greater than a linear term, such as $8x$. So $x^2 + 8x$ will probably not be as small as the smallest answer choice, -17, (A).

12. **(B)** $21^{60} = (3 \times 7)^{60}$, which equals $3^{60} \times 7^{60}$. This will be divisible by any number whose prime factorization contains only the primes 3 and/or 7, with each raised to a power of at most 60. Only choice (B), 3, works. The other choices all have 2 or 5 as a factor. When these choices are placed into the denominator as n, nothing in the numerator, $3^{60} \times 7^{60}$, will cancel with the 2 or 5, so the result is a non-integer fraction.

13. **(D)** Deduct the time of her rest breaks, $7 \times .5 = 3.5$ hours, from the 24 hours that she has available. $24 - 3.5 = 20.5$ hours. Then her average rate will be the distance traveled, 879 miles, divided by the time spent traveling, 20.5 hours. $\dfrac{879 \text{ miles}}{20.5 \text{ hours}} \approx 43 \dfrac{\text{miles}}{\text{hour}}$, (D).

14. **(B, D, E)** The domain of a function, $f(x)$, is the set of all possible x-values, or input values, for which the function is defined. (A) is not correct, because if $x = -4$, the denominator is 0, and division by 0 is undefined. (B) is correct, because the denominator $x^2 + 1$ is always greater than zero, so no division by zero error occurs. (C) is not correct, because if $x < 0$, then $4x^3 < 0$. This creates the square root of a negative, which is undefined within the real number system. (D) is correct, because squaring the quantity $(-4x)$ yields a value ≥ 0, and the square-root function is defined for all numbers ≥ 0. (E) is correct, because the cube-root function is defined for all real numbers, including negatives. For example $\sqrt[3]{-8} = -2$. The answer is (B), (D), and (E).

15. **(A, B)**

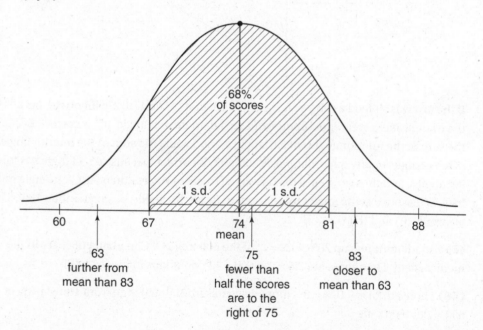

A normal curve is symmetrical about the mean. The number 63 is farther from the mean of 74 than is the number 83, because $74 - 63 = 11$, but $83 - 74 =$ only 9. Then 63 represents a more remote or extreme score, and fewer students score below 63 than above 83, making (A) correct. Alternately, there is less area in the tail to the left of 63 than in the tail to the right of 83. (B) is correct by the "rule of $68 - 95 - 99.7$." In a normal distribution, about 68% of the data falls within 1 standard deviation of the mean. The numbers $81 = 74 + 7$ and $67 = 74 - 7$ are exactly the values 1 standard deviation above and below the mean. So about 68% of students will score within that interval,

68% > 65%. Finally, (C) is not correct. In a normal distribution, 50% of the data is above the mean and 50% is below the mean. If about 50% of students score above 74, then fewer than 50% of students will score above the higher number, 75. A correct statement might have read, "More than half the students scored above 70." (Since 70 < 74 = the mean.) The answer is (A) and (B).

16. **(C, D)** Find the slope of the given line using the slope formula: $\frac{y_2 - y_1}{x_2 - x_1} = \frac{5-4}{6-3} = \frac{1}{3}$.

Parallel lines have the same slope, so the correct choices will be lines that also have slope = $\frac{1}{3}$. If the equation of a line is in the $y = mx + b$ form, then m, the number in front of x, is the slope. Choices (C) and (D) have $m = \frac{1}{3}$.

17. **(C, D)** Remember that geometry diagrams on the GRE are not drawn to scale and may be thought of as flexible, where not restricted by given information.

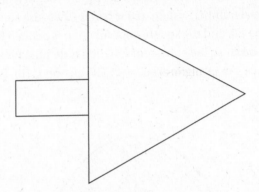

If the arrow is shaped as above, it is easy to see that (A) and (B) are incorrect, because the triangle has a greater perimeter and area than the rectangle. (C) is correct, because the sum of the interior angles of a triangle is 180°, while the sum of the interior angles of a rectangle, or any quadrilateral, is 360°. (D) is correct, because a rectangle has four 90° angles, and thus no angles that are acute (measuring less than 90°). A triangle must have at least two acute angles, or the sum of its angles would be greater than 180°. The answer is (C) and (D).

18. **(E)** Canadians make up 20% = .20 = .2 of the 600 total. Of Canadians, 35% are in the medical field. Then there are .35 × .2 × 600 = 42 Canadians in medical, (E).

19. **(48)** There are 24% – 16% = 8% more delegates from Brazil than from Tunisia. 8% of 600 = .08 × 600 = 48.

20. **(12%)** First, calculate that the number of Canadians in education is 20% of 20% of 600, or .2 × .2 × 600 = 24. There are .2 × 600 = 120 Canadian delegates altogether. Of the remaining 600 – 120 = 480 delegates from other nations, 10% are in education, which equals .1 × 480 = 48 delegates. This means that there are 24 (Canadian) + 48 (other nationalities) = 72 delegates from the field of education. This represents $\frac{72}{600}$ = .12 = 12% of all participants.

Practice Test 5

ANSWER SHEET
Practice Test 5

Section 2: Verbal Reasoning

1. Ⓐ Ⓑ Ⓒ Ⓓ Ⓔ
2. Ⓐ Ⓑ Ⓒ Ⓓ Ⓔ
3. Ⓐ Ⓑ Ⓒ Ⓓ Ⓔ Ⓕ
4. Ⓐ Ⓑ Ⓒ Ⓓ Ⓔ Ⓕ
5. Ⓐ Ⓑ Ⓒ Ⓓ Ⓔ Ⓕ
6. Ⓐ Ⓑ Ⓒ Ⓓ Ⓔ Ⓕ
   Ⓖ Ⓗ Ⓘ
7. Ⓐ Ⓑ Ⓒ Ⓓ Ⓔ

8. Ⓐ Ⓑ Ⓒ Ⓓ Ⓔ
9. Ⓐ Ⓑ Ⓒ Ⓓ Ⓔ
10. Ⓐ Ⓑ Ⓒ Ⓓ Ⓔ
11. Ⓐ Ⓑ Ⓒ
12. Ⓐ Ⓑ Ⓒ Ⓓ Ⓔ Ⓕ
13. Ⓐ Ⓑ Ⓒ Ⓓ Ⓔ Ⓕ
14. Ⓐ Ⓑ Ⓒ Ⓓ Ⓔ Ⓕ
15. Ⓐ Ⓑ Ⓒ Ⓓ Ⓔ Ⓕ

16. Highlight sentence in passage.
17. Ⓐ Ⓑ Ⓒ Ⓓ Ⓔ
18. Ⓐ Ⓑ Ⓒ Ⓓ Ⓔ
19. Ⓐ Ⓑ Ⓒ Ⓓ Ⓔ
20. Ⓐ Ⓑ Ⓒ Ⓓ Ⓔ

Section 3: Quantitative Reasoning

1. Ⓐ Ⓑ Ⓒ Ⓓ
2. Ⓐ Ⓑ Ⓒ Ⓓ
3. Ⓐ Ⓑ Ⓒ Ⓓ
4. Ⓐ Ⓑ Ⓒ Ⓓ
5. Ⓐ Ⓑ Ⓒ Ⓓ
6. Ⓐ Ⓑ Ⓒ Ⓓ
7. Ⓐ Ⓑ Ⓒ Ⓓ

8. Ⓐ Ⓑ Ⓒ Ⓓ
9. ☐
10. ☐
11. ☐
12. ☐
13. ☐
14. Ⓐ Ⓑ Ⓒ Ⓓ Ⓔ

15. ☐
16. Ⓐ Ⓑ Ⓒ Ⓓ Ⓔ
17. Ⓐ Ⓑ Ⓒ Ⓓ Ⓔ
18. Ⓐ Ⓑ Ⓒ Ⓓ Ⓔ
19. Ⓐ Ⓑ Ⓒ Ⓓ Ⓔ Ⓕ
20. Ⓐ Ⓑ Ⓒ Ⓓ Ⓔ Ⓕ

Section 4: Verbal Reasoning

1. Ⓐ Ⓑ Ⓒ Ⓓ Ⓔ
2. Ⓐ Ⓑ Ⓒ Ⓓ Ⓔ
3. Ⓐ Ⓑ Ⓒ Ⓓ Ⓔ Ⓕ
4. Ⓐ Ⓑ Ⓒ Ⓓ Ⓔ Ⓕ
5. Ⓐ Ⓑ Ⓒ Ⓓ Ⓔ Ⓕ
   Ⓖ Ⓗ Ⓘ
6. Ⓐ Ⓑ Ⓒ Ⓓ Ⓔ Ⓕ
   Ⓖ Ⓗ Ⓘ

7. Ⓐ Ⓑ Ⓒ Ⓓ Ⓔ
8. Ⓐ Ⓑ Ⓒ Ⓓ Ⓔ
9. Ⓐ Ⓑ Ⓒ
10. Ⓐ Ⓑ Ⓒ Ⓓ Ⓔ
11. Ⓐ Ⓑ Ⓒ
12. Ⓐ Ⓑ Ⓒ Ⓓ Ⓔ Ⓕ
13. Ⓐ Ⓑ Ⓒ Ⓓ Ⓔ Ⓕ
14. Ⓐ Ⓑ Ⓒ Ⓓ Ⓔ Ⓕ

15. Ⓐ Ⓑ Ⓒ Ⓓ Ⓔ Ⓕ
16. Ⓐ Ⓑ Ⓒ Ⓓ Ⓔ
17. Ⓐ Ⓑ Ⓒ Ⓓ Ⓔ
18. Ⓐ Ⓑ Ⓒ Ⓓ Ⓔ
19. Ⓐ Ⓑ Ⓒ Ⓓ Ⓔ
20. Ⓐ Ⓑ Ⓒ Ⓓ Ⓔ

Section 5: Quantitative Reasoning

1. Ⓐ Ⓑ Ⓒ Ⓓ
2. Ⓐ Ⓑ Ⓒ Ⓓ
3. Ⓐ Ⓑ Ⓒ Ⓓ
4. Ⓐ Ⓑ Ⓒ Ⓓ
5. Ⓐ Ⓑ Ⓒ Ⓓ
6. [   ]
7. [   ]

8. [   ]
9. [   ]
10. Ⓐ Ⓑ Ⓒ Ⓓ
11. Ⓐ Ⓑ Ⓒ Ⓓ
12. [   ]
13. Ⓐ Ⓑ Ⓒ Ⓓ Ⓔ
14. Ⓐ Ⓑ Ⓒ Ⓓ Ⓔ

15. Ⓐ Ⓑ Ⓒ Ⓓ Ⓔ
16. Ⓐ Ⓑ Ⓒ Ⓓ Ⓔ
17. Ⓐ Ⓑ Ⓒ Ⓓ Ⓔ Ⓕ
18. [   ]
19. Ⓐ Ⓑ Ⓒ Ⓓ Ⓔ
20. Ⓐ Ⓑ Ⓒ Ⓓ Ⓔ

SECTION 1—ANALYTICAL WRITING

TIME: 60 MINUTES—2 WRITING TASKS

TASK 1: ISSUE EXPLORATION

TIME: 30 MINUTES

The topic is presented in a one- to two-sentence quotation commenting on an issue of general concern.

Your essay will be judged on the basis of your skill in the following areas:

- response to the specific task instructions
- consideration of the complexities of the issue
- organization, development, and expression of your ideas
- support of your position with relevant reasoning and examples
- control of the elements of standard written English

TOPIC

Some believe the more comforts a society provides, the more likely it is to create people who cannot provide for themselves. Others believe such comforts are indicative of a society's self-sufficiency.

DIRECTIONS: Write a response in which you discuss which view more closely aligns with your own position and explain your reasoning for the position you take. In developing and supporting your position, you should address both the views presented.

TASK 2: ARGUMENT ANALYSIS

TIME: 30 MINUTES

Your essay will be judged on the basis of your skill in the following areas:

- identification and assessment of the argument's main elements
- organization and articulation of your thoughts
- use of relevant examples and arguments to support your case
- handling of the mechanics of standard written English

TOPIC

In a study of the music listening preferences of Hollyland residents, conducted by the University of Sunnyland, most respondents listed their favorite type of music as country. However, another study indicated that, in Hollyland, the most frequently downloaded songs were all in the popular music genre. Therefore, it can be assumed that the respondents in the initial study were not truthful about their music listening habits.

DIRECTIONS: Write a response in which you examine the stated and/or unstated assumptions of the argument. Be sure to explain how the argument depends on these assumptions and what the implications are for the argument if the assumptions prove unwarranted.

SECTION 2—VERBAL REASONING

TIME: 30 MINUTES—20 QUESTIONS

> **DIRECTIONS:** For Questions 1 to 6, select *one* entry for each blank from the corresponding column of choices. Fill all blanks in the way that best completes the text.

1. Once the new employees became accustomed to their supervisor's _____ wit, they felt at ease, but initially, many of them felt stung by his sharply-edged jibes.

Ⓐ	urbane
Ⓑ	jocular
Ⓒ	acerbic
Ⓓ	tumultuous
Ⓔ	convivial

2. Surprisingly, the most _____ student was also the first to volunteer to give a speech.

Ⓐ	lapidary
Ⓑ	brilliant
Ⓒ	natty
Ⓓ	audacious
Ⓔ	tremulous

3. Those who blithely advocate a tax increase on wealthier corporations, indicating that many such corporations volunteer to pay more taxes, are mistaken. Firstly, such corporations often have (i) _____, self-serving motives that many in the public cannot or do not notice. Secondly, whether the corporations are cognizant of the fact or not, such tax raises would undoubtedly (ii) _____ their global strength.

Blank (i)		Blank (ii)	
Ⓐ	openhanded	Ⓓ	sap
Ⓑ	ulterior	Ⓔ	buttress
Ⓒ	miserly	Ⓕ	supersede

4. There has been much written on the benefits of "studying abroad" while enrolled in a university. However, little has been discussed about the drawbacks of programs that offer this opportunity. The (i) _____ of most programs' curricula leaves much to be desired. Also, without supervision, many students (ii) _____ the culture of their adopted countries in favor of revelry.

Blank (i)	Blank (ii)
Ⓐ rigor	Ⓓ condemn
Ⓑ nuance	Ⓔ assimilate
Ⓒ advocacy	Ⓕ shun

5. The psychological costs of confinement become apparent when certain case studies involving prisoners-of-war are reviewed. Often, when granted freedom, former captives display a notable (i) _____ rejoining the outside world, and despite the (ii) _____ of their emancipators, prefer to remain inside their more familiar, and thus seemingly less threatening, prison cells.

Blank (i)	Blank (ii)
Ⓐ aversion to	Ⓓ nonchalance
Ⓑ reluctance about	Ⓔ exhortations
Ⓒ excitement about	Ⓕ faults

6. Ask an art critic whether the inherent value of a piece lies in its uniqueness, technical innovation, or cultural significance, and you might receive three different answers. This premise is the focus of Michaelson's compelling new paper, and he makes (i) _____ case that the (ii) _____ notion that an art critic's capability to assess the worth of a given piece is superior to a layman's is wrong. His new idea, that the untrained eye is usually unfettered by orthodoxy and can therefore see value (iii) _____ is supported by his oft quoted axiom: "visceral trumps rational."

Blank (i)	Blank (ii)	Blank (iii)
Ⓐ a convincing	Ⓓ conventional	Ⓖ logically
Ⓑ a questionable	Ⓔ belabored	Ⓗ universally
Ⓒ an undeserved	Ⓕ erroneous	Ⓘ instinctively

7. The election of a more restrictive government, rather than the availability of resources, is to blame for Country X's recent decline in manufacturing exports. Country Y suffers from the same shortage of resources, but its manufacturing exports have recently risen.

   Which of the following, if true, most seriously undermines the argument?

   Ⓐ Agricultural exports have also recently declined in Country X.
   Ⓑ Country X is much more accessible geographically for trade than is Country Y.
   Ⓒ Both countries have had trouble locating resources needed for manufacturing.
   Ⓓ The manufacturing exports from Country X are significantly different than those from Country Y.
   Ⓔ The government of Country X is trying to create an economy that will help distribute resources more fairly.

Questions 8 to 11 are based on the following reading passage:

Citizen participation has received increased attention since the 1950s, with the underlying assumption that if citizens become actively involved as participants in their democracy, the governance that emerges from this process will be more democratic
Line and more effective. Indeed, participation is considered to be a crucial element in our
(5) democratic process, capable of holding the government accountable to the public and, in the case of urban planning, creating an appropriate vision to guide development.

Engaging a diverse citizenry in long-term planning is frequently problematic as disadvantaged communities often experience barriers to participation, including language barriers, time restraints, lack of adequate knowledge of political systems, and lack of
(10) politically favorable relationships with those in power, among others. Moreover, the traditional model of planning can be daunting: planners often use jargon and theory that may be inaccessible to community members, and typical timelines for implementation exceed any relevant temporal horizon for many young residents and renters.

Despite the challenges associated with engaging diverse stakeholders in planning,
(15) studies suggest that inclusive processes may contribute to the creation of more robust plans with a greater likelihood of long-term success in both implementation and sustainability. Research has found that mandates requiring local governments to solicit public involvement resulted in enhanced citizen participation, while also affecting the level to which planners and city officials considered public input when designing plan-
(20) ning policies and procedures. Research further suggests that participation of a broad swath of community members can strengthen engagement in the democratic process and enhance support for local government. Moreover, culturally appropriate engagement of diverse audiences can encourage ongoing participation in implementation of development plans and improve communication between experts and community
(25) members.

However, if public plans are designed using an inclusive process but are inequitable or inept in their execution, community members may be nominally engaged in the short term but fail to be engaged meaningfully in the long term. Participatory planning should not only seek to understand and articulate community differences but also (30) provide inventive ways for interaction and negotiation of competing visions, interests, values, and identities. To ensure effective and comprehensive implementation of a community plan, research suggests that the development of relationships between and amongst members of existing local networks is essential. Consensus building requires developing relationships among diverse stakeholders to facilitate understanding and to (35) improve the quality of decision-making. Innes notes that consensus building "requires a full range of stakeholders, meaningfulness to participants, mutual understanding, dialogue with equal opportunity to participate, self-organization, and accessible information."

8. It can be inferred from the passage that which of the following would be a disadvantage associated with the traditional model of urban planning?

   Ⓐ Mixing urban groups unaccustomed to relating to each other often creates more conflicts than it solves.
   Ⓑ Members of disadvantaged communities often cannot afford the expenses associated with attending urban planning meetings.
   Ⓒ Often, those asked to attend urban planning sessions choose not to because the sessions' goals conflict with their political beliefs.
   Ⓓ The terminology used to convey planning goals is incomprehensible to some citizens.
   Ⓔ The lack of clear deadlines frustrates many participants.

9. In the final paragraph of the passage, the author is concerned primarily with

   Ⓐ answering critics who argue that the planning process is irretrievably flawed
   Ⓑ arguing that most urban planners are prone to ineptitude and incompetence
   Ⓒ suggesting that community members ultimately will fail to stay involved with the planning process
   Ⓓ discussing the advantages and disadvantages of participatory planning
   Ⓔ warning that mere involvement in a process must be accompanied by competent execution and providing examples of that execution

10. Which of the following is mentioned in the passage as a method by which to improve the urban planning process?

   Ⓐ including as many people as possible from the community in the planning process
   Ⓑ attempting to resolve community differences as they arise
   Ⓒ facilitating new ways by which different groups can discuss their goals
   Ⓓ dispersing existing local networks in favor of a more cohesive, unified group
   Ⓔ ignoring cultural difference in the engagement process so as to create a more equitable way to participate

For Question 11, consider each of the choices separately and select *all* that apply.

11. According to the passage, which of the following can be inferred about the "young residents and renters" (line 13)?

   Indicate *all* that apply.

   A Some young residents and renters will not live in the community long enough to see the results of certain planning projects.
   B Young residents and renters often cannot afford to take time out of their schedules to participate in planning processes.
   C Though young residents and renters are among the hardest groups to involve in the planning process, their involvement is especially important.

DIRECTIONS: For Questions 12 to 15, select the *two* answer choices that, when used to complete the sentence, fit the meaning of the sentence as a whole *and* produce completed sentences that are alike in meaning.

---

12. Those who dismiss the poetry of e.e. cummings as whimsy would do well to consider the depths of genuine meaning that he in fact _____ with exquisite care.

   A plumbs
   B fathoms
   C fashions
   D circumvents
   E circles
   F elucidates

13 Nitroglycerine is used in the manufacture of several explosives but must be handled with the utmost care due to its _____.

   A power
   B instability
   C potency
   D volatility
   E solvency
   F causticness

14. It was often his garrulous nature that exposed his infantile sense of humor: when a room would grow silent, he would often feel compelled to offer _____ anecdote.

   A a sophomoric
   B a cosmopolitan
   C a sophisticated
   D a grotesque
   E a puerile
   F an unsavory

15. Chosen not as much for his charm, or lack thereof, as for his _____ appearance, the singer's bodyguard proved to be an effective deterrent for many autograph-seekers.

   A placid
   B minatory
   C menacing
   D gargantuan
   E seedy
   F livid

DIRECTIONS: For Questions 16 to 20, select *one* answer choice unless otherwise instructed.

Question 16 is based on the following reading passage:

Research over the past two decades has established the centrality of social networks to the process of international migration. As social beings, humans are inevitably enmeshed in webs of strong ties to close friends and relatives and weak ties to more dis-
Line tant relatives, casual acquaintances, and friends of friends. The set of weak and strong
(5) ties to people with current or prior migratory experience constitutes a person's migrant network. Whenever an aspiring international migrant has a social tie to someone with prior migratory experience, that connection offers a potentially valuable source of social capital. By drawing on the tie, individuals can mobilize social capital embedded within it to gain access to valuable information, moral support, and material assistance
(10) that may reduce, often quite substantially, the costs and risks of international migration. As a result, people who have migrant friends and relatives display a much higher likelihood of migrating compared with those who do not.

16. Select the sentence in which the author defines a term.

Questions 17 to 19 are based on the following reading passage:

The least luminous known galaxies have historically been those closest to our own galaxy, the Milky Way. Whether visually or with automated searches, resolved stars reveal the presence of nearby dwarf galaxies with surface brightnesses too low to be
Line discovered by diffuse light alone. Even until recently, nearly all cataloged dwarfs resided
(5) within the Local Group (LG) of galaxies. In 1999, the LG contained 36 known members, of which 11 are Milky Way (MW) satellites. Four of these eleven MW dwarf galaxies are more than 10,000 times less luminous than the Milky Way itself. There is now a new class of "ultra-faint" dwarf companions to the Milky Way known to have even lower absolute magnitudes. The resolved stellar populations of these near-field cosmologi-
(10) cal laboratories have been used to derive their star formation and chemical evolution histories and to model their dark mass content in detail. The future will reveal whether we have yet seen the ultimate limit of galaxy formation. The possibilities remain that either the low luminosities of the ultra-faint dwarfs are an artifact of nature, rather than nurture, and/or the present survey data are not deep enough to reveal the very least
(15) luminous systems and a vast population of ultra-faint dwarfs lie just beyond our fingertips. Regardless, at least dozens of ultra-faint satellites will be discovered in the near future, with the possibility of hundreds or more.

17. The primary purpose of the passage is to

Ⓐ compare ultra-faint galaxies to galaxies with the normal range of luminosity
Ⓑ question whether current methods of data-gathering are sufficient
Ⓒ present evidence regarding a rare phenomenon
Ⓓ discuss the current status of research about a topic
Ⓔ outline the history of a unique stellar object

18. In the context in which it appears, "resolved" (line 2) most nearly means

Ⓐ decided
Ⓑ settled
Ⓒ separated
Ⓓ solved
Ⓔ strengthened

19. The author of the passage mentions the history of the least luminous known galaxies (line 1) primarily in order to

Ⓐ highlight the importance of the faint galaxies proximal to the Earth
Ⓑ suggest that, unlike other nearby galaxies, the Milky Way is particularly rich in faint galaxies
Ⓒ imply that this phenomenon is due in part to the limitations of current technology
Ⓓ indicate that the inherent brightness of the Milky Way is responsible for the difficulty in detecting faint galaxies
Ⓔ argue that the Milky Way spawns dozens of faint galaxies

Question 20 is based on the following reading passage:

Critics of Acme Electronics, a components distributor, cite its increasing inventory as evidence that **the company is acting unwisely.** However, **the critics' views are erroneous.** Although an increasing amount of inventory held at a distribution company *Line* is often a sign of over-production, Acme Electronics has increased its inventory in light (5) of significant new orders from several of its largest customers.

20.   In the argument given, the two portions in **boldface** play which of the following roles?

   Ⓐ The first states the position that the argument opposes; the second offers evidence to discredit the support of the position being opposed.

   Ⓑ The first states the position that the argument opposes; the second is evidence that was used to support the opposed position.

   Ⓒ The first states the position that the argument opposes; the second states the argument's conclusion.

   Ⓓ The first is evidence that was used to support a position that the argument opposes; the second provides data to weaken that evidence.

   Ⓔ The first is evidence that was used to support a position that the argument opposes; the second states the argument's conclusion.

SECTION 3—QUANTITATIVE REASONING

TIME: 35 MINUTES—20 QUESTIONS

> **DIRECTIONS:** For Questions 1 to 8, compare Quantity A and Quantity B, using the additional information given, if any, and select *one* of the following four answer choices:
>
> Ⓐ Quantity A is greater.
> Ⓑ Quantity B is greater.
> Ⓒ The two quantities are equal.
> Ⓓ The relationship cannot be determined from the information given.

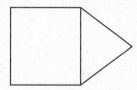

In the figure above, a square and an equilateral triangle share a common side.

	Quantity A	Quantity B
1.	The area of the square	Twice the area of the triangle

The price of an apple equals the price of a pear.
The price of a melon is twice the price of a pear.

	Quantity A	Quantity B
2.	The cost of eight apples, nine pears, and three melons	The cost of seven apples, four pears, and six melons

---

$$-2|x - 5| = -12$$

	Quantity A	Quantity B
3.	x	0

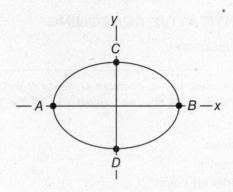

The equation of the curve shown in the
xy-plane above is $9x^2 + 16y^2 = 144$.
Points A, B, C, and D are the
x- and y-intercepts of the graph.

Quantity A	Quantity B
Length *AB*	Length *CD*

4.

Ed's three friends each live within 20 miles
of his house but more than 10 miles
from his house. Triangle *T* is the
triangle linking the three friends' houses.

Quantity A	Quantity B
The perimeter of triangle *T*	45 miles

5.

Quantity A	Quantity B
The distance traveled in 40 seconds by a marble rolling at a speed of 1.8 meters per second	The distance traveled in 4 minutes by a marble rolling at a speed of 35 centimeters per second

6.

Set $S = \{2, 4, 6, 11\}$ Set $T = \{50, 100, 200\}$

Quantity A	Quantity B
The number of distinct products that can be formed when an element of Set *S* is multiplied by an element of Set *T*	The number of distinct sums that can be formed when an element of Set *S* is added to an element of Set *T*

7.

Into empty Jar X, Jen places two black marbles and three white marbles.
Into empty Jar Y, she places five black marbles and four white marbles.
She then draws one marble at random from each jar.

Quantity A	Quantity B
8. The probability that both marbles drawn are black	The probability that both marbles drawn are white

---

DIRECTIONS: For Questions 9 to 13, enter your answer in the answer box below the question. Equivalent forms of the correct answer, such as 2.5 and 2.50, are all correct. Fractions do not need to be reduced to lowest terms.

Questions 9 and 10 are based on the following incomplete table, which shows the number of shirts sold by sleeve length and color in 1 year.

	Red	**Blue**	**Total**
Long Sleeve	423	591	
Short Sleeve		623	
Total			2,048

9. How many red short sleeve shirts were sold?

```
┌─────────────┐
│             │
│             │
└─────────────┘
```

10. If every shirt sold for $13.50, how much more money was earned from the sale of all short sleeve shirts than from the sale of all red shirts?

```
    ┌─────────────┐
 $  │             │
    │             │
    └─────────────┘
```

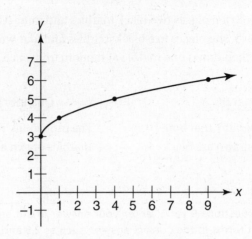

11.   The function $y = f(x)$ is graphed above. What is the value of $f(f(1))$?

12.   A nurse is combining one solution with an 8% concentration of acid in water with another solution that has a 15% concentration of acid in water. If the nurse uses 120 ml of the 8% solution, what volume of the 15% solution should be used to obtain a mixture with 12% concentration?

ml

13.   The cost c, in dollars, of buying shirts as a function of x, the number of shirts bought is given by $c(x) = 3.75x + 180$. The cost of buying 995 shirts is how much more than the cost of buying 775 shirts?

$

Questions 14 and 15 are based on the following table, which shows the weekly spending of a small business on office supplies.

Week Number	Dollars Spent
1	88
2	185
3	0
4	54
5	12
6	x

For Question 14, consider each of the choices separately and select *all* that apply.

14. For what values of x are *both* the mean (average) and the median weekly spending for the entire period between 60 and 70 dollars?

    Indicate *all* that apply.

    A 65
    B 72
    C 80
    D 83
    E 89

For Question 15, enter your answer in the answer box below the question.

15. If the Week 6 spending alone accounts for at least 80% of all spending for the entire period, what is the minimum value of x?

16. Machine A can produce a case of nails in 15 hours. Machine B can produce a case of nails in 12 hours. When both machines are running at the same time, how many hours will it take to produce nine cases?

Ⓐ 20
Ⓑ 40
Ⓒ 54
Ⓓ 60
Ⓔ 75

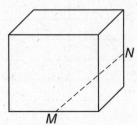

17. The cube above has a volume equal to 64 cubic feet. If Points M and N are the midpoints of two edges of the cube, what is length MN, in feet?

Ⓐ $4\sqrt{3}$
Ⓑ $3\sqrt{6}$
Ⓒ $4\sqrt{6}$
Ⓓ $6\sqrt{2}$
Ⓔ $2\sqrt{6}$

18. A boy is photocopying a rectangular poster. He sets the copier to increase the length of the poster by 30% and the width of the poster by 40%. The increase in the area of the poster is equal to x%. What is the value of x?

Ⓐ 68
Ⓑ 70
Ⓒ 75
Ⓓ 78
Ⓔ 82

For Questions 19 and 20, consider each of the choices separately and select *all* that apply.

19. Books sell for $5 to $10 each. Magazines sell for $3 to $5 each. Zoe bought four books and five magazines. Which of the following could be the amount of money she spent?

Indicate *all* that apply.

- A $30
- B $36.25
- C $48.50
- D $59.95
- E $64
- F $70

20. If $3x - 13 > -38$ and $4 - 5x > 38$, then x could equal which of the following?

Indicate *all* that apply.

- A −5.5
- B −6.5
- C −7.5
- D −8
- E −9
- F −10

DIRECTIONS: For Questions 1 to 6, select *one* entry for each blank from the corresponding column of choices. Fill all blanks in the way that best completes the text.

1. It seemed strange that the company trumpeted its _____ to the potential group of investors; a discussion of its forward direction might have been more relevant than one about its ability to pay back its debts.

Ⓐ solvency
Ⓑ liquidity
Ⓒ flexibility
Ⓓ usury
Ⓔ venerability

2. Ever a master of subtlety, the poet's _____ made others' depictions of mood and imagery seem heavy-handed.

Ⓐ bluntness
Ⓑ intimations
Ⓒ treachery
Ⓓ whispers
Ⓔ worldliness

3. Those who later studied the language of the embassy's missive agreed that though its wording was clearly designed to (i) _____ the leaders of the insurgency and to thereby prevent violence, its (ii) _____ tone was responsible for further inflaming their wrath.

Blank (i)	Blank (ii)
Ⓐ avoid	Ⓓ ebullient
Ⓑ incense	Ⓔ unfortunate
Ⓒ placate	Ⓕ condescending

4. The artist's technique is (i) _____ in that it combines (ii) _____ elements that seem to come from all over the world.

Blank (i)	Blank (ii)
Ⓐ a revolution	Ⓓ original
Ⓑ an amalgam	Ⓔ diverse
Ⓒ superlative	Ⓕ oceanic

5. Often the subject of an engineer's or manager's (i) _____, the conflict between those who design technology and those who market it is all too common. But despite workers' tendency to joke about this (ii) _____, for companies to function effectively, it is a chasm that must be bridged. Fortunately, a recent study has (iii) _____ ways by which companies can resolve some of their cross-departmental differences, so that they now have more of a blueprint for internal efficacy.

Blank (i)	Blank (ii)	Blank (iii)
Ⓐ woeful lament	Ⓓ pedagogy	Ⓖ researched
Ⓑ angry tirade	Ⓔ ineptitude	Ⓗ diffused
Ⓒ wry remark	Ⓕ schism	Ⓘ delineated

6. Athletic training regimens are most effective when they are designed for the athletes' intended sports. For triathletes, it is often desirable to (i) _____ endurance while strength is added, a dual goal that is usually (ii) _____ of the possible. A handful of triathletes have managed to add muscle mass while increasing their stamina and as a result, have performed at an elite level at competition. However, these athletes are clearly (iii) _____.

Blank (i)	Blank (ii)	Blank (iii)
Ⓐ extend	Ⓓ within the realm	Ⓖ reprehensible
Ⓑ augment	Ⓔ outside the bounds	Ⓗ critical
Ⓒ temper	Ⓕ among the options	Ⓘ anomalies

Questions 7 to 9 are based on the following reading passage:

Graf's primary interest is to describe and elaborate the basic premises of Wenders' film aesthetic. Although he admits that Wenders' meditations on the cinema "can sometimes leave an impression of puerile idealism," Graf generally refrains from staging a
Line full-scale critical interrogation and refutation of Wenders' premises. No doubt Wenders'
(5) film aesthetic is more of personal moral stance than a substantial theoretical position on the nature of cinema. Wenders' weighty statements about unmediated visual perception and the redemption of the real can strike the reader as naive, essentialist, and ahistorical, especially at a time when current theory emphasizes the inaccessibility of the real, and the constitutive process and mediating structures of representation.
(10) Wenders' belief that cinematography bears an unimpeachable witness to "things as they are," and provides an ontological bond between representation and what it represents, invokes a metaphysics of presence that leads to the misrecognition that images can exist somehow in an unmediated, nonmedialized, nonedited form. For Wenders, only film can redeem the real. The temporal and spatial separation of images from
(15) the realities they depict—making them reproductions, mere illusions of reality, and spectacle—seems to have little bearing on Wenders' desire for an unmediated representation of reality. Unlike Farber's special high tech camera in *Until the End of the World* (which records not optical images, but the neurological event of seeing), moving film images (even "true ones") do not automatically imprint on our brains—they are
(20) negotiated, mediated by our point of view, our experiences, our memories. Even if we grant that film images have a latent truth-telling potential and can preserve the real world, they are also, as Graf points out, highly fragile and open to abuse. Just like stories, they can be used to manipulate, distort, and tell lies.

7. The author's primary purpose in the passage is to

    Ⓐ explain the reasoning behind Graf's dismissal of Wenders' film aesthetic
    Ⓑ suggest that Wenders' films are childish and manipulative
    Ⓒ analyze Wenders' beliefs about the nature of film
    Ⓓ emphasize the importance of capturing reality in film
    Ⓔ affirm Wenders' reputation as a flawed yet groundbreaking modern filmmaker

8. In which of the following does the author discuss the implications of an idea put forward by Graf?

    Ⓐ The statement that Graf "refrains" from criticizing Wenders' premises.
    Ⓑ The description of Wenders' statements about perception as "weighty."
    Ⓒ The assertion that, for Wenders, "only film can redeem the real."
    Ⓓ The description of film images as "negotiated" and "mediated."
    Ⓔ The assertion that, like stories, images can "manipulate" and "distort."

For Question 9, consider each of the choices separately and select *all* that apply.

9. It can be inferred from the passage that the author would agree with which of the following statements about Wenders' beliefs about film?

   Indicate *all* that apply.

   A   For Wenders, the images of film serve to convey reality.
   B   Although Wenders believes film shows us what is real, he warns that it is also important for us to interpret its images.
   C   Wenders hopes that his films will be heralded as genuine representations of the world around us.

Questions 10 and 11 are based on the following reading passage:

Michael Walzer concluded the decade with a marvelous essay about participation in progressive politics. He made several key points. First, a citizen's choice not to participate does not constitute false consciousness. There are many legitimate reasons for citizens to disengage themselves from politics. Equally important, these nonpar-
(5) ticipants play an important role in democracy. They serve as audiences and critics of participants. Furthermore, they are citizens who have rights and interests that need to be represented. Walzer wrote, "Participatory democracy needs to be paralleled by representative democracy." Second, participatory democracy has a tendency to become "the rule of men with the most evenings to spare." Activists often turn participation
(10) into an onerous "duty" that entails constant meetings, discussions, deliberations, and decision-making. That duty may become so burdensome that most citizens cannot conceivably do it and many activists burn out trying. The "participatory" element in participatory democracy may disappear when the few activists who are willing to give 110 percent to the cause monopolize among themselves political initiative, strategy,
(15) and authority. Walzer warned that the most committed participants are the ones who need the strongest reminder that they are only part of the citizenry.

Line

10. The passage implies which of the following about the relationship between participatory and representative democracy?

   Ⓐ Those who actively urge others to participate are more valuable to the democratic process than those who do not.
   Ⓑ People who do not vote forfeit their right to a stake in the outcome of an election.
   Ⓒ Activists should devote some of their attention to ensure that those who do not vote are fairly represented.
   Ⓓ It is more valuable for most people to be an audience for those who participate in democracy than to participate themselves.
   Ⓔ The most committed activists would do well to allow others to have a greater role.

For Question 11, consider each of the choices separately and select *all* that apply.

11. The passage suggests which of the following about political activists?

    Indicate *all* that apply.

    A A minority of activists control a majority of political effort.
    B Activists use duty as a way of removing their political rivals from the participatory process.
    C Certain activists have shortsighted views regarding representation.

DIRECTIONS: For Questions 12 to 15, select the *two* answer choices that, when used to complete the sentence, fit the meaning of the sentence as a whole *and* produce completed sentences that are alike in meaning.

---

12. Claims that an atomic explosion could ignite the atmosphere had once been believed by some; however, after the first experimental atomic blast did not produce such an effect, the claims were widely regarded to be _____.

    A precocious
    B sacrosanct
    C immature
    D spurious
    E sound
    F apocryphal

13. Confused by his quarterly evaluation, which called his work ethic "phlegmatic" and "uninspired," the worker argued that he actually completed his tasks with _____.

    A chicanery
    B alacrity
    C zeal
    D meticulousness
    E transparency
    F artistry

14. The onscreen vampires of the current generation of film usually lack much feeling of being _____; they might better populate a soap opera than a horror movie.

    A belligerent
    B harmless
    C baleful
    D innocous
    E pernicious
    F bellicose

15. The saying that "a thousand truths are told in jest" would be well-heeded by those who are _____ about what their humor might imply to others.

A blithe
B demonstrative
C ardent
D debonair
E candid
F anxious

DIRECTIONS: For Questions 16 to 20, select *one* answer choice unless otherwise instructed.

Questions 16 and 17 are based on the following reading passage:

As with other areas of personal life now viewed as having larger public relevance, meat has traditionally been regarded as a "private" issue, in this case one's dietary choice—a matter of individual preference. The past few decades have witnessed *some* changes in
Line popular attitudes toward meat, yet most people see no connections between meat and
(5) general social problems. And these problems are indeed plentiful: resource depletion, pollution, food shortages, deforestation, global warming, and disease. *Worldwatch* magazine has observed: ". . . as environmental science has advanced, it has become apparent that the human appetite for flesh is a driving force behind virtually every category of environmental damage, including the growing scarcity of fresh water, loss of
(10) biodiversity, spread of toxic wastes and disease, even the destabilization of countries." This predicament is aggravated by the fivefold increase in global demand for meat in just the past four decades: with more than 6.2 billion humans on the planet, at least 90 percent consumers of meat, it takes no genius to see that the Earth's capacity for renewal is rapidly being outstripped. The source of astronomical profits for agribusi-
(15) ness, meatpackers, grocers, and the fast-food industry—in fact a bulwark of the entire corporate system—meat is today a decisive factor in altering planetary life.

16. In the context in which it appears, "popular" (line 4) most nearly means

Ⓐ widely appreciated
Ⓑ representative
Ⓒ humane
Ⓓ current
Ⓔ philosophical

17. The author of the passage suggests which of the following about the portrayal of meat consumption as "a matter of individual preference?"

   Ⓐ The portrayal is a direct result of corporate greed.
   Ⓑ If individuals form broader political groups, changes in meat consumption might become possible.
   Ⓒ Popular attitudes toward meat consumption have effected a shift in most people's perceptions of it.
   Ⓓ The portrayal is antiquated and needs modification.
   Ⓔ People should be free to consume meat, since eating it is a personal choice.

Questions 18 and 19 are based on the following reading passage:

Historically, Country A has imported much of its wheat from foreign sources. However, recent agricultural innovations have increased its ability to produce wheat and other grains. Country A's newly elected government has also flatly stated that it will devote
Line significant funds toward further developing the country's grain production. Therefore,
(5) Country A will soon rely less on wheat imports.

18. Which of the following, if true, would be useful in establishing the credibility of the argument?

   Ⓐ Will Country A's rice production ever exceed its wheat production?
   Ⓑ Does Country A rely more on wheat imports than its neighbors?
   Ⓒ What percentage of Country A's agricultural needs are met by soybeans?
   Ⓓ Is Country A's consumption of grain increasing?
   Ⓔ Have any of Country A's wheat fields been fallow in the past year?

19. In the context in which it appears, "flatly" (line 3) most nearly means

   Ⓐ clearly
   Ⓑ unemotionally
   Ⓒ absolutely
   Ⓓ emphatically
   Ⓔ evenly

20. Automobiles manufactured in Country J used to sell for high prices because they were usually higher in quality than automobiles manufactured in Country K. However, quality manufacturing technology is now so widespread that advantages in automobile manufacturing quality are rare. As a result, Country J's automobiles no longer offer higher quality or command higher prices than Country K's. Still, cars from Country J have a significant marketing advantage.

Which of the following, if true, best explains the contradiction presented in the passage?

Ⓐ Consumers believe that autos built in Country J have equal or better quality than those built in Country K.

Ⓑ Consumers realize that the quality of autos built in Country K can change.

Ⓒ When Country K adopted Country J's manufacturing technology, it was more concerned with imitating Country J's trucks than imitating its cars.

Ⓓ When quality advantages in automobile manufacturing were easier to possess, it was also easier to develop new automobile models.

Ⓔ When automobile sales decline, the automobile's account is usually offered to a new marketing agency.

SECTION 5—QUANTITATIVE REASONING

TIME: 35 MINUTES—20 QUESTIONS

DIRECTIONS: For Questions 1 to 5, compare Quantity A and Quantity B, using the additional information given, if any, and select *one* of the following four answer choices:

Ⓐ Quantity A is greater.
Ⓑ Quantity B is greater.
Ⓒ The two quantities are equal.
Ⓓ The relationship cannot be determined from the information given.

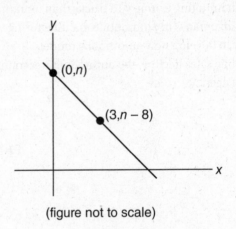

(figure not to scale)

The figure above shows the coordinates
of two points on a line in the *xy*-plane.

Quantity A	Quantity B
1. The slope of the line	$\dfrac{-17}{6}$

Ann earned a 25% raise to bring her salary to $20,000.
Bob received a 20% decrease in salary to bring his salary to $20,000.

Quantity A	Quantity B
2. The difference between Bob and Ann's salaries before these changes were made	$9,000

1,498 students are being assigned to classrooms that hold exactly 35 students each. *N* is the number of students left over when as many classrooms as possible are filled.

	Quantity A	Quantity B
3.	*N*	25

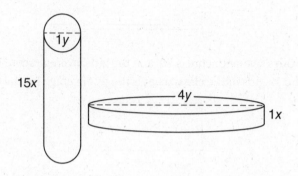

	Quantity A	Quantity B
4.	The volume of a right circular cylinder with height equal to 15*x* and diameter equal to 1*y*	The volume of a right circular cylinder with height equal to 1*x* and diameter equal to 4*y*

A man will choose two different flavors of ice cream for his sundae from the six flavors listed.

	Quantity A	Quantity B
5.	The number of different combinations of flavors that the man could possibly choose	15

DIRECTIONS: For Questions 6 to 9, enter your answer in the grid below the question. Equivalent forms of the correct answer, such as 2.5 and 2.50, are all correct. Fractions do not need to be reduced to lowest terms.

6. Adult tickets to a movie cost $9 each and children's tickets cost $5 each. When 44 tickets were bought, the total cost was $312. How many of the tickets purchased were adult tickets?

7. On a test, the boys' average score is 70, and the girls' average score is 80. If there are 18 boys and 12 girls in the class, what is the test average for the entire class?

8. The first five prime numbers in order are as follows: 2, 3, 5, 7, 11. The sum of the next four prime numbers in order is how much greater than the sum of the first five prime numbers?

9. The price of milk increased to $2.52 per gallon. If this represented a 12% increase in the price, what was the cost of buying nine gallons of milk before the increase?

$

Questions 10 to12 are based on the following table, which shows the vitamin content for three elements—iron, calcium, and zinc—contained in three different vitamin tablets. All units are in milligrams.

	Iron	Calcium	Zinc
Tablet X	17	40	14
Tablet Y	20	25	20
Tablet Z	45	20	15

For Questions 10 and 11, consider each of the choices separately, and select *all* that apply.

10. Which of the following statements are supported by the data?

    Indicate *all* that apply.

    A The tablet that contains the most iron contains the least zinc.
    B The tablet with the most total iron, calcium, and zinc combined is Tablet Z.
    C The tablet with the most calcium has less iron and less zinc than both of the other tablets.
    D By taking three of each tablet, a person will consume between 140 and 250 mg of all three elements.

11. A person wants to consume at least 120 mg but no more that 150 mg of each of the three elements. Which combination of tablets, considered individually, satisfy this requirement?

    Indicate *all* that apply.

    A two of Tablet X and two of Tablet Z
    B six of Tablet Y
    C three of Tablet Y and three of Tablet Z
    D one of Tablet X, four of Tablet Y, and one of Tablet Z

For Question 12, enter your answer in the answer box below the question.

12. What is the minimum number of tablets a person can take, using any combination of the three types of tablets, in order to obtain at least 140 mg of iron and at least 160 mg of calcium?

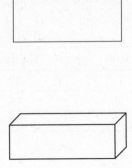

13. In the rectangular solid above, all edges have integer lengths. If the areas of three of the faces of the solid are 15, 33, and 55, what is its volume?

Ⓐ 103
Ⓑ 165
Ⓒ 495
Ⓓ 9,075
Ⓔ 27,225

14. The graphs $y = x^2 + 4$ and $y = |x| + 4$ have how many points in common?

Ⓐ none
Ⓑ one
Ⓒ two
Ⓓ three
Ⓔ four

15. A ball is launched from the ground with an initial height of zero meters. At t seconds after being launched, its height, h, in meters, as a function of time, t, is given by the equation $h(t) = -10t^2 + 40t$, for $0 \le t \le 4$. What is the height of the ball 3 seconds after being launched?

Ⓐ 10 meters
Ⓑ 20 meters
Ⓒ 30 meters
Ⓓ 980 meters
Ⓔ 1,020 meters

16. A *regular* polygon is defined as a polygon with all sides congruent and all angles congruent. In a regular polygon with n sides, the measure of one interior angle is equal to 168°. What is the value of n?

Ⓐ 12
Ⓑ 18
Ⓒ 24
Ⓓ 30
Ⓔ 36

For Question 17, consider each of the choices separately and select *all* that apply.

17. If $4^{x^2} = 8^{2x}$, then which of the following could be the value of x?

Indicate *all* that apply.

A −2
B 0
C 2
D 2.5
E 3
F 4

For Question 18, enter your answer in the answer box below the question. Equivalent forms of the correct answer, such as 2.5 and 2.50, are all correct. Fractions do not need to be reduced to lowest terms.

18. The area of circle C in square feet is equal to its circumference in feet. What is the circle's diameter?

| feet

Questions 19 and 20 are based on the following information: Maya flipped 24 coins, each of which landed with either a head face up or a tail face up, hereafter referred to as an outcome of "heads" or "tails."

For Question 19, consider each of the choices separately and select *all* that apply.

19.   Which of the following *could not be* the ratio of "heads" to "tails?"

Indicate *all* that apply.

A   1:1
B   2:1
C   3:1
D   4:1
E   5:1

20.   If all the coins are fair, in that the probability of "heads" = probability of "tails" = $\frac{1}{2}$

for every toss, which of the following events has the greatest probability?

Ⓐ Of the 24 tosses, the number of "heads" equals 11.
Ⓑ Of the 24 tosses, the number of "heads" equals 12.
Ⓒ Of the 24 tosses, the number of "tails" equals 14.
Ⓓ Of the 24 tosses, the number of "tails" is at most 3.
Ⓔ Of the 24 tosses, the number of "heads" is at least 22.

Section 2: Verbal Reasoning

1. **C**	8. **D**	15. **B, C**
2. **E**	9. **E**	16. **Sentence 3**
3. **B, D**	10. **C**	17. **D**
4. **A, F**	11. **A**	18. **C**
5. **B, E**	12. **A, B**	19. **C**
6. **A, D, I**	13. **B, D**	20. **C**
7. **D**	14. **A, E**	

Section 3: Quantitative Reasoning

1. **A**	8. **B**	15. **1,356**
2. **C**	9. **411**	16. **D**
3. **D**	10. **$2,700**	17. **E**
4. **A**	11. **5**	18. **E**
5. **D**	12. **160 ml**	19. **B, C, D, E**
6. **B**	13. **$825**	20. **C, D**
7. **B**	14. **B, C**	

Section 4: Verbal Reasoning

1. **A**	8. **E**	15. **A, D**
2. **B**	9. **A**	16. **B**
3. **C, F**	10. **C**	17. **D**
4. **B, E**	11. **A, C**	18. **D**
5. **C, F, I**	12. **D, F**	19. **C**
6. **B, E, I**	13. **B, C**	20. **A**
7. **C**	14. **C, E**	

Section 5: Quantitative Reasoning

1. **A**	8. **44**	15. **C**
2. **C**	9. **$20.25**	16. **D**
3. **A**	10. **B, C**	17. **B, E**
4. **B**	11. **B**	18. **4**
5. **C**	12. **5**	19. **D**
6. **23**	13. **B**	20. **B**
7. **74**	14. **D**	

ANSWER EXPLANATIONS

Section 2—Verbal Reasoning

1. **(C)** If the employees initially felt "stung by (the supervisor's) sharply-edged jibes," his humor must have been cutting. *Acerbic* (biting) would aptly describe that kind of humor.

2. **(E)** It would be surprising that a *tremulous* (timid) student would be the first to volunteer for public speaking.

3. **(B, D)** The author's critical stance and his description of the motives as ones that the public "cannot or do not notice" makes *ulterior* (beyond what is admitted) a good fit for blank (i). The author's critical tone also provides a clue for blank (ii), of the choices given, since only *sap* (weaken) would have a negative effect on the corporations.

4. **(A, F)** The author's critical tone and his use of the phrase "leaves much to be desired" makes it clear she is criticizing the *curricula* (courses) of the programs. Therefore, it would make sense for her to take issue with the *rigor* (exactness; difficulty) of the curricula. For blank (ii), if the students are doing something with the culture in favor of *revelry* (partying), they are choosing revelry over culture; i.e., they *shun* (avoid) the culture.

5. **(B, E)** Since the discussion of confinement focuses on its psychological costs, it can be expected that an unfortunate result will be discussed. A clue for the first blank is provided by the fact that the captives often "prefer to remain inside their . . . prison cells," i.e., they must display a *reluctance about* rejoining the world. The second blank must create a contrast between the actions of the *emancipators* (those who deliver freedom) and the captives' preference because of the shift the word *despite* creates. *Exhortations* (urgings) creates such a shift.

6. **(A, D, I)** Using *a convincing* for blank (i) is supported by the author's description of the paper as "compelling." Since Michaelson's new idea is highlighted, it would make sense that this new idea is taking the place of a more *conventional* (blank ii) one, which is described as "wrong." The clue for blank (iii) is at the end of the last sentence: "*visceral* (instinctive) trumps rational." This *axiom* (wise saying) is said to support his new idea, so *instinctively* would make sense to describe how the untrained person sees value.

7. **(D)** If the two countries have significantly different manufacturing exports, the same shortage of resources might affect Country X much more severely than it does Country Y; therefore this statement casts doubt that the shortage in Country X is caused by the government—it could very well be caused by the shortage of resources.

8. **(D)** The author, by saying that planners "often use jargon and theory that may be inaccessible to community members," is communicating that sometimes these members cannot comprehend the planners, making it more difficult for citizens to participate in the planning process since they don't understand some of the terms being used.

9. **(E)** In the beginning of the last paragraph, the author cautions that if an urban planning process is not well executed, then even if it is inclusive, it will not be effective in the long term. He then provides methods by which the process can be better executed.

10. **(C)** In the last paragraph, the author suggests that participatory planning "provide inventive ways for interaction and negotiation," therefore suggesting that planners should create new ways for different groups to discuss issues important to them.

11. **(A)** By saying that timelines for creation of planning projects sometimes "exceed any relevant temporal horizon" for young residents and renters, it can be inferred that a planning project will not be relevant to someone if he is no longer living in the community where it takes place.

12. **(A, B)** The phrase "in fact" signifies a shift in the sentence, so a logical shift from *whimsy* (imagination) would be to *plumb* (explore carefully) or *fathom* (probe) genuine meaning.

13. **(B, D)** If nitroglycerine must be handled with care and is used to make explosives, it would make sense that these are due to its *instability* or *volatility* (explosiveness).

14. **(A, E)** If the person's sense of humor is *infantile* (immature), then it follows that his anecdote will be *sophomoric* (immature) or *puerile* (childish).

15. **(B, C)** If the bodyguard's appearance is a *deterrent* (that which discourages), then he might look *minatory* (threatening) or *menacing*.

16. **(Sentence 3: The set of . . . network.)** In this sentence, the author provides a definition for the term "migrant network."

17. **(D)** Although the author makes a prediction in the last sentence and devotes the beginning of the passage to a description of faint galaxies' historical discovery, she spends most of the passage describing recent developments in the field as well as providing some current data about faint galaxies.

18. **(C)** Since the described stars are part of galaxies, the stars are resolved, or separated, from the galaxies so the stars can individually be observed.

19. **(C)** Since the author mentions the fact that historically most faint galaxies have been discovered close to our own galaxy, and later suggests that more galaxies may soon be discovered, it can be inferred that the historical prevalence of faint galaxies to our own is due partly to our technology's limits. Also, the author offers that "present survey data are not deep enough," again indicating that the reason faint galaxies have been discovered near the Milky Way is due to limitations of technology, not due to an astronomical phenomenon.

20. **(C)** The first portion in **boldface** is the critics' opinion, i.e., the position the argument opposes. The second portion in **boldface** is the argument's conclusion, that the critics are wrong, based on the evidence that the company's customers have placed orders that justify the inventory.

Section 3—Quantitative Reasoning

*Indicates an alternative way to solve the problem.

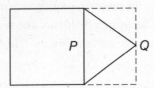

1. **(A)** Draw the dashed segments above and consider the rectangular region at right, made up of the three triangles together. The area of this rectangle equals twice the area of the original equilateral triangle and thus represents Quantity (B). This is because if $\overline{PQ}$ were drawn, the two exterior triangles could be paired with two congruent interior triangles. The rectangle has the same height as the square but a lesser width. So its area is less than that of the square, and (A) is greater.

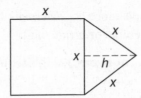

*Let x equal the length of each side in the figure. The area of the square (A), is x^2. Compute the area of the equilateral triangle by first drawing the dotted altitude, h, which will be used as the height, along with base x, to find the triangle's

$$\text{area} = \frac{\text{base} \times \text{height}}{2}.$$

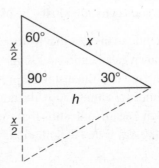

This altitude, h, creates a 30-60-90 triangle, and if you remember the $s - s\sqrt{3} - 2s$ pattern for the side lengths of these special triangles, you can quickly obtain

$h = \frac{x}{2} \times \sqrt{3} = \frac{x\sqrt{3}}{2}$. (Or find h by the Pythagorean theorem.) Then the area of the

original triangle is $\frac{x \times x\sqrt{3}}{2 \times 2} = \frac{x^2\sqrt{3}}{4}$. Twice this is $2 \times \frac{x^2\sqrt{3}}{4} = \frac{x^2\sqrt{3}}{2}$, which is less

than $1x^2$, because $\frac{\sqrt{3}}{2} < 1$. Then (A), x^2, is greater.

2. **(C)** Let x = price of apple = price of pear, and then $2x$ = price of melon. Quantity (A) is $8x + 9x + 3(2x) = 17x + 6x = 23x$. (B) is $7x + 4x + 6(2x) = 11x + 12x = 23x$, as well. So the quantities are equal, (C).

3. **(D)** Recall that absolute value equations generally have two solutions. Divide both sides by -2 to obtain $|x - 5| = 6$. Therefore, $x - 5 = 6$, or $x - 5 = -6$. Adding 5 to both sides in each equation yields $x = 11$ or $x = -1$. Since one possible x value is greater than 0, while the other is less than 0, there is not enough information to determine, and (D) is correct.

4. **(A)** Find the x-intercepts by setting $y = 0$, and the y term vanishes to leave $9x^2 = 144$, and so $x^2 = 16$. Then $x = \pm 4$, and $AB = 8$, the distance from $(-4, 0)$ to $(4, 0)$. Find the y-intercepts by setting $x = 0$, and the x term vanishes to leave $16y^2 = 144$, so $y^2 = 9$. Then $y = \pm 3$, and $CD = 6$, the distance from $(0, -3)$ to $(0, 3)$. Since $8 > 6$, (A) is correct.

5. **(D)**

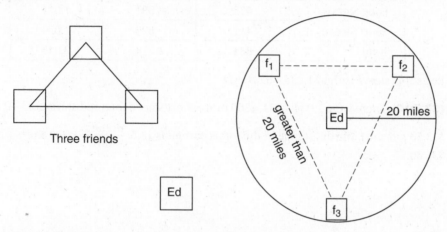

Three friends

Ed

As depicted at left, Ed's friends might live close to each other or even be neighbors, which would make the perimeter much less than 45 miles. On the other hand, in the diagram at right, the three friends live nearly 20 miles from Ed and much more than 20 miles from each other. This would make the perimeter greater than $3 \times 20 = 60 > 45$, and (D) is correct.

6. **(B)** Quantity (A) = $1.8 \frac{\text{meters}}{\text{second}} \times 40 \text{ seconds} = 72$ m. After converting 4 minutes to $4 \times 60 = 240$ seconds, Quantity (B) becomes $35 \frac{\text{centimeters}}{\text{seconds}} \times 240 \text{ seconds} = 8{,}400$ cm. Since 100 cm = 1 m, 8,400 cm = 84 m. Then (B) is greater, because $84 > 72$.

7. **(B)** It may appear that there are four choices for the element from Set S times three choices for the element from Set T, making both quantities equal $4 \times 3 = 12$, choice (C). But when you begin multiplying elements of S by elements of T, notice that many of the products formed are not distinct. For example, $2 \times 100 = 4 \times 50$. So Quantity (A) < 12. In Quantity (B), *there are* $4 \times 3 = 12$ distinct sums formed, because the large spread of values in Set T ensures no duplication. Thus, (B) must be greater.

8. **(B)** In Jar X, $\frac{2}{5}$ of marbles are black, and in Jar Y, $\frac{5}{9}$ are black, so the probability that both marbles drawn are black is $\frac{2}{5} \times \frac{5}{9} = \frac{10}{45}$ (A). In Jar X, $\frac{3}{5}$ of marbles are white, and in Jar Y, $\frac{4}{9}$ are white, so the probability that both marbles drawn are white is $\frac{3}{5} \times \frac{4}{9} = \frac{12}{45}$ (B). Since $12 > 10$, Quantity (B) is greater.

9. **(411)** Use your calculator to reconstruct all the values in the table, by first adding across the top row to obtain the total long sleeve shirts, 1,014, and then subtracting this sum from 2,048, the total of all shirts in the bottom right corner, to obtain the total short sleeves, 1,034.

	Red	**Blue**	**Total**
Long Sleeve	423	591	1,014
Short Sleeve	411	623	1,034
Total	834	1,214	2,048

Red short sleeve is then $1,034 - 623 = 411$.

10. **($2,700)** There were $1,034 - 834 = 200$ more short sleeve than red shirts sold. At $13.50 per shirt, the difference in the totals earned is $13.5 \frac{\text{dollars}}{-\text{shirt}} \times 200 \text{ shirts} = \$2,700$.

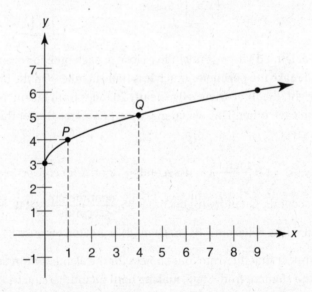

11. **(5)** First compute $f(1)$ by finding the point on the graph where $x = 1$, P, and then reading across horizontally to find the y-value associated with this point, 4. Then $f(f(1)) = f(4)$. Now find a point on the graph where $x = 4$, Q, by reading straight up vertically from the number 4 on the x-axis. The y-value associated with this point is 5.

12. **(160 ml)** The nurse uses 120 ml of the 8% solution, which must contain $120 \times .08 = 9.6$ ml of acid. Let $x =$ the volume of 15% solution that he or she uses. When the solutions are combined, there will be $120 + x$ total solution, of which $9.6 + .15x$ is acid. Since the combined solution is meant to have a 12% concentration, 12% of the total must equal the acid volume. That is, $.12(120 + x) = 9.6 + .15x$. Then $14.4 + .12x = 9.6 + .15x$. Combine like terms by subtracting 9.6 and $.12x$ from each side: $4.8 = .03x$. Finally, divide by .03 on each side to obtain 160 ml $= x$.

13. **($825)** The shortcut: the number in front of x—also called the coefficient of x—in the equation $c(x) = 3.75x + 180$ represents the per item cost. In other words, \$3.75 is the price per shirt. So when $995 - 775 = 220$ more shirts are bought, the cost differential is $3.75 \times 220 = \$825$.

    *The cost of 995 shirts is $c(995) = 3.75(995) + 180 = \$3,911.25$. The cost of 775 shirts is $c(775) = 3.75(775) + 180 = \$3,086.25$. The difference is $3,911.25 - 3,086.25 = \$825$.

14. **(B, C)** Start by arranging the five known numbers in order from least to greatest: 0, 12, 54, 88, 185. If $x > 88$, then 54 and 88 become the two middle values, and the median $= \dfrac{54 + 88}{2} = \dfrac{142}{2} = 71$. This is not between 60 and 70, so (E) is not correct.

    If $x = 65$, choice (A), then 54 and 65 become the two middle values, and the median $= \dfrac{54 + 65}{2} = \dfrac{119}{2} = 59.5$. So (A) is not correct. The average of six numbers will be between 60 and 70 when their sum, or total, is between $6 \times 60 = 360$ and $6 \times 70 = 420$. The sum of the weekly spending figures given is $0 + 12 + 54 + 88 + 185 + x = 339 + x$. Then $360 < 339 + x < 420$. Subtracting 339 from all three branches of the inequality yields $21 < x < 81$. (D) is incorrect, because $83 > 81$, so only choices (B) and (C) remain as correct.

15. **(1,356)** If x alone accounts for at least 80% of total spending, then $x \geq .80 \times (339 + x)$. Distribute the .8, and $x \geq 271.2 + .8x$. Subtract $.8x$ from both sides to obtain $.2x \geq 271.2$. Finally, divide both sides by .2, and $x \geq 1,356$.

16. **(D)** In 1 hour, Machine A produces $\dfrac{1}{15}$ of a case, and Machine B produces $\dfrac{1}{12}$ of a case. Working together, the machines produce $\dfrac{1}{15} + \dfrac{1}{12} = \dfrac{4}{60} + \dfrac{5}{60} = \dfrac{9}{60}$ of a case per hour, found by using the common denominator 60, because 60 is the least common multiple of 12 and 15. This implies that it will take the machines $\dfrac{60}{9}$ of an hour to produce one case, because $\dfrac{9}{60} \dfrac{\text{cases}}{\text{hour}} \times \dfrac{60}{9} \text{ hours} =$ one case. (A number times its reciprocal equals 1.) To produce nine such cases will require $9 \times \dfrac{60}{9} = 60$ hours, (D).

17. **(E)** If s is the side length of a cube, then the cube's volume = s^3. Here, $64 = s^3$, so $s = 4$, because $4 \times 4 \times 4 = 64$. Then $AB = 4$, and $MA = NB = 2$ in the figure below, because M and N are midpoints of two of the edges.

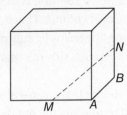

Now draw $\overline{MB}$ and form the two right triangles, MAB and MBN.

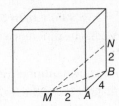

$\overline{MB}$ is the hypotenuse of a right triangle with legs equal to 2 and 4, so $MB = \sqrt{2^2 + 4^2} = \sqrt{4 + 16} = \sqrt{20}$ by the Pythagorean theorem. This length becomes a leg in the second right triangle MBN. Therefore, $\sqrt{20}^2 + 2^2 = MN^2$. Then $MN^2 = 20 + 4$, and $MN = \sqrt{24} = \sqrt{4 \times 6} = 2\sqrt{6}$, **(E)**.

18. **(E)** Let l and w be the poster's original length and width. When w is increased by 40%, the new width is $1w + .40w = 1.4w$. Similarly, the enlarged length equals $1.3l$. This makes the new area $1.4w \times 1.3l = 1.82lw$. Compared to the original area, lw, the change is $\dfrac{1.82lw - 1lw}{1lw} = \dfrac{.82lw}{1lw} = .82$, or 82%, **(E)**.

*Pick easy-to-use numbers for l and w, such as $l = 10 = w$. Then the poster's original area was $10 \times 10 = 100$. The new dimensions are $w = 14$ and $l = 13$, after the 40% and 30% increases in width and length. The new area is $14 \times 13 = 182$, which represents an increase of $\dfrac{182 - 100}{100} = \dfrac{82}{100} = 82\%$, **(E)**.

19. **(B, C, D, E)** Find the minimum Zoe could have spent by choosing the least price for both books and magazines. Then her total is $4 \times 5 + 5 \times 3 = 20 + 15 = \$35$. Find the maximum expenditure by choosing the greatest price for both books and magazines. Then her total is $4 \times 10 + 5 \times 5 = 40 + 25 = \$65$. So she spent from \$35 to \$65, (B), (C), (D), and (E).

20. **(C, D)** Except when multiplying or dividing by a negative number, you can work with inequalities in the same way that you work with equations:

$$
\begin{array}{ll}
3x - 13 > -38 & \qquad 4 - 5x > 38 \\
\underline{+13 \quad +13} & \qquad \underline{-4 \qquad -4} \\
\dfrac{3x}{3} > \dfrac{-25}{3} & \qquad \dfrac{-5x}{-5} > \dfrac{34}{-5} \\
x > -8.33 & \qquad x < -6.8
\end{array}
$$

Notice that the direction of the inequality reverses when you do multiply or divide by a negative (bottom right, above). This means $-8.33 < x < -6.8$. Choices (C) and (D) fall within this range.

Section 4—Verbal Reasoning

1. **(A)** Since the discussion was about the bank's "ability to pay back its debts," it must have been talking about its *solvency* (ability to meet financial obligations).

2. **(B)** If the poet is a master of "subtlety," and if he makes others seem *heavy-handed* (clumsy), then he would use *intimations* (implications).

3. **(C, F)** The *missive* (written message) was designed to "prevent violence," so its intention must have been to *placate* (soothe) the leaders. If it instead "inflamed their wrath," *condescending* would fit its tone.

4. **(B, E)** If the elements come from all over the world, it could be said that they are *diverse* (ii), and since this diversity describes the artist's technique, his technique could be said to be *an amalgam* (combination of diverse elements).

5. **(C, F, I)** A clue for blank (i) is provided by "despite workers' tendency to joke about this," which supports *wry* (drily humorous) *remark*. The passage described a "conflict," and refers to blank (ii) as a "chasm," supporting *schism* (separation). If the study is a blueprint for resolving differences, then it *delineates* (describes) how to do this.

6. **(B, E, I)** A clue for blank (i) is given by the phrase "dual goal" as well as by common sense; naturally, any athlete would want to *augment* (increase) endurance while building strength. For blank (ii), if only a "handful" of triathletes have managed to build both strength and endurance, then this goal is usually *outside the bounds* of the possible. Since the number of triathletes who have accomplished the dual goal is small, it would be fitting to describe these athletes as *anomalies* (exceptions).

7. **(C)** The author makes several statements about Wenders' beliefs about film. He suggests that Wenders' film aesthetic is a "personal moral stance," and says that for Wenders, "only film can redeem the real," among other such statements.

8. **(E)** In the preceding sentence, the author paraphrases Graf, saying that film images are open to abuse, and then proceeds to discuss the implications of that statement in the passage's last sentence, saying that the images can "manipulate, distort, and tell lies."

9. **(A)** The author states that "Wenders belie[ves] that cinematography bears an unimpeachable witness to 'things as they are,' " and later asserts that "for Wenders, only film can redeem the real," thereby arguing that Wenders believes film shows what is real.

10. **(C)** In discussing the importance of non-participants in the democratic process, the author suggests that these people have value, saying, "they are citizens who have rights and interests that need to be represented." This assertion supports the idea that participatory democracy should endeavor to represent those who choose not to be active.

11. **(A, C)** The author says that the "few" activists who do the most work "monopolize" the process, thus implying that a minority of them control most of the effort. He also says that this group of activists needs a "reminder that they are only part of the citizenry," implying some of their views are shortsighted in this regard.

12. **(D, F)** Since the claims were once believed until an experiment disproved them, and since the word "however" creates a shift, *spurious* (false) or *apocryphal* (of unlikely validity) would describe the claims.

13. **(B, C)** If the worker was surprised by his depiction as *phlegmatic* (unemotional) and *uninspired*, he must have thought he worked with *alacrity* (cheerful willingness) or *zeal* (enthusiasm).

14. **(C, E)** If the vampires would fit a soap opera better than they would a horror movie, then they are probably not very scary. Both *baleful* (threatening; ominous) or *pernicious* (deadly) would therefore describe them.

15. **(A, D)** Of the choices provided, those who are either *blithe* (carefree) or *debonair* (carefree) about their humor's effect would logically benefit from knowing its significance.

16. **(B)** In this sense, "popular" means "representative" because, in the sentence, the author is discussing the views of most people.

17. **(D)** The author compares attitudes about meat consumption to other personal choices with public relevance, but adds that the majority of people still see no link between meat and broader "problems." Since he then continues to explicate the problems that meat consumption engenders, he implies that the popular portrayal of meat consumption needs to be altered.

18. **(D)** In order to determine whether Country A will need to rely less on grain imports, it would be useful to know if its consumption of grains is increasing: if so, even if its own grain production increased, it still might have to maintain or even increase its imports.

19. **(C)** In this context, "flatly" means "without qualification or reservation," in other words, "absolutely" in that the government is saying it will not limit its promise.

20. **(A)** If automobile buyers base their decisions on the past, when Country J's autos were better than Country K's, then even though Country K's cars are now similar in quality to Country J's, Country J's would still enjoy a marketing advantage due to that outdated perception.

Section 5—Quantitative Reasoning

*Indicates an alternative way to solve the problem.

1. **(A)** Find the slope of the line by computing "rise over run." In moving along the line from n to $n-8$, the y-coordinate decreases by 8. In moving from 0 to 3, the x-coordinate increases by 3. So slope $= \dfrac{\text{change in } y}{\text{change in } x} = \dfrac{-8}{3}$. To compare to (B), multiply

the numerator and denominator by 2. $\frac{-8}{3} = \frac{-16}{6}$. This is greater than $\frac{-17}{6}$, which is "more negative," so (A) is correct.

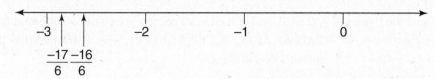

2. **(C)** If Ann's original salary was a, then $a + .25a = 20{,}000$, so $1.25a = 20{,}000$, and $a = 16{,}000$. If Bob's original salary was b, then $1b - .20b = 20{,}000$, so $.80b = 20{,}000$, and $b = 25{,}000$, after dividing both sides by .8. The difference in their original salaries was $25{,}000 - 16{,}000 = 9{,}000$, (C).

3. **(A)** When the 1,498 students are divided into classes of 35, the number of left over students, N, is simply the remainder when dividing 1,498 by 35. The easiest way is to use traditional long division, because your calculator will not give the remainder:

$$
\begin{array}{r}
42 \ \text{R } 28 \\
35\overline{)1498} \\
-140\!\downarrow \\
\hline
98 \\
-70 \\
\hline
28
\end{array}
$$

The remainder is 28, which is greater than 25, (A).

*You can also find the remainder on the calculator as follows. 1,498 divided by 35 = 42.8. Subtract the whole number part to get the decimal remainder: $42.8 - 42 = 0.8$. Multiply this result by the number you divided by: $0.8 \times 35 = 28$. This means that 28 is the remainder.

4. **(B)** The formula for the volume of a cylinder is Volume $= \pi r^2 h$. In (A), the height is 15 times as great, which would contribute 15 times to the volume. But in (B), the diameter, and hence the radius, is 4 times as great. Because radius is squared in the formula, multiplying r by 4 will multiply volume by $4^2 = 16$. In other words, $(4r)^2 = 16r^2$. Then (B) is greater by a factor of $\frac{16}{15}$.

*Use the Volume formula above, after you find the two radii, $\frac{1}{2}y$ and $2y$, by dividing the given diameters by 2. In (A), Volume $= \pi\left(\frac{1}{2}y\right)^2 (15x) = \frac{15}{4}\pi xy^2$. In (B),

Volume $= \pi(2y)^2(1x) = 4\pi xy^2$. Because $4 = \frac{16}{4} > \frac{15}{4}$, (B) is greater.

5. **(C)** Find the number combinations with the "choose" function, written as $_nC_k$ or $\binom{n}{k}$ and defined by the formula:

$$
\binom{n}{k} = \frac{n!}{k!(n-k)!} \quad \text{for } 0 \le k \le n.
$$

Recall that $n!$ means the product of all positive integers from 1 through n, inclusive. From six flavors, we are choosing two, so we want $_6C_2$, which equals

$$\frac{6\times5\times4\times3\times2\times1}{2\times1\times4\times3\times2\times1} = \frac{30}{2} = 15, \text{(C)}.$$

*Label the flavors A, B, C, D, E, and F, and list all combinations of two different flavors systematically: AB, AC, AD, AE, AF, BC, BD, BE, BF, CD, CE, CF, DE, DF, EF. There are $5 + 4 + 3 + 2 + 1 = 15$ combinations in all, (C).

6. **(23)** Let a = the number of adult tickets and c = the number of children's tickets. Since 44 tickets were sold, $a + c = 44$. Find the associated costs by multiplying the quantity of each type of ticket by the price per ticket. Then $9a + 5c = 312$. Multiply the first equation by -5 in order to eliminate the c variable:

$$
\begin{array}{rcl}
-5a - 5c &=& -220 \\
+\ \ 9a + 5c &=& 312 \\
\hline
4a &=& 92
\end{array}
$$

Dividing by 4 on each side shows $a = 23$.

7. **(74)** For 18 boys at 70 points per boy, there are $18 \times 70 = 1{,}260$ total points. For 12 girls at 80 points per girl, there are $12 \times 80 = 960$ total points. Then, the combined sum of test scores for the entire class is $1{,}260 + 960 = 2{,}220$ points. Divide this by 30 to obtain the average score per student, because there are $18 + 12 = 30$ students in the class. $2{,}220 \div 30 = 74$.

*Divide the number of boys and girls by 6, the greatest common factor of 18 and 12, in order to work with an equivalent ratio of children involving smaller numbers. The ratio of 18 boys to 12 girls is thus reduced to 3:2. For three boys at 70 points per boy, there are $3 \times 70 = 210$ total points. For two girls at 80 points per girl, there are $2 \times 80 = 160$ total points. This yields $210 + 160 = 370$ total points for all five students together (3 boys + 2 girls). Divide 370 by 5 to obtain the average score per student. $370 \div 5 = 74$.

8. **(44)** Prime numbers are numbers with exactly two positive integer factors, namely 1 and the number itself. The sum of the prime numbers given is $2 + 3 + 5 + 7 + 11 = 28$. The next four prime numbers in order are 13, 17, 19, 23. Their sum is $13 + 17 + 19 + 23 = 72$. This is $72 - 28 = 44$ greater.

9. **($20.25)** Let p = the original price of milk. Then p plus 12% of p becomes $p + .12p = 1.12p$. So $1.12p = \$2.52$, and by division $p = \$2.25$. The cost of nine gallons at this price is $9 \times 2.25 = \$20.25$.

10. **(B, C)** Tablet Z has the most iron, but it does not contain less zinc than Tablet X, so (A) is incorrect. Tablet Z has $45 + 20 + 15 = 80$ mg of the three elements combined, which is greater than any of the other row totals, so (B) is correct. Tablet X has the most calcium. But it has only 17 units of iron and 14 of zinc, which are less than the other tablets' contents, so (C) is correct. For (D), add the values in the middle column to find that one of each tablet would include $40 + 25 + 20 = 85$ mg of calcium. Then three of each tablet would contain $3 \times 85 = 255$ mg of calcium, which is not between 140 and 250, so (D) is not correct. The answer is (B) and (C).

11. **(B)** Combination (A) has insufficient zinc. Combination (B) contains either 120 or 150 milligrams of each element, as desired. Combination (C) has too much iron. Combination (D) contains too much calcium. Only (B) works.

12. **(5)** We are trying to arrive at 140 mg of iron and 160 mg of calcium efficiently, so we might as well not consume any of Tablet Y, which is highest in zinc, the one element we have no interest in. Notice that 3 of Tablet X and 2 of Tablet Y would contain $3 \times 40 + 2 \times 20 = 120 + 40 = 160$ mg of calcium exactly. This same combination contains $3 \times 17 + 2 \times 45 = 51 + 90 = 141$ mg of iron, which is greater than 140, as required. This combination of $3 + 2 = 5$ tablets achieves the desired quantities with very little wastage. No combination of four tablets will have sufficient amounts of both iron and calcium, so 5 is the minimum.

13. **(B)** Try to find the three edge lengths of the solid. The areas of the rectangular faces are 15, 33, and 55, so the pairwise products of the edges (the edge lengths multiplied two at a time) must equal these values. Trial and error reveals that $3 \times 5 = 15$, $3 \times 11 = 33$, and $5 \times 11 = 55$. This implies that the side lengths of the solid are 3, 5, and 11.

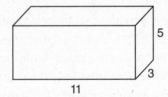

Notice that the top and bottom faces of the solid have area 33, while the front and back have area 55, and the right and left faces have area 15. Then Volume $= l \times w \times h = 11 \times 3 \times 5 = 165$, (B).

14. **(D)**

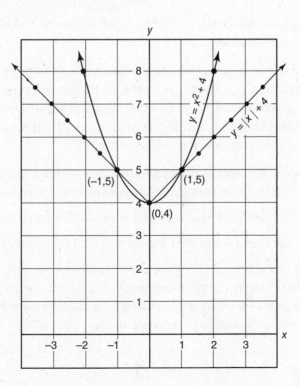

Graph both equations. Each represents a standard graph, $y = x^2$ or $y = |x|$, shifted vertically upward by 4 units. The three points of intersection are $(0, 4)$, $(1, 5)$, and $(-1, 5)$, so (D) is correct. Note that $x^2 > |x|$, except on the interval from -1 through 1. To understand why the graphs are equal when $x = 0$, 1, or -1, observe that $0^2 = 0 = |0|$, while $1^2 = 1 = |1|$, and $(-1)^2 = 1 = |-1|$.

15. **(C)** This is a problem on the basic use of a function in math. We know $t = 3$, so we can plug in 3 as t anywhere that t appears in the given function, to obtain $h(3) = -10 \times 3^2 + 40(3)$. Evaluate the right side, remembering to compute the exponent 3 squared before multiplying by -10, as per the order of operations. Then $-10 \times 9 + 40 \times 3 = -90 + 120 = 30$. This means that $h(3)$, which is the height of the ball at 3 seconds, is equal to 30 meters, choice (C).

16. **(D)** The sum of the measures of the interior angles on an n-sided polygon is given by the formula Angle Sum $= 180(n - 2)$ degrees. A polygon with n sides also has n angles, and if each angle measures $168°$, then the sum of all angles equals $168n$. So we can set $180(n - 2) = 168n$. Distribute 180, and $180n - 360 = 168n$. Subtract $168n$ and add 360 to each side to obtain $12n = 360$. Divide by 12, and $n = 30$, (D).

17. **(B, E)** The key to this type of exponent problem is to get a common base. Note that $4 = 2 \times 2 = 2^2$, and that $8 = 2 \times 2 \times 2 = 2^3$. Substituting these into the original equation, we obtain $(2^2)^{x^2} = (2^3)^{2x}$. The "power to a power" rule dictates that exponents are multiplied here, so $2^{2x^2} = 2^{6x}$. Since both sides have the common base of 2, we can set the exponents equal. Then $2x^2 = 6x$, and $2x^2 - 6x = 0$. Take out the common factor, and $2x(x - 3) = 0$, implying that $2x = 0$ or $x - 3 = 0$. So $x = 0$ or 3, (B) and (E).

*See the Introduction to this book, Math Section, Basic Strategy #6 for an alternative approach.

18. **(4)** If area equals circumference, then $\pi r^2 = 2\pi r$. Divide both sides by πr to obtain $r = 2$. If radius $= 2$, then diameter $= 2 \times 2 = 4$.

19. **(D)** Test the answer choices. If the ratio of heads to tails were 1:1, choice (A), then for some integer x, $1x + 1x = 24$, so $2x = 24$, and $x = 12$. This would mean 12 heads and 12 tails, which is permissible. The choice that could not be the ratio of heads to tails is (D), 4:1, because then $4x + 1x$ would equal 24. If $5x = 24$, x is not an integer. Specifically, we could not have 4.8 tosses that resulted in "tails."

20. **(B)** To compute these probabilities directly is beyond the scope of this book or the timeframe of the GRE. Treat this as a concept question. If the probability of heads is $\frac{1}{2}$, we expect $\frac{1}{2}$ of the 24 tosses to result in heads. The actual number of heads will vary if this experiment is repeated, but since $\frac{1}{2} \times 24 = 12$, the result of 12 heads will be the most probable single outcome and will represent the long-term average number of heads. (B). While choice (E) represents three distinct outcomes—22 heads, 23 heads, or 24 heads—it is extremely unlikely to obtain that many heads on 24 tosses, as these numbers are remote from the mean of 12.

$$1$$
$$1 \quad 1$$
$$1 \quad 2 \quad 1$$
$$1 \quad 3 \quad 3 \quad 1$$
$$1 \quad 4 \quad 6 \quad 4 \quad 1$$
$$1 \quad 5 \quad 10 \quad 10 \quad 5 \quad 1$$

*A reader familiar with *Pascal's Triangle* may be aware that the values in the triangle can be used to find the values of $_nC_r$, the "choose function" for obtaining the number of combinations when r objects are chosen from n. For example, in the small portion of Pascal's Triangle above, the six numbers in the bottom line represent $_5C_0$, $_5C_1$, $_5C_2$, $_5C_3$, $_5C_4$, and $_5C_5$, in order. In Pascal's Triangle, the largest values always occur in the middle of each line, which implies that $_{24}C_{12}$ is greater than $_{24}C_n$, for any value of n other than 12, so (B) is correct.

Practice Test 6

ANSWER SHEET
Practice Test 6

Section 2: Verbal Reasoning

1. Ⓐ Ⓑ Ⓒ Ⓓ Ⓔ

2. Ⓐ Ⓑ Ⓒ Ⓓ Ⓔ

3. Ⓐ Ⓑ Ⓒ Ⓓ Ⓔ Ⓕ

4. Ⓐ Ⓑ Ⓒ Ⓓ Ⓔ Ⓕ

5. Ⓐ Ⓑ Ⓒ Ⓓ Ⓔ Ⓕ
   Ⓖ Ⓗ Ⓘ

6. Ⓐ Ⓑ Ⓒ Ⓓ Ⓔ Ⓕ
   Ⓖ Ⓗ Ⓘ

7. Ⓐ Ⓑ Ⓒ

8. Highlight sentence in passage.

9. Ⓐ Ⓑ Ⓒ Ⓓ Ⓔ

10. Ⓐ Ⓑ Ⓒ Ⓓ Ⓔ

11. Ⓐ Ⓑ Ⓒ Ⓓ Ⓔ

12. Ⓐ Ⓑ Ⓒ Ⓓ Ⓔ Ⓕ

13. Ⓐ Ⓑ Ⓒ Ⓓ Ⓔ Ⓕ

14. Ⓐ Ⓑ Ⓒ Ⓓ Ⓔ Ⓕ

15. Ⓐ Ⓑ Ⓒ Ⓓ Ⓔ Ⓕ

16. Ⓐ Ⓑ Ⓒ Ⓓ Ⓔ

17. Ⓐ Ⓑ Ⓒ

18. Ⓐ Ⓑ Ⓒ Ⓓ Ⓔ

19. Ⓐ Ⓑ Ⓒ Ⓓ Ⓔ

20. Ⓐ Ⓑ Ⓒ

Section 3: Quantitative Reasoning

1. Ⓐ Ⓑ Ⓒ Ⓓ

2. Ⓐ Ⓑ Ⓒ Ⓓ

3. Ⓐ Ⓑ Ⓒ Ⓓ

4. Ⓐ Ⓑ Ⓒ Ⓓ

5. Ⓐ Ⓑ Ⓒ Ⓓ

6. Ⓐ Ⓑ Ⓒ Ⓓ

7. Ⓐ Ⓑ Ⓒ Ⓓ

8. Ⓐ Ⓑ Ⓒ Ⓓ

9. ☐

10. ☐

11. ☐

12. Ⓐ Ⓑ Ⓒ Ⓓ Ⓔ

13. Ⓐ Ⓑ Ⓒ Ⓓ Ⓔ

14. Ⓐ Ⓑ Ⓒ Ⓓ Ⓔ

15. Ⓐ Ⓑ Ⓒ Ⓓ Ⓔ

16. Ⓐ Ⓑ Ⓒ Ⓓ Ⓔ

17. Ⓐ Ⓑ Ⓒ Ⓓ Ⓔ

18. Ⓐ Ⓑ Ⓒ Ⓓ Ⓔ

19. Ⓐ Ⓑ Ⓒ Ⓓ Ⓔ

20. Ⓐ Ⓑ Ⓒ Ⓓ Ⓔ

ANSWER SHEET
Practice Test 6

Section 4: Verbal Reasoning

1. Ⓐ Ⓑ Ⓒ Ⓓ Ⓔ
2. Ⓐ Ⓑ Ⓒ Ⓓ Ⓔ
3. Ⓐ Ⓑ Ⓒ Ⓓ Ⓔ Ⓕ
4. Ⓐ Ⓑ Ⓒ Ⓓ Ⓔ Ⓕ
5. Ⓐ Ⓑ Ⓒ Ⓓ Ⓔ Ⓕ
   Ⓖ Ⓗ Ⓘ
6. Ⓐ Ⓑ Ⓒ Ⓓ Ⓔ Ⓕ
   Ⓖ Ⓗ Ⓘ

7. Ⓐ Ⓑ Ⓒ
8. Ⓐ Ⓑ Ⓒ Ⓓ Ⓔ
9. Ⓐ Ⓑ Ⓒ Ⓓ Ⓔ
10. Ⓐ Ⓑ Ⓒ
11. Ⓐ Ⓑ Ⓒ Ⓓ Ⓔ
12. Ⓐ Ⓑ Ⓒ Ⓓ Ⓔ Ⓕ
13. Ⓐ Ⓑ Ⓒ Ⓓ Ⓔ Ⓕ
14. Ⓐ Ⓑ Ⓒ Ⓓ Ⓔ Ⓕ

15. Ⓐ Ⓑ Ⓒ Ⓓ Ⓔ Ⓕ
16. Ⓐ Ⓑ Ⓒ Ⓓ Ⓔ
17. Ⓐ Ⓑ Ⓒ Ⓓ Ⓔ
18. Ⓐ Ⓑ Ⓒ Ⓓ Ⓔ
19. Ⓐ Ⓑ Ⓒ
20. Ⓐ Ⓑ Ⓒ Ⓓ Ⓔ

Section 5: Quantitative Reasoning

1. Ⓐ Ⓑ Ⓒ Ⓓ
2. Ⓐ Ⓑ Ⓒ Ⓓ
3. Ⓐ Ⓑ Ⓒ Ⓓ
4. Ⓐ Ⓑ Ⓒ Ⓓ
5. Ⓐ Ⓑ Ⓒ Ⓓ
6. [ ]
7. [ ]

8. [ ]
9. [ ]
10. Ⓐ Ⓑ Ⓒ Ⓓ Ⓔ
11. Ⓐ Ⓑ Ⓒ Ⓓ Ⓔ
12. Ⓐ Ⓑ Ⓒ Ⓓ Ⓔ
13. Ⓐ Ⓑ Ⓒ Ⓓ Ⓔ
14. Ⓐ Ⓑ Ⓒ Ⓓ Ⓔ

15. Ⓐ Ⓑ Ⓒ Ⓓ Ⓔ Ⓕ
16. Ⓐ Ⓑ Ⓒ Ⓓ Ⓔ
17. Ⓐ Ⓑ Ⓒ Ⓓ Ⓔ
18. Ⓐ Ⓑ Ⓒ Ⓓ Ⓔ
19. Ⓐ Ⓑ Ⓒ Ⓓ Ⓔ
20. Ⓐ Ⓑ Ⓒ Ⓓ Ⓔ

SECTION 1—ANALYTICAL WRITING

TIME: 60 MINUTES—2 WRITING TASKS

TASK 1: ISSUE EXPLORATION

TIME: 30 MINUTES

The topic is presented in a one- to two-sentence quotation commenting on an issue of general concern.

Your essay will be judged on the basis of your skill in the following areas:

- response to the specific task instructions
- consideration of the complexities of the issue
- organization, development, and expression of your ideas
- support of your position with relevant reasoning and examples
- control of the elements of standard written English

TOPIC

All cities should devote at least five percent of their budgets to programs that preserve and protect existing parks.

DIRECTIONS: Write a response in which you discuss the extent to which you agree or disagree with the recommendation and explain your reasoning for the position you take. In developing and supporting your position, describe specific circumstances in which adopting the recommendation would or would not be advantageous and explain how these examples shape your position.

TASK 2: ARGUMENT ANALYSIS

TIME: 30 MINUTES

Your essay will be judged on the basis of your skill in the following areas:

- identification and assessment of the argument's main elements
- organization and articulation of your thoughts
- use of relevant examples and arguments to support your case
- handling of the mechanics of standard written English

TOPIC

The following was written as part of a study weighing the benefits of a new construction project in the city of Winterville:

Car racing is extremely popular in the city of Winterville: over 20,000 Winterville residents attended the state's annual 500-lap race last summer, and the highest-rated television program in Winterville is "Race Talk," which is broadcast every night. Also, many successful race-car drivers live in Winterville. However, the nearest racetrack is over 150 miles away from Winterville. Given the popularity of car racing in Winterville, and a recent report indicating that the average race fan spends close to $500 per year attending car races, a new racetrack in Winterville would be very profitable.

DIRECTIONS: Write a response in which you discuss what questions would need to be answered in order to decide whether the recommendation is likely to have the predicted result. Be sure to explain how the answers to these questions would help to evaluate the recommendation.

SECTION 2—VERBAL REASONING

TIME: 30 MINUTES—20 QUESTIONS

> **DIRECTIONS:** For Questions 1 to 6, select *one* entry for each blank from the corresponding column of choices. Fill all blanks in the way that best completes the text.

1. The ski resort employee was a pleasant mix of the _____ and the urbane; despite his rustic clothing and rural accent, he was the epitome of politeness and composure.

Ⓐ bucolic
Ⓑ sophisticated
Ⓒ artless
Ⓓ churlish
Ⓔ disparate

2. Far from the cacophony bubbling out the 9th graders' music room, the _____ melodies of the more skilled 12th graders drifted pleasingly down the hall.

Ⓐ monotonous
Ⓑ impassive
Ⓒ gregarious
Ⓓ bilious
Ⓔ dulcet

3. A skilled though (i) _____ speaker, the party chairman was lauded for the sophistication by which he conveyed its message but increasingly criticized for the bombast that, in the end, (ii)_____ all but his most loyal followers from supporting him.

   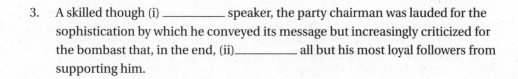

Blank (i)	Blank (ii)
Ⓐ unschooled	Ⓓ dissuaded
Ⓑ eloquent	Ⓔ atrophied
Ⓒ grandiloquent	Ⓕ hailed

4. The butterfly's (i) _____, though (ii) _____, allowed the entomologist ample time with which to fashion a quick sketch of its markings.

Blank (i)	Blank (ii)
Ⓐ pulchritude	Ⓓ camouflaged
Ⓑ verisimilitude	Ⓔ short-lived
Ⓒ quiescence	Ⓕ fragile

5. The magician, not immune to his own (i) _____ daydreams in which his entire audience stood spellbound at his feet, was nevertheless (ii) _____ when, apropos of nothing, a fan mailed him an oil painting in which the magician stood atop a stormy mountain, lightning bolt in hand, while below, throngs of admirers lay prostrate in (iii) _____ his depicted magnificence.

Blank (i)	Blank (ii)	Blank (iii)
Ⓐ transitory	Ⓓ flabbergasted	Ⓖ conjunction with
Ⓑ mysterious	Ⓔ bamboozled	Ⓗ homage to
Ⓒ fanciful	Ⓕ rattled	Ⓘ defiance of

6. Knowing the direction of his research would be condemned by his colleagues, the scientist did not realize the (i) _____ of mixing human and insect DNA until the twisted, suffering offspring of his trials came to life. Later, when such experimentation had been outlawed and the general public was more (ii) _____ its depravity, the scientist became even more (iii) _____.

Blank (i)	Blank (ii)	Blank (iii)
Ⓐ permutation	Ⓓ inured to	Ⓖ reviled
Ⓑ immensity	Ⓔ cognizant of	Ⓗ oblivious
Ⓒ enormity	Ⓕ tarnished by	Ⓘ chary

Questions 7 to 9 are based on the following reading passage:

In 2000, Oxford University Press gave C. Wright Mills' classic statement in political sociology, *The Power Elite* (1956), a face-lift. Gone from its cover were the somber black-
and-white and clichéd Davy Crocket-like floating hats of yesteryear. The New Edition's
Line fresh look is given by a cover wallpapered with photographs of The White House, Pen-
(5) tagon, and Wall Street, the hyper-ascendancy and anti-democratic integration of each
sphere of national power therein symbolized described by Mills 50 years ago as having
formed an emergent mid-century institution, a now-hidden, now-visible, American
power elite that, swollen with hubris, often played God. In a wobbly lexicon that would
become characteristically his own, Mills not only described a sociology of power in an
(10) increasingly bureaucratized United States, he also proceeded to identify the baleful,
sobering consequences of this development, including particularly a world-histor-
ical irrationality of bureaucratic rationality that he believed stood back of the rapid,
unchecked movement of the United States—together with its partner in nuclear brink-
manship, the Soviet Union—toward a perverse socio-political convergence and, quite
(15) possibly, finally, to each other's mutually assured destruction. The sympathetic reader
might simply note that, in 1956, it was understandably difficult for the then 40-year-old
Mills to see through the shadows cast back and forth between Max Weber and the coming Cuban Missile Crisis.

For Question 7, consider each of the choices separately and select *all* that apply.

7. Which of the following can be inferred that the author of the passage believes
   regarding Mills's depiction of the "power elite?"

   Indicate *all* that apply.

   A Mills based some of his description of the power elite on those who worked on
      Wall Street.
   B Mills always portrayed the relationship between the U.S. and the Soviet Union
      as a dangerous one.
   C For at least some of the factors surrounding the power elite, Mills was
      ill-informed.

8. Select the sentence in the passage in which the author comments on Mills's use
   of language.

9. In the context in which it appears, "played" (line 8) most nearly means

Ⓐ wagered on
Ⓑ competed against
Ⓒ acted as
Ⓓ fiddled with
Ⓔ exploited

Question 10 is based on the following reading passage:

On a certain deep space mission, the vessel's computer indicated that there was insufficient oxygen in the ship's atmosphere to keep all six crew members alive until they reached the closest space station. The ship's doctor reasoned that the amount of oxygen
Line needed by the crew had been underestimated. However, **this reasoning was incorrect.**
(5) The ship's biologist checked the oxygen records and, in fact, **more than enough oxygen had been budgeted for the mission.** Additionally, the ship's engineer confirmed that the ship was not leaking air. Therefore, something other than the crew members must have been responsible for the oxygen shortage.

10. In the argument given, the two portions in **boldface** play which of the following roles?

Ⓐ The first is an assertion made by the argument in support of a certain position; the second is that position.
Ⓑ The first is an opinion made by the argument about a certain explanation; the second is that explanation.
Ⓒ The first is the argument's dismissal of an objection to the position it tries to establish; the second is that position.
Ⓓ The first summarizes the argument's position with regard to a certain hypothesis; the second provides support for that position.
Ⓔ The first is an admission by the argument that its position is flawed; the second corrects the flaw in the argument's position.

Question 11 is based on the following reading passage:

Convective clouds and storms represent one of the most important and challenging problems for forecasters. The severe local storms and deep convective clouds are characterized by the enhanced transport of heat and moisture in the upper layers, very
Line strong self-organized flow fields, very complex microphysical transformations and
(5) stratospheric penetrations, and rapid evolution and dissipation processes. The precipitation processes are activated in very limited time intervals and space, and their intensities are manifested by a large natural variability. Supercell storms are perhaps the most violent of all convective storm types and are capable of producing damaging winds, large hail, and weak to violent tornadoes. They are most common during
(10) the spring across the mid-latitudes when moderate to strong atmospheric wind fields, vertical wind shear, and instability are present. The degree and vertical distribution of moisture, instability, lift, and especially wind shear have a profound influence on

convective storm types. It is generally recognized that the environmental buoyancy and vertical wind shear have an important effect on the characteristics of convective

(15) storms. Much of our understanding of the sensitivity of convective storms to these environment parameters has been derived from modeling studies that tested a variety of, but often idealized, environmental conditions.

11.   According to the passage, which of the following is NOT a characteristic of convective storms?

Ⓐ increased movement of heat and moisture
Ⓑ powerful flow-fields
Ⓒ intricate transformations and penetrations
Ⓓ rapid evolution processes
Ⓔ persistence over certain geographical areas

DIRECTIONS: For Questions 12 to 15, select the *two* answer choices that, when used to complete the sentence, fit the meaning of the sentence as a whole *and* produce completed sentences that are alike in meaning.

---

12.   The tranquility experienced by those who live in a country that enjoys _____ over its neighbors often hides the conflicts created by this state of dominance.

A hegemony
B intractability
C ascendancy
D obstinacy
E derision
F equilibrium

13.   The football coach's reputation for _____ his players was well-deserved; his halftime speeches were usually filled with scathing rebukes.

A coddling
B indulging
C debilitating
D enfeebling
E excoriating
F upbraiding

14.   In its _____ stages, before anyone knew about its imperialist designs, the foreign infrastructure bill won bipartisan approval.

A callow
B embryonic
C tertiary
D primary
E nascent
F terminal

15.   Befitting one of whom gravity and repose was a requirement rather than a desired attribute, the funeral director's _____ nature helped soothe the mourners, comforting them with silence rather than chatter.

    A garrulous
    B exacting
    C severe
    D taciturn
    E laconic
    F gregarious

DIRECTIONS: For Questions 16 to 20, select *one* answer choice unless otherwise instructed.

Questions 16 to 18 are based on the following reading passage:

Since the emergence of the automobile as a mass commodity in the early twentieth century, natural themes and imagery have been used to flesh out and concretize these two principles of spatial epistemology—the pursuit of spatial novelty and a spatial
Line phenomenology that privileges spectacle—by attaching a utopian flavor to movement
(5) through space. "We shall solve the city problem," Henry Ford once quipped, "by leaving the city." From the 1920s onward, car advertising has invoked the fantasy of leaving behind the constraints of a crowded, mundane and polluted urban environment for the wide-open spaces offered by nature. Charting the evolution of automotive promotional discourse, Andrew Wernick argues that the reliance upon natural imagery intensified
(10) in the 1970s and 1980s as people grew disenchanted with technology (and its militaristic overtones) and expressed concerns over growing traffic congestion, energy consumption and road construction. Among the easiest tactics for advertisers wishing to deflect the negative associations invoked by the car was, and remains, an image-based rearticulation of cars with nature. For both producers and consumers, the association
(15) of automobiles with (travel to) pristine natural environments helps to forget the vast resources and infrastructure required to support car-based societies as well as the enormous ecological consequences that accompany their mass production. In an American context, the use of natural imagery also taps deeply into core national myths. Thomas Jefferson, for example, famously idealized the authenticity and moral supremacy of life
(20) in the country, an idea that has been replayed in countless texts and venues over the past two centuries in which a redemptive arc is traced from the corruption of the city to the honesty, virtue, and community of the small town. Frederick Jackson Turner's "frontier thesis," which has become deeply embedded in popular culture (if somewhat discredited in academic scholarship) traces a similar trajectory in defining the essential
(25) strength and vigor of U.S. moral character and democracy as a product of the struggle to carve a new life out of the wilderness and, conversely, suggesting the likely atrophy of such virtues in an urban environment. The recent popularity of sentimental and often melancholy tributes to the declining role that nature plays in everyday life, best expressed perhaps in Bill McKibben's bestsellers *The End of Nature* and *The Age of Miss-*

(30) *ing Information*, confirm the ongoing purchase that this dream of escaping the city for the sensual bliss of nature has on the popular imagination.

The flight from urban to natural space looms large in automobile ads of today, ranging from the carefully crafted stories of big budget national campaigns to generic foot-age of vehicles racing through natural landscapes that populate spots for local deal-

(35) ers. Cities or, more accurately, the monotonous routines that often seem to dominate urban and suburban existence are regularly targeted by advertisers. A typical ad for Saab, for instance, paints an Orwellian portrait of social life as characterized by end-less sameness: row upon row of identical suburban homes, identical suitcases on an airport trolley, identical office cubicles, identical dresses in a clothing store and, lastly,

(40) identical black sedans in a parking garage. Puzzled, confused, and disoriented, the commercial's protagonists shuffle about aimlessly in a bland, urban dystopia of com-plete homogeneity. Finally, salvation arrives in the form of a silver Saab convertible that offers its young driver the opportunity to stand out from the crowd. As the growl of its engine mixes with the chorus "I'm free" sung by The Who, the vehicle slowly pulls

(45) out of a parking garage, leaving a stunned onlooker speechless with wonder. "In a world of sameness, you can still maintain your identity." It is a familiar refrain, dupli-cated *ad nauseam* since marketers discovered the counterculture in the 1960s, yet still a popular formula in marketing discourse.

16. The primary purpose of the passage is to

   Ⓐ compare the different methods by which advertisers attempt to influence consumers

   Ⓑ question whether connecting automobile advertisements to nature imagery is ethical

   Ⓒ present evidence suggesting that advertising using images of nature is more effective than ads without those types of images

   Ⓓ discuss the benefits associated with living outside of an urban area

   Ⓔ analyze the reasoning behind and implications of a certain type of marketing

For Question 17, consider each of the answer choices separately and select *all* that apply.

17. The passage implies which of the following about Frederick Jackson Turner's "frontier thesis?"

Indicate *all* that apply.

   Ⓐ It is more a part of American culture than is Jefferson's idealization of country life.

   Ⓑ Academics who write about the thesis often do so in a critical manner.

   Ⓒ It attributes certain values to the effort expended on the American frontier.

18. In the context in which it appears, "purchase" (line 30) most nearly means

(A) allure
(B) security
(C) exchange
(D) hold
(E) dominance

Questions 19 and 20 are based on the following reading passage:

Despite numerous investigations, the debate concerning whether Neanderthals became extinct because of climate change or competition with modern humans is still unresolved. Some researchers argue that competition alone cannot be the cause of
Line Neanderthal extinction. By contrast, other authors support the existence of competi-
(5) tive exclusion for the same niche and argue that competition played a major role in the demise of the Neanderthal population. Some analyses, which are based on mathematical modeling, lack plausibility because they are too theoretical; others, which are based on more integrative simulations or which take into account archaeological and ethnologic examples, are more convincing.

(10) The modeling approach is used to understand complex systems by working on a simplified model of these systems. Thus, this process involves the choice of certain parameters and variables, which, if they are simplified, are controlled in such a way that they are capable of representing the system as a whole. Therefore, the models used so far do not attempt to determine the kind of food that Neanderthals and modern humans
(15) consumed but to highlight the potential differences in dietary habits characteristic of these two populations.

19. The author of the passage most likely cites "archaeological and ethnologic examples" in order to

(A) suggest that the authors of most Neanderthal extinction investigations failed to use integrative simulations
(B) offer an explanation for the paradox involved in explaining the extinction of Neanderthals
(C) provide examples of additional parameters that can be included in Neanderthal studies
(D) suggest that providing archaeological and ethnological examples makes research about extinct populations more convincing
(E) provide support for the idea that theoretical modeling of extinct populations is an outdated concept

For Question 20, consider each of the answer choices separately and select *all* that apply.

20. Which of the following statements about the "modeling approach" is supported by the passage?

    Indicate *all* that apply.

    A   Studies that simplify parameters cannot adequately represent entire systems.
    B   Attempting to determine what kind of food Neanderthals ate is more complex than theorizing the differences between Neanderthal and modern diets.
    C   Models of systems representing the behavior of complex systems are necessarily also complex.

SECTION 3—QUANTITATIVE REASONING

TIME: 35 MINUTES—20 QUESTIONS

DIRECTIONS: For Questions 1 to 8, compare Quantity A and Quantity B, using the additional information given, if any, and select *one* of the following four answer choices:

Ⓐ Quantity A is greater.

Ⓑ Quantity B is greater.

Ⓒ The two quantities are equal.

Ⓓ The relationship cannot be determined from the information given.

$$4^n = 256$$

	Quantity A	Quantity B
1.	3^n	$\frac{3}{2}n^3$

	Quantity A	Quantity B
2.	The greatest possible area of a triangle with side lengths 4, 5, and x	11

$$m = 3n$$
$$n = 5p$$

	Quantity A	Quantity B
3.	m	p

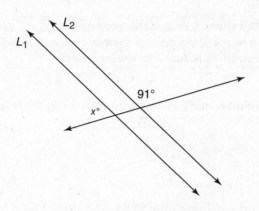

Lines L_1 and L_2 are parallel.

Quantity A	Quantity B
4. | x | 91 |

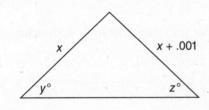

Quantity A	Quantity B
5. | y | z |

$$(m+5)(m-5) = 0$$
$$(k+4)(k-4) = 0$$

Quantity A	Quantity B
6. | m^2 | k^2 |

Quantity A	Quantity B
The number of meters	The number of square
in 10 kilometers	centimeters in 1 square meter

7.

Quantity A	Quantity B
The area of a quadrilateral	The area of a quadrilateral
with perimeter equal to P	with perimeter equal to $2P$

8.

9.   The average of a number and 20% of the number is 660. What is the number?

10.   A store raises the price of bread from $1.99 to $2.49 per loaf. A family buys 22 loaves of bread per month from the store. As a result of the price increase, the family's monthly expenditure for bread will increase by x%. What is the value of x? *Round* your answer to the *nearest whole number*.

11.   If $\frac{1}{8}$ of a certain number is 15 greater than $\frac{1}{9}$ of the same number, then what is $\frac{1}{10}$ of the number?

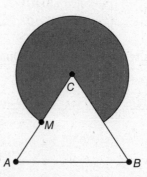

12.   In equilateral triangle *ABC*, above, *AB* = 12, and *M* is the midpoint of *AC*. Point *C* is the center of the circle. What is the shaded area?

ⓐ   6π

ⓑ   7.2π

ⓒ   10π

ⓓ   24π

ⓔ   30π

13. If $\dfrac{x-y}{2.25} = \dfrac{\sqrt{3}}{7}$, then which of the following must be true?

Ⓐ $x = y$

Ⓑ $x > y$

Ⓒ $x < y$

Ⓓ $x = 2y$

Ⓔ $y = 2x$

14. How many 4-digit numbers have the following two properties? The first and last digits of the number are both prime numbers, and the number is divisible by 2 or 5.

Ⓐ 800

Ⓑ 900

Ⓒ 1,000

Ⓓ 1,200

Ⓔ 1,600

15. For all positive real numbers, x and y, let $x \star y = \sqrt{x} - 2y^2$. What is the value of $9 \star 2$?

Ⓐ −13

Ⓑ −8

Ⓒ −7

Ⓓ −5

Ⓔ −3

16. If a is the greatest common factor of 111 and 141, and b is the least common multiple of 8 and 10, what is the value of ab?

Ⓐ 60

Ⓑ 80

Ⓒ 120

Ⓓ 160

Ⓔ 240

For Question 17, consider each of the choices separately and select *all* that apply.

17. If $x = 2y$ and $y = 4z$, then which of the following must equal z?

Indicate *all* that apply.

☐A 4y

☐B $\dfrac{1}{4} y$

☐C 8x

☐D $\dfrac{1}{8} x$

☐E 2x

Questions 18 to 20 refer to the following graph:

Value of Exports of Country X, 2000–2012
(in U.S. Dollars)

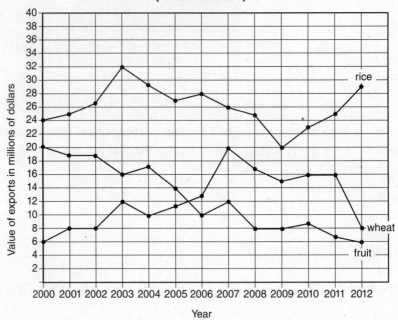

18. In which year did the value of rice exports roughly equal the value of the other two types of exports combined?

Ⓐ 2000
Ⓑ 2002
Ⓒ 2003
Ⓓ 2006
Ⓔ 2012

19. For the 3-year period from 2009 through 2011, inclusive, the total value of rice exports exceeded the total value of wheat exports by how many million dollars?

Ⓐ 20
Ⓑ 20.5
Ⓒ 21
Ⓓ 21.5
Ⓔ 22

20. In what year did the value of fruit exports decrease by the highest percentage from the year before?

Ⓐ 2003
Ⓑ 2006
Ⓒ 2008
Ⓓ 2011
Ⓔ 2012

SECTION 4—VERBAL REASONING

TIME: 30 MINUTES—20 QUESTIONS

> **DIRECTIONS:** For Questions 1 to 6, select *one* entry for each blank from the corresponding column of choices. Fill all blanks in the way that best completes the text.

1. Only by studying the transcripts of the conversations between the diplomat and the senator did the investigator realize that the foreign emissary's _____ nature used a barrage of verbiage to divert rather than to discuss.

   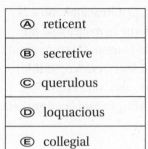

Ⓐ	reticent
Ⓑ	secretive
Ⓒ	querulous
Ⓓ	loquacious
Ⓔ	collegial

2. Each successive _____ of a fractal, by repetition, beautifully describes shapes that Euclidean geometry cannot.

   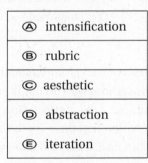

Ⓐ	intensification
Ⓑ	rubric
Ⓒ	aesthetic
Ⓓ	abstraction
Ⓔ	iteration

3. It seemed ironic that the very (i) _____ with which the cheetah (ii) _____ its rival was its undoing; in its eagerness to fight, it charged too quickly and was pushed off of a cliff by its foe.

   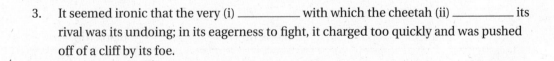

Blank (i)	Blank (ii)
Ⓐ truculence	Ⓓ assailed
Ⓑ wavering	Ⓔ skirted
Ⓒ maladroitness	Ⓕ harrowed

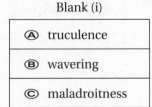
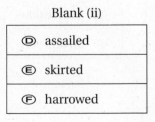
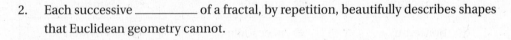

PRACTICE TEST 6

4. Though initially (i) _____ the lack of precedent with which the battle unfolded, the general soon recovered and initiated (ii) _____ strategy.

Blank (i)	Blank (ii)
Ⓐ debased by	Ⓓ a shrewd
Ⓑ nonplussed by	Ⓔ an ingenuous
Ⓒ buoyed by	Ⓕ an overwhelming

5. Puffed up with (i) _____ pride, the callow young scientist trumpeted his preliminary results to the world in a voluminous paper. Unfortunately, he was not experienced enough with the fickle politics of academe to realize that the experimental successes of the uninitiated are often held to more exacting standards. His colleagues, who were more aware of this critical tendency, cringed at the self-congratulatory (ii) _____ that riddled the work, and were even more (iii) _____ when criticism of the paper started trickling in, implicating their entire institution in the process.

Blank (i)	Blank (ii)	Blank (iii)
Ⓐ auspicious	Ⓓ conceits	Ⓖ apposite
Ⓑ boisterous	Ⓔ peccadillos	Ⓗ abrogated
Ⓒ overweening	Ⓕ preening	Ⓘ chagrined

6. The assertion that people who receive slightly higher doses of background radiation than the national average are less (i) _____ harm than those who do not is based on the assumption that this background radiation has (ii) _____ effect. However, no reliable studies have been conducted to support the notion that these low levels of background radiation (iii) _____; in fact, most studies have indicated that every additional increase in dosage brings a corresponding increase in the chances of cell damage.

Blank (i)	Blank (ii)	Blank (iii)
Ⓐ susceptible to	Ⓓ a negligible	Ⓖ act as a tonic
Ⓑ protected from	Ⓔ a salubrious	Ⓗ threaten health
Ⓒ concerned with	Ⓕ an injurious	Ⓘ can be discounted

Questions 7 and 8 are based on the following reading passage:

The discovery of penicillin by Fleming in 1929 opened an entire new way to control bacterial infections. The industrial production of penicillin in 1940 and the subsequent introduction of new antibiotics into medical application saved many lives and raised
Line hopes for permanent control of pathogens. However, the continuous and increasing
(5) use of antibiotics led to the emergence of pathogenic bacteria resistant to many of these anti-infectiva. During antibiotic treatment, these resistances are probably generated by hypermutating strains. An elevated number of strains exhibiting high mutation frequencies have recently been reported in the population of many pathogenic bacteria, for example, *Pseudomonas aeruginosa* in the cystic lung. The
(10) majority of naturally occurring strong mutators possessing up to 1,000-fold higher than the normal mutation rates have an advantage against normal strains for the selection of some antibiotic-resistant mutations. Horizontal gene transfer is also enhanced in mismatch repair-defective mutators, facilitating the spread of drug resistance in bacteria. However, hypermutators have a price to pay for their fitness, which is not
(15) the case for weak mutators found in many clinical isolates. Furthermore, the sewage systems are loaded with antibacterials excreted by humans and animals treated for prophylactic and therapeutic reasons. Several classes of chemotherapeutics have been found in the outlets of sewage treatment plants and can be detected in rivers. It has been hypothesized that these pharmaceuticals as well contribute to the increasing
(20) number of resistant pathogens.

For Question 7, consider each of the choices separately and select *all* that apply.

7. It can be inferred from the passage that the author agrees with which of the following about pathogens?

    Indicate *all* that apply.

    A The hypermutation of pathogenic organisms supports the notion that many antibiotics do more harm than good.
    B Some of the measures that people take to preserve their health in fact threaten their health.
    C Pharmaceuticals contribute to the resistance of pathogenic bacteria.

8. It can be inferred that the author of the passage mentions "a price to pay" (line 14) primarily in order to

Ⓐ help explain why hypermutators are usually the most harmful pathogens
Ⓑ identify one weakness in the argument that all pathogens create disease
Ⓒ indicate how hypermutators' resistance to antibiotics has been steadily increasing
Ⓓ help account for how weak mutators generally outnumber hypermutators
Ⓔ suggest that hypermutators' resistance to antibiotics does not always help them thrive

Question 9 is based on the following reading passage:

Compared to the old equipment used by factory workers to assemble circuit boards, the new equipment allows for faster assembly by allowing the worker to rotate the board 360 degrees in any direction. Therefore, by replacing the old equipment with this new equipment, factories will quickly realize cost savings.

9. Which of the following, if true, most undermines the argument?

Ⓐ Workers who use both the old and new equipment report greater difficulty switching to the old equipment from the new equipment than switching to the new equipment from the old equipment.
Ⓑ Manufacturing costs for the new equipment are similar to those for the old equipment.
Ⓒ The number of factories that use the new equipment has increased every year for the past 5 years.
Ⓓ The more time an employee has spent using the old equipment, the more expensive it is to teach that employee to use the new equipment.
Ⓔ New workers can learn to use the new equipment in the same amount of time that it takes them to learn to use the old equipment.

Questions 10 and 11 are based on the following reading passage:

Karl Marx, writing in the *Grundrisse* in 1857, anticipated how the contradictions of capital could spur on the "annihilation of space by time." He wrote, "While capital . . . must strive to tear down every barrier . . . to exchange and conquer the whole earth for its
Line markets, it strives on the other side to annihilate this space with time." Certainly, adver-
(5) tising has done its best to equate gains in speed with general notions of progress—how often have ads referred to gaining time by using a particular product? In a world seemingly packed to capacity with things to do and places to be, the technology of speed promises to deliver us to a better place.

Breaking speed-barriers is not a new obsession. Speed of movement not only signals
(10) our capacity for overcoming the fixity of geographical distance (space), it also has come to suggest the possibility for increased flexibility, efficiency, and productivity. Since its inception, capitalism has measured value in terms of time inputs since the amount of labor required to produce a commodity could most easily be measured in units of time.

So it stands to reason that our "common-sense" understanding of technologies of speed

(15) connote a future liberation from material scarcity. In contemporary society, where time itself has become perceived as a scarce resource, appeals to instantaneity and immediacy are seductive. Has speed annihilated spatial distance? Paul Virilio writes that one of the most revolutionary transformations occurring today "is the invention of a perspective of real time."

For Question 10, consider each of the choices separately and select *all* that apply.

10.   Which of the following inferences about Marx's opinions of capital are supported by the passage?

Indicate *all* that apply.

- [A] Marx, more than any other philosopher, was critical of capitalism's destructive nature.
- [B] Marx was critical about the means by which capitalism accomplished its ends.
- [C] Marx believed that capitalism should be discarded and replaced with a more equitable economic framework.

11.   In the eighth sentence ("So it stands . . . scarcity"), the author of the passage is most likely suggesting that

- Ⓐ speed will be more valuable than material wealth in the future
- Ⓑ scholarship focused on technology will pay more attention to the speed advantages such technology produces than to the technology itself
- Ⓒ material wealth, not speed, is the most important aspect of capital
- Ⓓ the current understanding of speed implies that someday speed will help offset the lack of materials
- Ⓔ the focus of many advertisements on speed is deceptive

> **DIRECTIONS:** For Questions 12 to 15, select the *two* answer choices that, when used to complete the sentence, fit the meaning of the sentence as a whole *and* produce completed sentences that are alike in meaning.

12.   Advice columns written for women in the 1950s seem almost laughable by today's more equitable standards: housewives were instructed to, among other things, make sure their responses to their husbands were _____ so as to promote a harmonious household.

- [A] coquettish
- [B] agreeable
- [C] antiquated
- [D] chauvinistic
- [E] flirtaceous
- [F] felicitous

13. Criticism of the direction of his research as _____ failed to perturb the scientist, who knew that his experiments on water molecules, though admittedly quite commonplace and even unoriginal, still would produce helpful results.

[A] quotidian
[B] trifling
[C] frivolous
[D] impractical
[E] pedestrian
[F] eccentric

14. Its coffers full with another round of investment funding, the fledgling company was inexperienced enough to adopt _____ spending policy, and it quickly exhausted its erstwhile surplus.

[A] a spendthrift
[B] an impecunious
[C] a miserly
[D] a profligate
[E] a stringent
[F] a meticulous

15. By surrounding himself with _____, the monarch was shielded from any criticism and was thus blind to the shortsightedness of many of his decrees until their effects were manifest.

[A] opulence
[B] sycophants
[C] toadies
[D] diversions
[E] distractions
[F] gadflies

> **DIRECTIONS:** For Questions 16 to 20, select *one* answer choice unless otherwise instructed.

Questions 16 to 18 are based on the following reading passage:

Maria Helena P.T. Machados's bilingual edition of *Brazil Through the Eyes of William James* expertly gathers and examines James's sketches, written correspondence, and diaries produced during the Thayer Expedition to the Amazon basin in 1865 and 1866,
Line offering a fascinating glimpse into the formative voyage of one of North America's pre-
(5) eminent thinkers. While adding to an important body of travel literature set in Brazil that spans from the early colonial era (Hans Staden) to the 20th century (Claude Levi-Strauss), the handsomely illustrated volume offers a comprehensive cultural and

historical critique of the expedition and its participants, contributing to a greater understanding of U.S.–Brazilian relations amid the contentious political climate of the (10) U.S. Civil War era.

James's letters and journal entries are both typical of the era in which they were written and, as Machados argues in her lengthy introduction (comprising half the volume), highly idiosyncratic documents to the point of being mildly subversive. Consisting primarily of correspondence to his parents, brother Henry, and sister Alice, James's (15) missives raise considerable doubts about the expedition's defining goals, namely, to find evidence supporting the creationist agenda of leader and Harvard luminary Louis Agassiz. As Machados points out, Agazziz was one of Charles Darwin's most formidable and charismatic critics as well as one of the foremost U.S. public intellectuals of the period. As such, the Swiss-born scientist received a great deal of financial backing and (20) accolades from both the U.S. South and imperial Brazilian government.

Although on a number of occasions, James, in his letters, declares admiration for his professor, in his journal entries he reveals the full range of his sentiments: that he abhors the tedious work of collecting species after new species, each new discovery evidence, in Agazziz's mind, of the stasis of nature and therefore a repudiation of evolutionary (25) theory. James clearly considers his mentor intellectually impressive and physically tireless yet something of a self-righteous blowhard. "Never," he writes, "did a man utter a greater amount of humbug." James's amusing caricatures of Agazziz and fellow voyagers reinforce his irreverent attitude toward their central mission, and provide a clear indication as to why he chose to abort the Thayer Expedition after 8 months of travel.

16. Which of the following can be inferred from the passage regarding James's communication with his family?

   Ⓐ James, for fear of criticism from Agazziz, had to be implicit about the contents of his journal entries.

   Ⓑ James used the correspondence with his family to voice his disillusion with his work.

   Ⓒ It was necessary for James to create the illusion that he admired Agazziz so as not to raise his professor's suspicions.

   Ⓓ James was secretly a critic of Darwin's theory of evolution.

   Ⓔ James, unlike his creationist professor, was a staunch atheist.

17. In the passage, the author is primarily concerned with

Ⓐ summarizing the results of a study
Ⓑ analyzing the reasoning behind an argument
Ⓒ considering an opinion
Ⓓ speculating about a set of circumstances
Ⓔ defining categories

18. In the context in which it appears, "body" (line 5) most nearly means

Ⓐ organism
Ⓑ carcass
Ⓒ trunk
Ⓓ consistency
Ⓔ collection

Question 19 is based on the following reading passage:

A quark-nova is the explosion driven by phase transition of the core of a neutron star to the quark matter phase (i.e., neutron star core collapse) leading to the formation of a quark star. The gravitational potential energy released (plus latent heat of phase transi-
Line tion) during this event is converted partly into internal energy and partly into outward
(5) propagating shock waves, which impart kinetic energy to the material that forms the ejecta (i.e., the outermost layers of the neutron star crust). The ejection of the outer layers of the neutron star is driven by the thermal fireball generated as the star cools from its birth temperature down to ~7.7 MeV. The fireball expands without losing or gaining heat, while pushing the overlaying crust and cooling fairly rapidly. The energy needed
(10) to eject the crust is less than 1% of the fireball energy, which is thought to be one of the most powerful explosions in the universe.

For Question 19, consider each of the choices separately and select *all* that apply.

19. According to the passage, which of the following occurs during a quark-nova?

Indicate *all* that apply.

Ⓐ The crust of a neutron star is driven into the core of the star.
Ⓑ The ejecta are expelled by the shock waves generated by the fireball.
Ⓒ The fireball produced by a quark-nova contains 99% of its energy.

Question 20 is based on the following reading passage:

People native to islands far from major land masses usually subsist mainly on fish and vegetables, and eat very little red meat. Few of them develop heart disease, and their risk for heart disease does not increase as they get older, unlike people living in less
Line isolated countries. These islanders do often develop heart disease if they move to cities
(5) and begin eating diets high in red meat. However, these facts do not prove red meat is the reason they develop heart disease in these instances because _____.

20. Which of the following most logically completes the passage?

Ⓐ such islanders might be genetically predisposed to not contract heart disease

Ⓑ people who eat high amounts of red meat in cities of countries that are not isolated tend to develop heart disease

Ⓒ some people live in cities of countries that are not isolated and do not develop heart disease

Ⓓ other aspects of diet are altered when islanders move to cities such as these

Ⓔ red meat provides iron, which is essential for health

SECTION 5—QUANTITATIVE REASONING

TIME: 35 MINUTES—20 QUESTIONS

DIRECTIONS: For Questions 1 to 5, compare Quantity A and Quantity B, using the additional information given, if any, and select *one* of the following four answer choices:

Ⓐ Quantity A is greater.

Ⓑ Quantity B is greater.

Ⓒ The two quantities are equal.

Ⓓ The relationship cannot be determined from the information given.

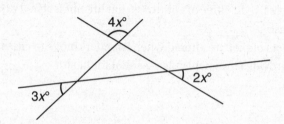

Quantity A	Quantity B
$5x$	100

1.

In the xy-plane, P is the point of intersection
of the two lines given by the following equations:

$$y = 2x - 6 \qquad y = \frac{1}{2}x + 6$$

Quantity A	Quantity B
The x-coordinate of point P	The y-coordinate of point P

2.

Quantity A	Quantity B
The area of a square with perimeter equal to 64	The area a circle with diameter equal to 18

3.

	Quantity A	Quantity B
4.	$2x + 3y$	$3x + 4y$

	Quantity A	Quantity B
5.	The daily rent of a man who pays $975 rent per month	The daily rent of a man who pays $11,650 rent per year

DIRECTIONS: For Questions 6 to 9, enter your answer in the grid below the question. Equivalent forms of the correct answer, such as 2.5 and 2.50, are all correct. Fractions do not need to be reduced to lowest terms.

6. The number 980,000,000 is equal to 9.8×10^n, for some integer n. What is the value of n?

7. A basketball player scores an average of 26.5 points per game for an 82-game season. A second player who averages 28 points per game during the same season scores how many more points than the first player, in the full season?

8. In the xy-plane, the coordinates of the three vertices of a triangle are given by $(0, 0)$, $(0, a)$, and $(b, 0)$. The triangle's area is 6, and all three of its sides have integer length. What is the triangle's perimeter?

9. When the whole numbers from 1 through 200, inclusive, are written on a page, how many individual digits are written?

10. The diameters of the smaller and larger circles above are 6 and 8, respectively. The two circles have the same center. What is the shaded area?

Ⓐ 4π

Ⓑ 7π

Ⓒ 8π

Ⓓ 9π

Ⓔ 16π

11. Jim is now 15 years older than Ted. 18 years ago, Jim was twice Ted's age. Jim is now how many years old?

Ⓐ 33

Ⓑ 35

Ⓒ 47

Ⓓ 48

Ⓔ 51

	Quiz 1	Quiz 2	Quiz 3
Wendy	8	9	10
Yuri	7	10	6
Zoe	9	9	6

12. One quiz score is chosen at random from each of the three students, Wendy, Yuri, and Zoe. What is the probability that all three numbers chosen are even?

Ⓐ $\frac{2}{27}$

Ⓑ $\frac{4}{27}$

Ⓒ $\frac{8}{27}$

Ⓓ $\frac{1}{9}$

Ⓔ $\frac{2}{9}$

13. A car leaves New York at 12:00 driving due west at an average speed of 54 miles per hour. A second car leaves New York 2 hours later, driving due west on the same road, at an average speed of 66 miles per hour. If both cars continue to move at the same rates, at what time will the second car reach the first?

Ⓐ 9:00
Ⓑ 10:00
Ⓒ 10:30
Ⓓ 11:00
Ⓔ 11:30

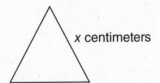
x centimeters

14. The area of an equilateral triangle, in square centimeters, is equal to its perimeter, in centimeters. What is its side length?

Ⓐ $2\sqrt{3}$ cm

Ⓑ $4\sqrt{3}$ cm

Ⓒ $8\sqrt{3}$ cm

Ⓓ $4\sqrt{2}$ cm

Ⓔ $3\sqrt{3}$ cm

For Questions 15 to 17, consider each of the choices separately and select *all* that apply.

15. When Leila buys six sandwiches for her family, she always pays from $29.70 to $38.70, depending on what types of sandwiches she orders. One day, she buys 20 sandwiches of the same types, at the same prices per sandwich. Which of the following could be her total cost?

   Indicate *all* that apply.

   A $95
   B $98
   C $100
   D $125
   E $130
   F $132

16. The set of numbers, S, has the following two properties: the product of any two numbers in set S is also an element of set S, the sum of any two numbers in set S is also an element of set S. Which of the following could be set S?

   Indicate *all* that apply.

   A $S = \{$all even integers$\}$
   B $S = \{$all odd integers$\}$
   C $S = \{$all real numbers$\}$
   D $S = \{$all positive real numbers$\}$
   E $S = \{$all negative real numbers$\}$

17. If $0 < \dfrac{1}{x} < 1$, then which of the following must be true?

   Indicate *all* that apply.

   A $0 < x < 1$
   B $1 < x < 1000$
   C $\dfrac{1}{x} < x$
   D $x > 1$
   E $\dfrac{1}{x} > \dfrac{1}{x^2}$

Questions 18 to 20 refer to the following graph;

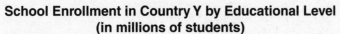

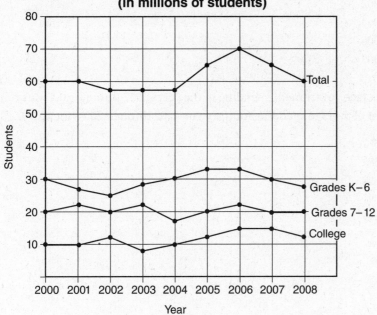

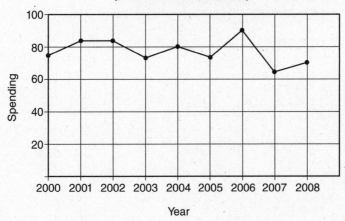

18. In 2007, what was the ratio of students enrolled in College to students enrolled in Grades 7–12?

    Ⓐ 3:2

    Ⓑ 2:3

    Ⓒ 3:4

    Ⓓ 4:3

    Ⓔ 5:8

19. In what year was government spending on education the highest *per student* enrolled at any level?

Ⓐ 2001

Ⓑ 2002

Ⓒ 2004

Ⓓ 2006

Ⓔ 2007

20. The average government spending in the years 2007 through 2008 was roughly what percent of average spending for the years 2002 through 2004, inclusive?

Ⓐ 56%

Ⓑ 65%

Ⓒ 72%

Ⓓ 78%

Ⓔ 84%

Section 2: Verbal Reasoning

1. **A**	8. **Sentence 4**	15. **D, E**
2. **E**	9. **C**	16. **E**
3. **C, D**	10. **D**	17. **B, C**
4. **C, E**	11. **E**	18. **D**
5. **C, D, H**	12. **A, C**	19. **C**
6. **C, E, G**	13. **E, F**	20. **B**
7. **A, C**	14. **B, E**	

Section 3: Quantitative Reasoning

1. **B**	8. **D**	15. **D**
2. **B**	9. **1,100**	16. **C**
3. **D**	10. **25%**	17. **B, D**
4. **B**	11. **108**	18. **B**
5. **A**	12. **E**	19. **C**
6. **A**	13. **B**	20. **D**
7. **C**	14. **A**	

Section 4: Verbal Reasoning

1. **D**	8. **E**	15. **B, C**
2. **E**	9. **D**	16. **B**
3. **A, D**	10. **B**	17. **A**
4. **B, D**	11. **D**	18. **E**
5. **C, D, I**	12. **B, F**	19. **B**
6. **A, E, G**	13. **A, E**	20. **D**
7. **B**	14. **A, D**	

Section 5: Quantitative Reasoning

1. **C**	8. **12**	15. **C, D**
2. **B**	9. **492**	16. **A, C, D**
3. **A**	10. **B**	17. **C, D, E**
4. **D**	11. **D**	18. **C**
5. **A**	12. **B**	19. **B**
6. **8**	13. **D**	20. **E**
7. **123**	14. **B**	

ANSWER EXPLANATIONS

Section 2—Verbal Reasoning

1. **(A)** The descriptive phrasing after the semicolon provides clues. "Epitome of politeness and composure" is similar to *urbane* (polite; sophisticated), and "rustic" and "rural" fit *bucolic* (rustic; simple).

2. **(E)** If the 12th graders have "melodies," which "drifted pleasingly," then those melodies could be described as *dulcet* (melodious; pleasing).

3. **(C, D)** The word "though" signifies a shift from "skilled," so blank (i) must be negative, and since the speaker is criticized for *bombast* (pompousness), then he could be *grandiloquent* (pompous; self-important). This unflattering self-importance would understandably have *dissuaded* (deterred) many of his followers.

4. **(C, E)** If a butterfly had *quiescence* (the quality of being still), the entomologist might have time to sketch it. Blank (ii) could be *short-lived* because of the shift that the word "though" creates; the shift is from "short-lived" to "*ample* (plentiful) time."

5. **(C, D, H)** If the magician is daydreaming about his entire audience being spellbound, those daydreams could be described as *fanciful* (whimsical; imaginary). If he is "not immune" to those daydreams, he could be described as susceptible to them. Then the word "nevertheless" creates a shift from the expected result; therefore, blank (ii) could be *flabbergasted* (astounded), since one would expect the magician to be used to fantasizing about his effect. If the "throngs of admirers" are *prostrate* (lying face down), they could be so in *homage* (public respect) to him.

6. **(C, E, G)** The scientist knew he would be condemned, and *enormity* (excessive wickedness) would fit blank (i) if he realized the enormity only after seeing that the offspring were "twisted" and "suffering." *Reviled* (hated) fits blank (iii): the scientist was already condemned, so "even more" signifies a higher degree of that condemnation. Logically, if the public was *cognizant* (aware) of the experiments' *depravity* (having low moral values), they would revile him.

7. **(A, C)** Choice (A) is supported because the author describes the cover of the book's new version, commenting on the photos of the White House, Pentagon, and Wall Street, and remarks that "each sphere of national power therein symbolized described by Mills," thereby saying that Mills described each of these three places and in doing so, naturally implies that Mills described some of the people working in these places. Choice (C) is supported because the author says that a "sympathetic reader" might understand that Mills had trouble "see[ing] through the shadows."

8. **(Sentence 4: In a wobbly . . . destruction.)** By calling Mills's *lexicon* (vocabulary) "wobbly," the author implies that Mills's use of language is uneven.

9. **(C)** Since the power elite are described as "swollen with *hubris*" (excessive pride), "played God" means "acted as God."

10. **(D)** The first statement in **boldface** summarizes the argument's position toward the hypothesis that not enough oxygen was budgeted, saying that the hypothesis is wrong.

The second statement in **boldface** provides support for that statement by indicating that according to the records, enough oxygen was budgeted.

11. **(E)** The author says that the convective storms have rapid evolution and dissipation processes, so it can be inferred that they come and go quickly and therefore do not persist for very long.

12. **(A, C)** The country has "tranquility" and a "state of dominance"; therefore, it could be enjoying *hegemony* (dominance) or *ascendancy* (decisive advantage) over its neighbors.

13. **(E, F)** If the coach gave speeches filled with *scathing* (harshly critical) *rebukes* (sharp criticisms), then he would be either *excoriating* (strongly condemning) or *upbraiding* (scolding) his players.

14. **(B, E)** The described stages are "before anyone knew," so *embryonic* (being of a beginning stage) or *nascent* (coming into existence) would fit here.

15. **(D, E)** If the funeral director had *gravity* (a solemn presence) and *repose* (tranquility), and if he "soothed" the mourners with silence, then he could be *taciturn* (silent) or *laconic* (using few words).

16. **(E)** The author describes and analyzes some trends in car advertising, and also speculates about the implications of these advertisements.

17. **(B, C)** The author says that the thesis is "somewhat discredited" in academia. This statement supports choice (B). The author also says the thesis asserts that the "strength and vigor" of the U.S. comes from the "struggle" to make a new life in the wilderness, thereby supporting choice (C).

18. **(D)** In this context, "purchase" is on imagination; it means the hold, or grasp, that the dream has on popular imagination.

19. **(C)** In the first paragraph, archaeological and ethnologic examples are mentioned as examples of additional criteria that studies can include.

20. **(B)** The author, in the second paragraph, explains that complex systems are modeled by choosing parameters to encompass the complexity of the systems in a manageable way; the discussion of how studies explore potential differences between Neanderthal and modern human diets instead of determining Neanderthal food types is used as an example of this simplification.

Section 3—Quantitative Reasoning

1. **(B)** Solve $4^n = 256$ by multiplying fours on your calculator until you reach 256 as a product. Note that $4 \times 4 \times 4 \times 4 = 16 \times 16 = 256$, meaning that the exponent n equals 4. Then (A) is $3^4 = 3 \times 3 \times 3 \times 3 = 9 \times 9 = 81$. Quantity (B) is greater, because

$$\frac{3}{2} \times 4^3 = \frac{3}{2} \times 64 = 96, \text{ and } 96 > 81.$$

2. **(B)**

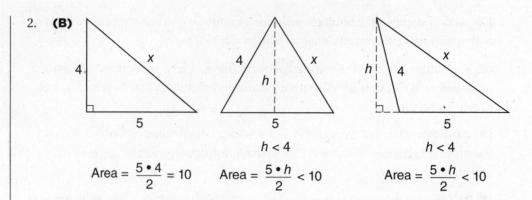

$$\text{Area} = \frac{5 \cdot 4}{2} = 10 \qquad \text{Area} = \frac{5 \cdot h}{2} < 10 \qquad \text{Area} = \frac{5 \cdot h}{2} < 10$$

If the two known sides of length 4 and 5 are placed perpendicular to each other, they can be used as the base and height to compute the triangle's area as $\frac{5 \times 4}{2} = 10$, by the formula area $= \frac{\text{base} \times \text{height}}{2}$. Now imagine using the side of length 5 as the base and swiveling the side of length 4, about a hinge at the vertex of the triangle where these sides intersect. The resulting height, h, in the figures above, is less than 4, whether the triangle is acute or obtuse. (It should be obvious that $h < 4$ in the two diagrams at right, above, but if you are not sure why, observe that h is the leg of a smaller right triangle, which has hypotenuse $= 4$.) Then the area of the right triangle, 10, is the maximum possible, and (B), 11 is greater.

3. **(D)** By substitution, $m = 3(5p) = 15p$. This means that m is 15 times p. It looks as if m, Quantity (A), is greater, but if the variables are negative, p is greater, so (D) is correct.

4. **(B)**

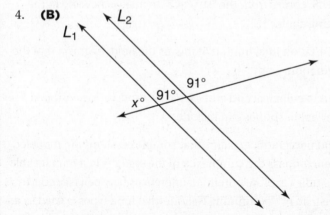

When the lines are parallel, corresponding angles are congruent. So the angle adjacent to x, measures 91°. This makes $x = 180 - 91 = 89$. (B) is greater.

5. **(A)** In a triangle, the larger sides are across from the larger angles, and the smaller sides are across from the smaller angles. Since the side length $x + .001 > x$, the angle opposite $x + .001$ is greater than the angle opposite x. So $y > z$, (A).

6. **(A)** Expand $(m+5)(m-5)$ as $m^2 - 5m + 5m - 25 = m^2 - 25$. If this equals 0, then $m^2 = 25$. Similarly, $(k+4)(k-4) = k^2 - 4k + 4k - 16 = k^2 - 16 = 0$. Add 16 to both sides, and $k^2 = 16$, (A) is greater.

7. **(C)**

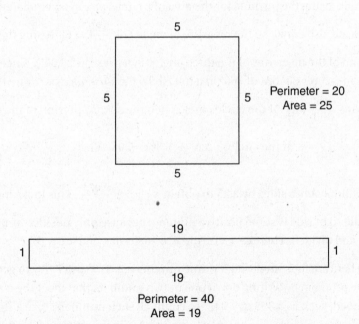

1 m

1 m

100 cm

100 cm

Area = 1 square meter *or*
100 × 100 = 10,000 cm²

One kilometer is 1,000 meters, so 10 km = 10,000 m, making (A) 10,000. There are 100 centimeters in a meter, but 100 × 100 square cm in 1 m² of area. So (B) is 100 × 100 = 10,000, as well. The answer is (C). Note that

$$100 \, \frac{\text{cm}}{\text{m}} \times 100 \, \frac{\text{cm}}{\text{m}} = 10,000 \, \frac{\text{cm}}{\text{m}} \,.$$

8. **(D)**

5

5

5

5

Perimeter = 20
Area = 25

19

1

19

1

Perimeter = 40
Area = 19

A quadrilateral is any four-sided polygon. When the perimeter of one quadrilateral is twice that of another, it will usually have a greater area. But consider the two quadrilaterals above. The long thin rectangle has twice the perimeter of the square but less area. (D) is correct.

9. **(1,100)** Let n = the number, and then $.2n$ represents 20% of the number. If the average of these is 660, then $\frac{n+.2n}{2} = \frac{1.2n}{2} = 0.6\ n = 660$. Divide each side by .6, and $n = 1,100$.

10. **(25%)** Find the percent change in the prices by finding the change or difference in the prices and dividing this by the original price: $\frac{2.49-1.99}{1.99} = \frac{.50}{1.99} \approx .2513$, or 25.13%. This rounds to $x = 25\%$. The number of loaves the family buys per month, 22, does not matter when considering the *percentage* change in the family's bill for bread.

11. **(108)** Translate the words into math symbols: $\frac{1}{8}x = 15 + \frac{1}{9}x$, for some number x.

    Subtract $\frac{1}{9}x$ from each side in order to combine like terms: $\frac{1}{8}x - \frac{1}{9}x = 15$. Since the least common multiple of 8 and 9 is 72, use 72 as the common denominator and combine the fractions: $\frac{1}{8}x - \frac{1}{9}x = \frac{9}{72}x - \frac{8}{72}x = \frac{1}{72}x = 15$. Then $x = 15 \times 72 = 1,080$.

    Finally, $\frac{1}{10}$ of this number is $1,080 \div 10 = 108$.

12. **(E)** Since the triangle is equilateral, all sides are equal, and $AC = 12$. M is the midpoint of AC, so $MC = \frac{1}{2}$ of $AC = \frac{1}{2} \times 12 = 6$. Then the circle's radius is 6, and its area is $\pi 6^2 = 36\pi$, using the formula for the area of a circle: πr^2. In an equilateral triangle, all angles are also equal, so the measure of angle C is $\frac{180}{3} = 60°$ (using the fact that the sum of the measures of the three angles in a triangle is 180°). Since the central angle measures 60° out of 360° in a full circle, the *unshaded* portion of the circle contains $\frac{60°}{360°} = \frac{1}{6}$ of the circle's area. Then the *shaded* portion of the circle contains $1 - \frac{1}{6} = \frac{6}{6} - \frac{1}{6} = \frac{5}{6}$ of the circle's area. $\frac{5}{6} \times 36\pi = 30\pi$, (E).

13. **(B)** Multiply both sides by 2.25 to obtain $x - y = \frac{2.25\sqrt{3}}{7}$. This looks messy, but note that the right side is some positive number, because only positive numbers are multiplied and divided. Then $x - y > 0$. Add y to each side, and $x > y$, (B).

14. **(A)** There are four single-digit prime numbers: 2, 3, 5, and 7. Try to get a feeling for the problem by writing down one or two numbers that meet the conditions described, such as 3,895 or 7,042. To count all such numbers, take a "fill-in-the-blank" approach. Use four blanks to represent the four digits of the number, and in each blank write the number of possible choices for the digit corresponding to that blank: _____ _____ _____ _____.

    Any of the four primes listed above may begin the number, but of these, only the digits 2 or 5 may end the number, to ensure that the number is divisible by 2 or 5. So we have __4__ _____ _____ __2__ combinations so far. There are no restrictions on the middle two digits of the number, so they can be any of the 10 digits, 0 through 9, in our base 10 system. The diagram becomes __4__ __10__ __10__ __2__. The *basic counting principle* dictates that we multiply the number of possibilities at each juncture to obtain the total number of combinations. $4 \times 10 \times 10 \times 2 = 800$, (A).

15. **(D)** Substitute 9 and 2 for x and y in the definition of the "star" operation, and $9 \star 2 = \sqrt{9} - 2 \times 2^2 = 3 - 8 = -5$, (D). When evaluating 2×2^2, be sure to square first and then multiply by 2, since the order of operations dictates that exponents are performed before multiplication.

16. **(C)** To find the greatest common factor (GCF) of 111 and 141, you could divide each by various numbers on the calculator and look for common factors. Or you can short-cut the process by recalling the divisibility test for the number 3: if the sum of the digits of an integer is divisible by 3, then the integer itself is divisible by 3. 111 and 141 are both divisible by 3 because the sums $1 + 1 + 1 = 3$ and $1 + 4 + 1 = 6$ are both multiples of 3. Dividing 111 and 141 by 3 on the calculator shows that $111 = 37 \times 3$ and that $141 = 47 \times 3$. Since 37 and 47 are prime numbers with no additional factors in common, the GCF is 3.

    The easiest way to find the least common multiple (LCM) of 8 and 10 is to list multiples of the larger number until you reach one that is also a multiple of the smaller number: 10, 20, 30, 40. Since 40 equals 8×5, 40 is the LCM of 8 and 10. Then $a = 3$ and $b = 40$, so $ab = 120$, choice (C).

17. **(B, D)** If $y = 4z$, then $z = \frac{y}{4} = \frac{1}{4}y$, and (B) is correct. By substitution, $x = 2(4z) = 8z$. So $z = \frac{1}{8}x$, and (D) is correct. The answer is (B) and (D).

18. **(B)** *In Questions 18 to 20, note that each box on the y-axis represents $2 million dollars, and so each half-box represents $1 million.* For choice (A), the rice exports in 2000 were $24 million, which is close to $20 million for fruit + $6 million for wheat, but not roughly equal. For choice (B), the rice exports were between $26 million and $27 million, which *is* roughly equal to $19 million (fruit) + $8 million (wheat). For the other three choices, it should be easy to see at a glance that rice exports alone exceeded the sum of the other two exports. Imagine a vertical bar stretching up from the x-axis to each graph. For the 3 years listed in (C), (D), and (E), the rice bar is taller than the other two bars stacked end to end.

19. **(C)** Save time by "counting boxes" to find the difference in value between rice and wheat exports, rather than finding each individual value. For example, in 2009 rice is 2.5 boxes above wheat, which represents $2.5 \times \$2$ million $= \$5$ million. Similarly, the 3.5 and 4.5 boxes that separate rice and wheat in 2010 and 2011, respectively, correspond to $7 million and $9 million. The total difference in export value for the 3-year period is then $5 + 7 + 9 = \$21$ million, (C).

20. **(D)** Scan along the fruit curve for years in which the value of exports decreased greatly from the year before. In 2006 and 2008, fruit exports dropped significantly—by two

boxes, or \$4 million—from the year before. In 2008, this \$4 million decrease represented a larger percent change, because the change occurred from a lower starting value. Specifically, in 2008 the decrease was $\frac{4}{12} = \frac{1}{3} \approx 33.3\%$ from the year before, while in 2006 the decrease was $\frac{4}{14} \approx 28.6\%$ from the year before. (D) is correct.

Section 4—Verbal Reasoning

1. **(D)** If the emissary used a barrage of *verbiage* (excessive wordiness) to divert, then he could have been described as *loquacious* (talkative).

2. **(E)** A clue for the blank is provided by "repetition," which implies that the fractal describes via *iteration* (repetition).

3. **(A, D)** A clue for blank (i) is provided by the description of the cheetah as eager to fight; *truculence* (disposed to fight) fits. If the cheetah is ready to fight, it makes sense that the cheetah *assailed* (violently attacked) its rival.

4. **(B, D)** The word "though" creates a shift from blank (i) to "soon recovered," so blank (i) could be *nonplussed* (perplexed) by. Blank (ii), then, needs to contrast with the general's initial confusion, so designing *a shrewd* (cunning) plan would create such a contrast.

5. **(C, D, I)** If the scientist is "puffed up," "*callow*" (inexperienced), and if he "trumpeted" his results, his pride could be described as *overweening* (arrogant). If his colleagues "cringed," the paper could have self-congratulatory *conceits* (unduly high self-opinions). The phrase "even more" indicates an increase in a description's intensity, so *chagrined* (dismayed) would logically be an increase from the colleagues' initial cringing.

6. **(A, E, G)** The phrase at the end of the passage is useful because it indicates that studies have connected increased dosage with increased harm. The word "however" creates a shift to this assertion, thus the portion of the passage before the assertion must imply the opposite—that the radiation has a positive effect. Blank (i) can be *susceptible to* (vulnerable to), since if the doses make people less susceptible to something, the effect is positive. Blank (ii) continues this direction, so *salubrious* (healthful) would fit, and blank (iii) is being criticized by the passage's argument, so it could be *acts as a tonic* (aid).

7. **(B)** The author, by saying that drugs and *prophylactics* (things designed to prevent) create resistant pathogens, implies that at least some of the things people do to protect their health actually endangers their health because of the creation of these resistant pathogens.

8. **(E)** By saying that hypermutators have "a price to pay," the author implies that although their mutations increase their immunity to drugs, these mutations also have a downside.

9. **(D)** If it is more expensive to teach workers to use the new equipment if they have spent a long time using the old equipment, then this undermines the argument that switching to the new equipment will quickly allow factories to realize cost savings since, initially, there will be expenses associated with the teaching.

10. **(B)** The use of words like "annihilate" and "conquer" by Marx to describe the process of capitalism provides support for the notion that Marx was critical of capitalism's means.

11. **(D)** By saying that "understanding of technologies of speed connote a future liberation from material scarcity," the author is arguing that our understanding of speed suggests that it will, in the future, deliver us from the scarcity, or lack of needed materials.

12. **(B, F)** If the advice to the housewives was designed to facilitate "harmonious households," then it could have instructed them to be *agreeable* or *felicitous* (agreeable).

13. **(A, E)** Admittedly, the experiments are "commonplace" and "unoriginal," so criticism of them could call them *quotidian* (everyday) or *pedestrian* (dull; common).

14. **(A, D)** If the company exhausted its *erstwhile* (former) surplus, it must have been either *spendthrift* (reckless with money) or *profligate* (wasteful).

15. **(B, C)** *Sycophants* (flatterers) and *toadies* (yes-men) would not criticize a monarch.

16. **(B)** The author of the passage indicates that most of James's *missives* (letters) were to his family, and that these letters raised doubts, or disillusions, about the expedition.

17. **(A)** The author is discussing another author's book about James during James's expedition in South America; in doing so, he is summarizing the results of that author's study of James.

18. **(E)** Since "body" is describing travel literature, it must mean "collection," i.e., the entire collection of James's travel literature.

19. **(B)** The passage indicates that the shock wave created by a quark-nova ejects the outer layers, which become the ejecta, of the neutron star, and that the fireball "pushes" these layers.

20. **(D)** This statement explains the apparent contradiction in the passage by introducing another explanation for the fact that these people tend to develop heart disease—other dietary changes.

Section 5—Quantitative Reasoning

*Indicates an alternative way to solve the problem.

1. **(C)** When lines intersect, the *vertical angles*, those directly across from each other, are equal. This means that we can label the three angles *within* the triangle $2x°$, $3x°$, and $4x°$. By the triangle sum theorem, $2x° + 3x° + 4x° = 180°$. Then $9x = 180$, and $x = 20$. So $5x = 100$, (C).

2. **(B)** Find the point of intersection of the lines by setting the equations equal to each other. That is, if $y = 2x - 6$, and $y = \frac{1}{2}x + 6$, then $2x - 6 = \frac{1}{2}x + 6$, by *substitution*.

   Adding 6 and subtracting $\frac{1}{2}x$ from each side yields $\frac{3}{2}x = 12$ (or $1.5x = 12$). Multiply both sides by $\frac{2}{3}$ (or divide by 1.5) to obtain $x = 8$. Substitute this x-value into one of the original equations to obtain $y = 2(8) - 6 = 10$. Since $10 > 8$, (B) is greater.

3. **(A)** If the perimeter of a square is 64, then the length of each side is $\frac{64}{4} = 16$. The square's area is $16^2 = 256$. If a circle has diameter 18, then radius is $\frac{18}{2} = 9$. The circle's area is $\pi 9^2 = 81\pi$. $81\pi \approx 254.5$, so (A) is greater.

4. **(D)** Quantity (B) "seems greater" by exactly $1x + 1y$, because $(3x + 4y) - (2x + 3y) = 1x + 1y$. Though (B) appears greater, x and y may be negative numbers, so (D) is correct. For example, if $x = y = 1$, then (A) $= 5 <$ (B) $= 7$, but if $x = y = -1$, then (A) $= -5 >$ (B) $= -7$.

5. **(A)** Don't be misled by the word *daily* into finding the actual daily rent of the man in column A, by dividing his monthly rent by the number of days in a month. You may waste a lot of time deciding whether to divide by 31, 30, or 30.25 to obtain a messy figure you don't need. Since you know there are 12 months in a year, multiply 975 by 12 to obtain \$11,700 as the annual rent in (A), which is greater than quantity (B), \$11,650. A man who pays more rent per year will also pay more rent per day.

6. **(8)** $980\ \underset{2}{\overgroup{}}\,000\ \underset{3}{\overgroup{}}\,000\ \underset{3}{\overgroup{}} \Rightarrow 2 + 3 + 3 = 8$. This question involves the concept of *Scientific Notation*. The decimal point must be shifted 8 times to make the number 980,000,000—with its invisible decimal point at the end—look like the number 9.8. That is $980,000,000 = 9.8 \times 10^8$. The exponent of the base 10 determines the number of times the decimal point is shifted.

7. **(123)** The second player scored $28 - 26.5 = 1.5$ points per game more than the first player. For an 82-game season, this would amount to $1.5\ \frac{\text{points}}{\cancel{\text{game}}} \times 82\ \cancel{\text{games}} = 123$ more points, in total.

8. **(12)**

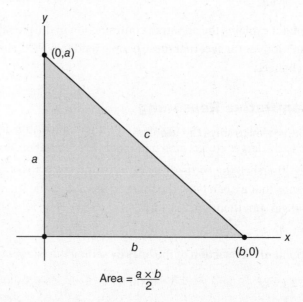

$$\text{Area} = \frac{a \times b}{2}$$

The unknowns a and b can be thought of as two of the triangle's side lengths. Because the x- and y-axes are perpendicular, the triangle is a right triangle and its area is given by $\frac{ab}{2}$, which is given as 6. Then $ab = 6 \times 2 = 12$. Since a and b are integers, we can list all possible pairs of whole numbers for a and b whose product is twelve: $(1, 12)$, $(2, 6)$, $(3, 4)$. The length of the third side of the triangle is determined by the Pythagorean theorem: $a^2 + b^2 = c^2$, which implies $c = \sqrt{a^2 + b^2}$. If c represents the remaining, unknown side length here, there are three possible values for c, one for each of the three pairs listed above. That is, $c = \sqrt{1^2 + 12^2} = \sqrt{145}$ or $c = \sqrt{2^2 + 6^2} = \sqrt{40}$, or $c = \sqrt{3^2 + 4^2} = \sqrt{25}$. However, only the last, $\sqrt{25} = 5$, is an integer as required, so $c = 5$, $a = 3$, and $b = 4$. This makes the perimeter $3 + 4 + 5 = 12$. The values of a and b may be interchanged, but the perimeter is still 12.

9. **(492)** When a list contains consecutive integers, use a simple but helpful formula for determining how many numbers there are from some first number, F, through some last number, L, inclusive. The formula is $L - F + 1$. Here, the 200 consecutive integers 1, 2, 3, . . . 200 are written on a page. Of these, there are nine single-digit numbers written, because $9 - 1 + 1 = 9$ (using $F = 1$ and $L = 9$ in the formula). The two-digit numbers written include from 10 through 99, and thus include $99 - 10 + 1 = 90$ numbers. The three-digit numbers written on the page include from 100 through 200, and thus include $200 - 100 + 1 = 101$ whole numbers. So the total number of *digits* written is $(9 \times 1) + (90 \times 2) + (101 \times 3) = 9 + 180 + 303 = 492$.

10. **(B)**

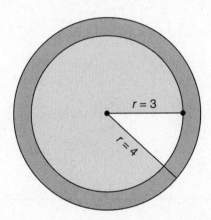

If the diameters are 6 and 8, divide by 2 to obtain the radii: 3 and 4. The area of each circle is given by the formula $A = \pi r^2$, for radius $= r$. Then the smaller circle has area $\pi 3^2 = 9\pi$, while the larger circle has area $\pi 4^2 = 16\pi$. The shaded area between the two circles is equal to the larger circle's area minus that of the smaller. $16\pi - 9\pi = 7\pi$, (B).

11. **(D)** Let $x =$ Jim's age now. Then Ted is now $x - 15$ years old, since he is 15 years younger. 18 years ago, Jim was $x - 18$ years old, and Ted's age was $(x - 15) - 18 = x - 33$. Since Jim was twice Ted's age then, $x - 18 = 2(x - 33)$, or $x - 18 = 2x - 66$. Subtract $1x$ and add 66 to each side, to obtain $48 = x$, (D).

*Let the ages now be J and T. Then the ages 18 years ago, the ages were $J - 18$ and $T - 18$. Set up one equation for present ages, $J = T + 15$, and one equation for past ages: $J - 18 = 2(T - 18)$. Now substitute $T + 15$ for the J in the second equation: $T + 15 - 18 = 2(T - 18)$. Therefore, $T - 3 = 2T - 36$. Finally, subtract T and add 36 to each side to find $33 = T$. Don't forget, the question asked for *Jim's* age, which is $T + 15 = 33 + 15 = 48$, (D).

12. **(B)** Wendy's list of three quiz scores contains two even scores, 8 and 10, so the probability that an even number is selected from her quiz scores is $\frac{2}{3}$. Yuri's list contains the two even numbers, 10 and 6, so there is also a $\frac{2}{3}$ probability that an even number is selected from his list. Zoe has only one even quiz score out of three scores total, so the probability that an even number is selected from her list is $\frac{1}{3}$. Find the probability that all three numbers chosen are even by multiplying these independent probabilities: $\frac{2}{3} \times \frac{2}{3} \times \frac{1}{3} = \frac{4}{27}$ (B).

13. **(D)** Use the formula $D = r \times t$, or distance = rate × time. When the second car leaves New York, the first car is ahead by $54 \frac{\text{miles}}{\text{hour}} \times 2 \text{ hours} = 108 \text{ miles}$. The second car travels faster by $66 - 54 = 12$ miles per hour, meaning that it catches up by 12 miles every hour. Then by the $D = rt$ formula again, $108 = 12 \times t$, and $t = 9$. This means that the second car will require 9 hours to close the distance of 108 miles. Since it departed at 2:00 (2 hours after 12:00), it reaches the first car at 2:00 + 9 hours = 11:00, (D).

14. **(B)**

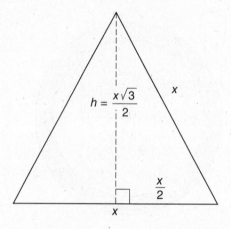

$$\text{Area} = \frac{1}{2} \times x \times \frac{x\sqrt{3}}{2} = \frac{x^2\sqrt{3}}{4}$$

Perimeter = $3x$

The triangle's perimeter is simply $3x$ because it has three equal sides of length x. To find its area, first draw the altitude or height (call it h), and note that this divides the base into two congruent segments of length $\frac{x}{2}$. By the Pythagorean theorem, $\left(\frac{x}{2}\right)^2 + h^2 = x^2$. Then $h^2 = x^2 - \frac{x^2}{4} = \frac{3x^2}{4}$. Take the square root of each side to obtain $h = \frac{\sqrt{3}x}{2}$. (You can also get h quickly by the $s - s\sqrt{3} - 2s$ pattern for side lengths of a 30-60-90 triangle, with s here set equal to $\frac{x}{2}$.) Since the area of a triangle is given by $\frac{1}{2} \times \text{base} \times \text{height}$, the area here is $\frac{1}{2} \times \frac{x}{1} \times \frac{\sqrt{3}x}{2} = \frac{x^2\sqrt{3}}{4}$. Set this equal to the perimeter: $3x = \dfrac{x^2\sqrt{3}}{4}$. Multiply by 4, and $12x = x^2\sqrt{3}$. Since $x \neq 0$, we can divide by x on both sides to obtain $12 = x\sqrt{3}$. Divide by $\sqrt{3}$, and $x = \dfrac{12}{\sqrt{3}}$. Finally, simplify and get rid of the square root on the bottom, by multiplying both the numerator and denominator by $\sqrt{3}$. That is, $\dfrac{12 \times \sqrt{3}}{\sqrt{3} \times \sqrt{3}} = \dfrac{12\sqrt{3}}{3} = \dfrac{4\sqrt{3}}{1} = 4\sqrt{3}$, (B).

15. **(C, D)** Set up ratios to determine her costs. $\dfrac{\text{sandwiches}}{\text{price}} : \dfrac{6}{29.7} = \dfrac{20}{x}$. Cross-multiply to obtain $6x = 594$, and $x = 99$. This means that Leila will spend at least \$99. Similarly, $\dfrac{\text{sandwiches}}{\text{price}} : \dfrac{6}{38.7} = \dfrac{20}{x}$. Cross-multiply again to obtain $6x = 774$, and $x = \$129$ is the most she will spend. Choices **(C)** and **(D)** fall within this range.

16. **(A, C, D)** (A) is correct because the sum of two even integers is even, and the product of two even integers is even. For example, $2 + 4 = 6$, $10 + -8 = 2$, $12 \times 4 = 48$. (B) is not correct because the sum of two odd integers is not odd. For example, $1 + 3 = 4$. (C) is correct: the Real number system is *closed* under addition and multiplication, meaning that any two real numbers when added or multiplied will produce another real number. (D) is correct, because when positive numbers are added or multiplied, the result is positive. (E) is not correct, because the product of two negative real numbers is not negative but positive. The answer is (A), (C), and (D).

17. **(C, D, E)** (A) is not correct, because if $0 < x < 1$, then $\dfrac{1}{x}$ will be greater than 1. For example, if $x = \dfrac{1}{2}$, then $\dfrac{1}{x} = \dfrac{1}{\frac{1}{2}} = 1 \times \dfrac{2}{1} = 2$. (B) is not correct, because x does not have to be less than 1,000. For example, if $x = 1{,}000{,}000$, then $0 < \dfrac{1}{x} < 1$, as required. (D) is correct, because $\dfrac{1}{x}$ will be both positive and less than 1, whenever x is greater than 1. (C) is correct as follows: we are given $\dfrac{1}{x} < 1$. We know $1 < x$ as described in (D), above. These inequalities can be put together as $\dfrac{1}{x} < 1 < x$, which implies $\dfrac{1}{x} < x$. (E) is correct, because when a fraction or decimal between 0 and 1 is squared, the result is smaller than the starting number. Here, $\left(\dfrac{1}{x}\right)^2 = \dfrac{1}{x^2}$ will be strictly less than $\dfrac{1}{x}$, or equivalently, $\dfrac{1}{x} > \dfrac{1}{x^2}$. The answer is (C), (D), and (E).

18. **(C)** In 2007, there were 15 students in college for every 20 students in grades 7–12, so the ratio was 15:20. (You may drop the "millions" when considering these figures as a ratio.) Dividing through by 5, the greatest common factor of 15 and 20, yields the reduced form, 3:4, (C).

19. **(B)** Eliminate choices (C) and (E), years in which government spending was relatively low. Comparing choices (A) and (B), spending was the same in both years, but in 2001, there were more total students, so the per student spending was less. This

eliminates (A). In 2002, choice (B), $85 was spent for every 57.5 students, which amounts to $\frac{85}{57.5} \approx \$1.48$ per student. In 2006, choice (D), $90 was spent for every 70 students, which amounts to $\frac{90}{70} \approx \$1.29$ per student. (B) is correct.

20. **(E)** The average government spending in the years 2007 through 2008 was $\frac{65+70}{2} = \$67.5$ million. The average government spending in the years 2002 through 2004 was $\frac{85+75+80}{3} = \$80$ million. The former is $\frac{67.5}{80} = .84375 = 84.375\%$ of the latter. This is roughly 84%, (E).

Acknowledgments

INTRODUCTION

Page 4: Excerpt from Thilo Hinterberger: "The Sensorium: A Multimodel Neurofeedback Environment," *Advances in Human-Computer Interaction,* vol. 2011, Article ID 724204, 10 pages, 2011. doi:10.1155/2011/724204.

PRACTICE TEST 1

Page 31: Excerpt from Michael J. Pauers, "One Fish, Two Fish, Red Fish, Blue Fish: Geography, Ecology, Sympatry, and Male Coloration in the Lake Malawi Cichlid Genus Labeotropheus (Perciformes: Cichlidae)," *International Journal of Evolutionary Biology,* vol. 2011, Article ID 575469, 12 pages, 2011. doi:10.4061/2011/575469.

Page 35: Excerpt from Karen E. H. Skinazi, "A Cosmopolitan New World: Douglas Coupland's Canadianation of AmLit," *AmeriQuests,* vol. 4, no. 1, 2007.

Page 45: Excerpt from Ron Coleman, "Long Memory of Pathfinding Aesthetics," *International Journal of Computer Games Technology,* vol. 2009, Article ID 318505, 9 pages, 2009. doi:10.1155/2009/318505.

Page 46: Excerpt from Katherine Garrett and Gintaras Dŭda, "Dark Matter: A Primer," *Advances in Astronomy,* vol. 2011, Article ID 968283, 22 pages, 2011. doi:10.1155/2011/968283.

Page 47: Excerpt from Christine Photinos, "The Tramp in American Literature, 1873–1939," *AmeriQuests,* vol. 5, no 1, 2008.

Page 48: Excerpt from Frank van der Velde, "Where Artificial Intelligence and Neuroscience Meet: The Search for Grounded Architectures of Cognition,"*Advances in Artificial Intelligence,* vol. 2010, Article ID 918062, 18 pages, 2010. doi:10.1155/2010/918062.

Page 50: Excerpt from Dana A. Williams, "Review of *A Killing in This Town,*" *AmeriQuests,* vol. 6, no 1, 2008.

PRACTICE TEST 2

Page 86: Excerpt from Robert D. Young, Bertrand Desjardins, Kirsten McLaughlin, Michel Poulain, and Thomas T. Perls, "Typologies of Extreme Longevity Myths," *Current Gerontology and Geriatrics Research,* vol. 2010, Article ID 423087, 12 pages, 2010. doi:10.1155/2010/423087.

Page 87: Excerpt from Daniel Berrar, Naoyuki Sato, and Alfons Schuster, "Quo Vadis, Artificial Intelligence?," *Advances in Artificial Intelligence*, vol. 2010, Article ID 629869, 12 pages, 2010. doi:10.1155/2010/629869.

Page 90: Excerpt from Bala Ramasamy and Matthew Yeung, "Customer Satisfaction and the Consumption Function," *Economics Research International*, vol. 2010, Article ID 202014, 5 pages, 2010. doi:10.1155/2010/202014.

Page 90: Excerpt from Philip McVeigh, Colin O'Dowd, and Harald Berresheim, "Eddy Correlation Measurements of Ozone Fluxes over Coastal Waters West of Ireland," *Advances in Meteorology*, vol. 2010, Article ID 754941, 7 pages, 2010. doi:10.1155/2010/754941.

Page 98: Excerpt from Vedat Sar, "Epidemiology of Dissociative Disorders: An Overview," *Epidemiology Research International*, vol. 2011, Article ID 404538, 8 pages, 2011. doi:10.1155/2011/404538.

Page 99: Excerpt from Sue Marasco, "Many Identities, One Nation: The Revolution and Its Legacy in the Mid-Atlantic," *AmeriQuests*, vol. 5, no. 1, 2008, Vanderbilt University.

Page 100: Excerpt from Alan Lightman, *AmeriQuests*, vol. 3, no. 2, 2006.

Page 102: Excerpt from Danielle I. Harrow, Jill M. Felker, and Katherine H. Baker, "Impacts of Triclosan in Greywater on Soil Microorganisms," *Applied and Environmental Soil Science*, vol. 2011, Article ID 646750, 8 pages, 2011. doi:10.1155/2011/646750.

Page 103: Excerpt from L. Joe Moffitt, John K. Stranlund, and Craig D. Osteen, "Securing the Border from Invasives: Robust Inspections Under Severe Uncertainty," *Economics Research International*, vol. 2010, Article ID 510127, 9 pages, 2010. doi:10.1155/2010/510127.

PRACTICE TEST 3

Page 137: Excerpt from Som B. Ale and Henry F. Howe, "What Do Ecological Paradigms Offer to Conservation?," *International Journal of Ecology*, vol. 2010, Article ID 250754, 9 pages, 2010. doi:10.1155/2010/250754.

Page 151: Excerpt from Paul Hegarty, "The Hallucinatory Life of Tape," *Culture Machine*, vol. 9, 2007, ISSN 1465–4121.

Page 152: Excerpt from Trevor Paglen, "Unmarked Planes and Hidden Geographies," *Vectors Journal*.

Page 155: Excerpt from Niv Horesh, "The People's or the World's: RMB Internationalisation in Longer Historic Perspective," *Economics Research International*, vol. 2011, Article ID 161074, 13 pages, 2011. doi:10.1155/2011/161074.

PRACTICE TEST 4

Page 189: Excerpt from Robert G. Mogull, "A Contrast of U.S. Metropolitan Demographic Poverty: Chicago, Los Angeles, and New York," *International Journal of Population Research*, vol. 2011, Article ID 860684, 5 pages, 2011. doi:10.1155/2011/860684.

Page 193: Excerpt from Marc Ebner and Stuart Hameroff, "Lateral Information Processing by Spiking Neurons: A Theoretical Model of the Neural Correlate of Consciousness,"

Computational Intelligence and Neuroscience, vol. 2011, Article ID 247879, 17 pages, 2011. doi:10.1155/2011/247879.

Page 203: Excerpt from Mark Poster, The Aesthetics of Distracting Media, *Culture Machine*, vol. 4, 2002.

Page 204: Excerpt from Dave Boothroyd, Deconstruction and Everyday Life, or How Deconstruction Helped Me Quit Smoking, *Culture Machine*, vol. 6, 2004.

Page 206: Excerpt from Gillian Fuller, Perfect Match: Biometrics and Body Patterning in a Networked World, *The Fibreculture Journal*, Issue 1, 2003.

Page 208: Excerpt from Lisa Gye, Halflives, a Mystory: Writing Hypertext to Learn, *The Fibreculture Journal*, Issue 2, 2003.

PRACTICE TEST 5

Page 243: Excerpt from Molly Oshun, Nicole M. Ardoin, and Sharon Ryan, "Use of the Planning Outreach Liaison Model in the Neighborhood Planning Process: A Case Study in Seattle's Rainier Valley Neighborhood," *Urban Studies Research*, vol. 2011, Article ID 687834, 12 pages, 2011. doi:10.1155/2011/687834.

Page 246: Excerpt from Douglas S. Massey and María Aysa-Lastra, "Social Capital and International Migration from Latin America," *International Journal of Population Research*, vol. 2011, Article ID 834145, 18 pages, 2011. doi:10.1155/2011/834145.

Page 247: Excerpt from Beth Willman, "In Pursuit of the Least Luminous Galaxies," *Advances in Astronomy*, vol. 2010, Article ID 285454, 11 pages, 2010. doi:10.1155/2010/285454.

Page 258: Excerpt from Peter Ruppert, "The Perils and Possibilities of Story, on Alexander Graf The Cinema of Wim Wenders: The Celluloid Highway," *Film-Philosophy*, Vol. 8, No. 1 (2004).

Page 259: Excerpt from Mark E. Kann, "From Participatory to Digital Democracy," *Fast Capitalism* (2005).

Page 261: Excerpt from Carl Boggs, "Corporate Power, Ecological Crisis, and Animal Rights," *Fast Capitalism* (2007).

PRACTICE TEST 6

Page 299: Excerpt from Steven P. Dandaneau, "The Power Elite at 50: Wright Mills's Political Sociology in Midlife Crisis," *Fast Capitalism* (2006).

Page 300: Excerpt from V. Spiridonov, Z. Dimitrovski, and M. Curic, "A Three-Dimensional Simulation of Supercell Convective Storm," *Advances in Meteorology*, vol. 2010, Article ID 234731, 15 pages, 2010. doi:10.1155/2010/234731.

Page 302: Excerpt from Shane Gunster, "'Second Nature': Advertising, Metaphor, and the Production of Space," *Fast Capitalism* (2006).

Page 304: Excerpt from Virginie Fabre, Silvana Condemi, Anna Degioanni, and Estelle Herrscher, "Neanderthals versus Modern Humans: Evidence for Resource Competition from Isotopic Modelling," *International Journal of Evolutionary Biology*, vol. 2011, Article ID 689315, 16 pages, 2011. doi:10.4061/2011/689315.

Page 313: Excerpt from Wolf-Rainer Abraham, "Megacities as Sources for Pathogenic Bacteria in Rivers and Their Fate Downstream," *International Journal of Microbiology*, vol. 2011, Article ID 798292, 13 pages, 2011. doi:10.1155/2011/798292.

Page 314: Excerpt from Robert Goldman, Stephen Papson, and Noah Kersey, "Speed—Through, Across, and In—The Landscapes of Capital," *Fast Capitalism* (2005).

Page 316: Excerpt from Jason Borge, "Vanderbilt University," *Ameriquests*, Vol. 5, No. 1 (2008).

Page 318: Excerpt from Rachid Ouyed, Denis Leahy, Jan Staff, and Brian Niebergal, "Quark-Nova Explosion Inside a Collapsar: Application to Gamma Ray Bursts," *Advances in Astronomy*, vol. 2009, Article ID 463521, 10 pages, 2009. doi:10.1155/2009/463521.

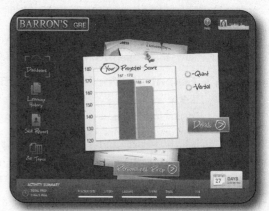

GRAMMAR GRAMMAR & MORE GRAMMAR

For ESL courses . . . for remedial English courses . . . for standard instruction in English grammar and usage on all levels from elementary through college . . . Barron's has what you're looking for!

501 English Verbs, 3rd Ed., w/CD-ROM

Thomas R. Beyer, Jr., Ph.D.

An analysis of English verb construction precedes 501 regular and irregular verbs presented alphabetically, one per page, each set up in table form showing indicative, imperative, and subjunctive moods in all tenses.

ISBN 978-1-4380-7302-6, paper, $18.99, *Can$21.99*

Grammar in Plain English, 5th Ed.

H. Diamond, M.A. and P. Dutwin, M.A.

Basic rules of grammar and examples clearly presented, with exercises that reflect GED test standards.

ISBN 978-0-7641-4786-9, paper, $14.99, *Can$16.99*

Painless Grammar, 3rd Ed.

Rebecca Elliott, Ph.D.

Focused mainly toward middle-school students, this book takes a light, often humorous approach to teaching grammar and usage.

ISBN 978-0-7641-4712-8, paper, $9.99, *Can$11.99*

E-Z Grammar, 2nd Ed.

Dan Mulvey

Barron's E-Z Grammar is written primarily for high school seniors and college freshmen and emphasizes the simple logic underlying correct grammar and clear expression. The author covers all parts of speech and correct sentence structure.

ISBN 978-0-7641-4261-1, paper, $14.99, *Can$16.99*

Prices subject to change without notice.

Available at your local book store or visit **www.barronseduc.com**

Barron's Educational Series, Inc.
250 Wireless Blvd.
Hauppauge, NY 11788
Order toll-free: 1-800-645-3476
Order by fax: 1-631-434-3217

In Canada:
Georgetown Book Warehouse
4 Armstrong Ave.
Georgetown, Ont. L7G 4R9
Canadian orders: 1-800-247-7160
Fax in Canada: 1-800-887-1594

(#90) R8/14